The New Sciences of Religion

The New Sciences of Religion

Exploring Spirituality from the Outside In and Bottom Up

William Grassie

palgrave
macmillan

First published in 2010 by
PALGRAVE MACMILLAN®
in the United States—a division of St. Martin's Press LLC,
175 Fifth Avenue, New York, NY 10010.

Where this book is distributed in the UK, Europe and the rest of the world,
this is by Palgrave Macmillan, a division of Macmillan Publishers Limited,
registered in England, company number 785998, of Houndmills,
Basingstoke, Hampshire RG21 6XS.

Palgrave Macmillan is the global academic imprint of the above companies
and has companies and representatives throughout the world.

Palgrave® and Macmillan® are registered trademarks in the United States,
the United Kingdom, Europe and other countries.

ISBN: 978–0–230–10877–6

Library of Congress Cataloging-in-Publication Data

Grassie, William, 1957–
    The new sciences of religion : exploring spirituality from the outside in and
    bottom up / by William Grassie.
        p. cm.
    Includes bibliographical references and index.
    ISBN 978–0–230–10877–6 (alk. paper)—ISBN 978–0–230–10876–9 (alk. paper)
        1. Religion—Study and teaching. 2. Religion and science. I. Title.
    BL41.G72 2010
    201'.6—dc22   2010014275

A catalogue record of the book is available from the British Library.

Design by Newgen Imaging Systems (P) Ltd., Chennai, India.

First edition: November 2010

10 9 8 7 6 5 4 3 2 1

Printed in the United States of America.

CONTENTS

ACKNOWLEDGMENTS

This book is long overdue in two senses. First, the book has been needed to help shape an important field of research and the public understanding of that field, that is, the scientific study of religious and spiritual phenomena. Second, the book has also had a long gestation in my life, really going back over thirty years when I first began to study religion as an undergraduate student at Middlebury College in 1975, including a voyeuristic junior year abroad at the Hebrew University as a "participant observer" of religions in Jerusalem in 1977–1978. In the ensuing decades, my studies and reflections on these big questions continued through formal and informal education, through many encounters and much travel, and through the many personal, political, and practical challenges of life. Given this long and ponderous intellectual and spiritual journey, there are a lot of people whom I should acknowledge. My life has been touched and transformed by them in myriad ways; this book is a result of those transformations.

Starting at the beginning, I want to thank my extraordinary mother, May Hatchard. She does not remember anymore, but we remember for her. I acknowledge also my father, Vernon Grassie (deceased), whom I barely knew, and my stepfather, William Hatchard (deceased), whom I came to love. To these giants in my life, I add a large, extended, blended family of siblings, their spouses, and aunts, uncles, cousins, nieces, nephews, and others scattered across Canada and the United States.

In the same vein, I need to thank Babette Jenny, my former wife, and our two very special daughters, Maisy Grassie and Gillian Grassie. They put up with me before, during, and after graduate school. For the first few years, Metanexus and its staff worked out of our home at Laurels Forge Farm in Unionville, Pennsylvania, so they were all intimately acquainted with the work, the staff, and the trials and tribulations of this long process of studying, traveling, organizing, and reflecting.

Thanks also to my new wife and partner, Rashmini Yogaratnam. We prove not only that opposites attract, but also that the whole is more than the sum of the parts. Rashmini propped me up in the sometimes lonely struggle to finish this book. My love and appreciation grows with compounded interest.

I need to acknowledge the original board members of Metanexus—Peter Dodson, Sol Katz, Andy Newberg, and Stephen Dunning—as well as all of those who have joined the organization since, but especially Kathleen Duffy, Ed Devinney, Ed Berkowitz, Theodore Friend, and many more. Thank you.

I acknowledge the first staff of Metanexus—Carol Urbanc, Julia Loving—and the others who have join the staff since then—Barbara Bole, John Witcoski, and the whole team—who have come and gone and remain. I especially need to acknowledge Eric Weislogel and Greg Hansell, whom I have supervised and been supervised by in return. Great minds and great people think differently and learn from one another to accomplish greater things.

I would like to thank my many teachers and mentors—David Rosenberg, Steven Rockefeller, John Elder, and Paul Nelson, with whom I studied at Middlebury College many years ago. There then followed a whole slew of Quaker colleagues who profoundly shaped my life as a spiritual activist and late-blooming scholar. I would also thank Gibson Winter (deceased), Norbert Samuelson, and John Raines with whom I studied in graduate school at Temple University, as well as others such as Holmes Rolston, John Haught, Thomas Berry, Brian Swimme, Paul Ricouer, Donna Haraway, and others, whose writings I have intensively studied and from whom I have learned so much. Acknowledged and not, the voices and insights of many others have shaped this book in profound ways.

Other mentors, some I should better call friends, include Phil Clayton, George Ellis, Scott Gilbert, Ursula Goodenough, Phil Hefner, William Hurlbut, Nancey Murphy, Ted Peters, Varadaraja Raman, Mark Richardson, Robert Russell, Jeff Schloss, Stephen Post, Wentzel van Huÿssteen, and many unmentioned.

I also need to thank my colleagues around the world. I have been blessed with many opportunities to travel to a number of countries, including Canada, China, France, Germany, India, Indonesia, Iran, Israel-Palestine, Lebanon, Mexico, Spain, Sri Lanka, Thailand, the United Kingdom, and many parts of the United States. Without these opportunities to get outside, look around, look back, and look in at myself and the universe, I would not have been able to attempt this ambitious project.

In particular, I need to acknowledge the U.S.-Sri Lanka Fulbright Commission and its executive director, Tissa Jayatilika, who sponsored me for an important sabbatical year as a Senior Fulbright Fellow in the Department of Buddhist Studies at the University of Peradeniya. The first drafts of this book began as a series of lectures given in Sri Lanka. I have left a number of references to Sri Lanka in the text because this resplendent island is an interesting case study and microcosm of a troubled world. I would like to acknowledge several colleagues in Sri Lanka, including Professor P. D. Premasiri, the Venerable Muwaetagama Gnanananda, Dr. Maya Shobrook, and Harsha Navaratne, who helped make my sabbatical year informative, pleasant, and productive.

I need to thank Sir John Templeton, now deceased, for his vision and generosity, which made so much of this work possible. Sir John provided both the ideas and the means, the fulcrum and the lever, to transform religions and the world in many positive ways. I would also like to thank the trustees, advisers, and staff of the John Templeton Foundation,. Working with the foundation has always been fascinating and rewarding work. I have learned so much and met so many wonderful people through this collaboration. Sir John's program for "Progress in Religion" and "Humility-in-Theology" is very much part of the intellectual and spiritual matrix that I seek to advance in the book and in my life. Sir John took a special interest in me. Consider this book then a modest repayment on a great debt owed.

I need to especially thank Holmes Rolston and John Haught for reading earlier drafts of the manuscript and making many critical comments and suggestions. Thanks also to the anonymous peer reviewers for your critical comments and endorsements. I am grateful for the suggestions and support. I need to also thank Mary Lou Bertucci and Meenakshi Venkat for editing the manuscript. My dyslexia is certainly a source of creativity and insight in my life, but also a real challenge for me as a writer and for any copy editor of my writing. And I thank my editor at Palgrave Macmillan, Burke Gerstenschlager, for shepherding this book into its final form.

Finally, my cybernetic self needs to also acknowledge the MacBook Pro on my lap running Microsoft Word with the help of FileMaker and Endnotes to keep track of citations and references. To this I add the assistance provided by my "personal" librarians, Google and Amazon. Without these prosthetics, I could never have produced this book.

This book is a constructive and synthetic exercise, bringing together the research, philosophy, and perspectives of many different people, so credit goes to all of those who have gone before and on whom this endeavor is constructively parasitic and productively symbiotic. These other voices have helped me learn a little bit more about God-by-whatever-name and this amazing universe in which we are privileged to live and think for a brief and remarkable sojourn. What remains then are the mistakes for which I alone accept responsibility.

PERMISSIONS

"The New Sciences of Religion" was a lecture presented at Nanjing University, China, October 2006, and other venues over the years. It was published online by Metanexus in May 2007 and edited and republished in print by *Zygon: Journal of Religion and Science* in March 2008. This book expands on this essay. Many parts of this argument and some sections of the book have been copied and adapted into chapters one, two, eight, and nine. The project has expanded from a 15,000-word essay into a 100,000-word book.

Chapter three, "The Economics of Religion," was presented at the Society for the Integration of Science and Human Values (SiSHVa) at the University of Peradeniya, Kandy, Sri Lanka, on October 17, 2007.

Chapter four, "The Evolution of Religion," was also presented at the University of Peradeniya, Kandy, Sri Lanka, November 1, 2007.

Chapter five, "The Neurosciences of Religion," was presented at the University of Peradeniya, Kandy, Sri Lanka, on November 22, 2007. This essay was published in *Metanexus* (January 2008) and is available online at http://www.metanexus.net/magazine/tabid/68/id/10260/Default.aspx as well as on my personal website. The essay was later translated into Spanish and published in *Tendencias21* http://www.tendencias21.net/m/index.php#3. This essay is substantially revised and edited for this book.

Chapter six, "The Medicine of Religion," was presented for the Society for the Integration of Science and Human Values at the University of Peradeniya, Kandy, Sri Lanka, on January 31, 2008.

Chapter seven, "The Narratives of Religion," is based in part on research on hermeneutics that was published in William Grassie's dissertation in 1994, as well as an adaptation of an essay entitled "Entangled Narratives: Competing Visions of the Good Life" presented at a symposium of the US-Sri Lankan Fulbright Commission in Colombo, Sri Lanka, on January 4, 2008. It was published in *Sri Lanka Journal of the Humanities* 34, nos. 1&2 (2008). The essay was then republished by Metanexus at http://www.metanexus.net/magazine/tabid/68/id/10473/Default.aspx. Chapter seven is significantly revised and edited for this book.

Other bits and pieces, here and there, have appeared in other essays online and in a collection of my essays: *Politics by Other Means: Science and Religion in the Twenty-First Century.* (Philadelphia: Metanexus Institute, 2010.)

Cover image: The dome of the Church of the Holy Sepulcher, Jerusalem. Photograph by Jeff Lefever © 2009. www.lefever.com.

Introduction

What is religion? What is spirituality? Both are involved in family and society, killing and eating, cooperating and competing, education and labor, values and norms, hierarchies and anarchies. Religions and spiritualities touch many intimate parts of our lives—at birth, during adolescence, in marriage, and at death, as well as at other transformative moments in the lives of individuals and societies.

We proceed at first from the common language uses of the terms without precise definitions. We note the historical ubiquity, the emotional valence, and the cultural diversity of religious and spiritual phenomena. Whatever religions and spiritualities may be, they certainly manifest themselves in a multitude of faiths and practices, behaviors and adaptations, and moods and motivations. They sometimes present themselves as naive superstitions and sometimes as profound metaphysical insights. Religions and spiritualities are involved in narratives and ideologies, philosophies and theologies. They are implicated in economic markets and in neural networks. They can inspire sublime emotions as well as ugly passions. The best and the worst things that humans do in life are often religiously motivated.

The serious study of religion cannot be disentangled from the diversity of disciplines that defines the modern university. The humanities, the social sciences, and the natural sciences are all implicated in the serious study of religious and spiritual phenomena. Whatever "a science of religion" might entail, it is necessarily interdisciplinary. Depending on what verities lie at the heart of the religious impulse, the study of religion may also be transdisciplinary in the sense that the religious insight precedes and transcends all disciplines and expertise, or at least many believers maintain.

A quick search on Google for the word *spirituality* returns over 54 million Internet sites that feature the term. The same search for the word *religion* returns 374 million Internet sites. A search for *God* gives an even higher count—487 million sites—but not as high as *sex*—733 million sites—or *money*, which registers over a billion Internet sites. These comparisons are not incidental, because, as we will learn, whatever religion is, it is not unrelated to sex and money.[1]

For the time being, I will use the term *religion* to denote many different religions and spiritualities. Later I will tease out some distinctions between the terms *religion* and *spirituality*. When I mean to emphasize the diversity of religions thereof, I will shift from the abstract singular, religion, to the plural, religions, knowing that the plural form also involves many layers of abstractions. Diversity exists not only between religions but also within each religious tradition that might be named—Hinduism, Buddhism, Judaism, Christianity, Islam, and so forth, down a list of many thousands of distinct creeds and cults.

Traditionally, one practices a particular religion and seeks spiritual verities inside an inherited tradition, as a member of a group, inhabiting a group's ethos and sacred history. Traditionally, one studies the sacred scriptures, sages, and saints, *inside* a particular worldview and culture. Committed scholars and students of a particular religion study the interpretation of sacred texts and history, the philology of ancient languages, the translation thereof into contemporary idioms, and the correct practice of rituals and liturgies. The purpose of this traditional study is to understand the authentic meaning of a particular revelation and to obtain a normative orientation to that which is called transcendent and divine.

In this book, I will start instead from the outside looking in, imagining myself to be detached and objective, even if such a standpoint is ultimately illusory. I imagine adopting this perspective from the outside, even though we are always self-implicated in that which we presume to study, perhaps religion most of all. No one can truly be objective, particularly about something so metaphysically, politically, and emotionally laden as religion, though people can certainly be wrong in how they read the evidence. I will, however, bracket the truth claims of religion for the time being and work instead with tentative naturalist and secularist assumptions. In this pursuit, I will employ numerous sciences—sociology, psychology, anthropology, economics, biology, neuroscience, and philosophy. I will also necessarily touch on ethics, politics, hermeneutics, and metaphysics. Working initially from the outside in and later from the bottom up, I seek to build a coherent scientific interpretation of religion that turns into a religious interpretation of science. In this manner, I will try to narrow the gap between religion and science, but not so far as to validate any particular revealed religion. I will argue against mythological literalism and for symbolic realism. The foundational stories of religions may not be true in a literal sense, but they are in some sense profound and precious. And while not true in every sense of the word, religions turn out to be extremely practical. Religion stands at the center of a remarkable human drama.

The metaphoric use of these directional adverbs—outside in and bottom up—captures the unique approach of this book. By imagining ourselves to stand outside a particular tradition and worldview, we end up with the possibility of returning to a particular tradition and worldview with a more robust understanding, one that is more wholesome and more plausible.

Because I start with science, I also start with a sense of scale and perspective. I assume the latest consensus on cosmology and evolution, including the macrohistory of human origins and the ten-thousand-year rise of human civilizations. I appreciate the remarkable cultural and technological evolution of our species. Science gives us a rigorous body of knowledge established through careful evidence-based research over many centuries. I understand humans to be a special symbolic species living at a remarkable moment in the natural history of our planet and of our own species' curious cultural evolution. This scientific consensus is the stage and setting for our exploration of religious and spiritual phenomena.

So, I ask again: What is religion? What is spirituality? How does one study this complex? How does one teach it? Are religions healthy and functional for individuals and societies, or are they unhealthy and dysfunctional? What does it mean to take a scientific approach to the study of religion? Does a scientific study of religion disprove the existence of God, the reality of nirvana, the possibility of miracles, and the hope of a life beyond death? These are difficult questions at the center of some of the most challenging controversies of the twenty-first century.

The scientific study of religion is not new. The idea of a "science of religion" was first proposed as such in 1872 by the German-born Oxford professor Friedrich Max Müller. The founders of the fields of psychology, sociology, and anthropology all had a lot to say about religion, most of it quite negative. And the last few years have witnessed a steady stream of new books by noted scientists and philosophers, the so-called New Atheists, purporting to explain religion scientifically, mostly with the intentions of explaining religion away.[2] This is not such a book. I have no expectation that religions will or should disappear. I do expect that religions will change and evolve in new times as they have always done in the past. I hope that the religions of the world, large and small, old and new, will contribute in many powerful and positive ways to crafting a safer and healthier world. I also recognize that many evil things are done in the name of religion and that these terrible things may not be incidental to the nature of religion or the nature of humanity. I predict religion to be the real wild card in future economic development, environmental health, and political well-being of the world. I believe that these new sciences of religion can help religions adapt to a rapidly changing world in more wholesome and indeed more authentic ways. A careful, far-reaching, and fair-minded science of religion will also help transform the sciences to be more objective and wholesome, appropriately metaphysical, and less blindly seduced by fashionable ideologies and prejudices.

A New Paradigm

The scientific approach to religion that I advocate in this book is *nonreductive functionalism*.[3] By "nonreductive," I mean that there is no single scientific paradigm or analytic framework from which to understand the complex phenomena of religion. I am not against employing reductionist explanations as a strategy. This is critical to any science. Religions, however, are multivariable and multileveled phenomena. No single analytic theory is adequate. We have to consider sociological, psychological, and anthropological theories of religion. These are the old sciences of religion, though they too have evolved in the last century. Today, we can supplement these with new economic, evolutionary, and neuroscientific theories of religion. These are the new sciences of religion, which I will explore in this book. To these, I will add a dose of the medicine of religion not only for good measure and better health but also because studies of spirituality and health help us better understand the challenges of studying religion as an independent variable. I will explicitly address the new hermeneutics of ancient scriptures in light of contemporary historical science. In this book, I will try on many different reductionist approaches to religion, knowing that each one acts as an epistemological filter for what we see and what we do not see. None of these approaches will be adequate, though all together will enlarge our understanding of religion and give us a new appreciation of this enduring dimension of human life.

In using the term "nonreductive," I will also make a larger metaphysical claim about the structure and limits of science. Science is not a unified epistemology, though it turns out to be a unified body of knowledge. It is better to talk about many different sciences, each with its own methods of inquiry and validation determined by the nature of the phenomena studied as adjudicated through the rigors of peer review. Science is a complex, diverse, and multileveled enterprise. An adequate philosophy of science today recognizes that there are emergent phenomena and that different methodologies need to be employed to account for different levels of complexity. Religion is also a complex and emergent phenomenon and, therefore, must be studied with multiple methodologies, none of which exhausts the meaning of the phenomenon.

That science is nonetheless a unified body of knowledge, knowledge that is progressively factual, requires, however, that we abandon mythological literalism in any plausible reinterpretation of religion. This is not really a problem, because these revelations were never intended to be understood as scientific textbooks, documentary movies on the History Channel, or the nightly reports on Fox News and Al Jazeera.

In employing the term "functionalism," I mean that religions exist and persist in part because they serve diverse human purposes. These functions work on the level of both individuals and groups. The sciences of religion must be open to understanding how religions differentially benefit individuals and groups and why they arose and thrived in the past and continue to do so in our contemporary world. Of course, to say that religions can be functional also implies that they can be dysfunctional, so I will explore the dark side of religion as well. Function and dysfunction often turn out to be closely related and context-specific. In social-scientific terminology, religions operate as both dependent and independent variables in human history and in individual lives.

When we do a functional analysis of religion rather than a comparison of different creeds, we notice that there may be as much functional diversity within a major tradition as there is between traditions. The typical focus on dogmas, doctrines, and stories by philosophers, theologians, and historians of religion blinds us to these many functional similarities that cut across cultural boundaries. This bias toward dividing religions by doctrinal differences is not a surprise, because, as we will learn, one of the many functions of religion is to maintain the boundaries of group identity. This question of boundaries also turns out to be a major preoccupation in the sciences and the philosophy of sciences, so border wars between science and religion, as well as between different religions, are to be expected and demand a new kind of diplomacy, supplemented also by a new kind of commerce and exchange between the cultures and domains of religions and sciences in our increasingly globalized civilization.

I argue that this new religion of science and the new sciences of religion do not necessarily threaten the core truth claims of the world's religions. The assumption that the scientific study of religion somehow discredits religion and supports atheism needs to be examined critically. Too many researchers are motivated by an ideological agenda of "explaining religion away." In other instances, the researchers are motivated by an apologetic agenda of revalorizing religion. These apologetic studies further distort the field because they invariably promote a particular tradition and worldview, for instance, taking Christianity to be normative. Science works best when it does not include strong biases for or against whatever the scientists study. Setting out to prove that religions are dysfunctional and regressive or that a particular religion is useful and superior is not going to result in good science or an adequate philosophy of religion.

What is called for is a phenomenological approach that brackets the truth claims of religions. A careful consideration of the complexity, diversity, commonality, and function of religion without regard to "truth" is the first step toward developing a descriptive science of religion. In this phenomenology of religion, however, we can only temporarily bracket these questions because part of the phenomenon is a deep commitment to a particular way of thinking and acting in the world. The truth of religion is not just a question for philosophers and theologians but a recurrent concern for clerics and lay people around the world and throughout history. So, we must ultimately ask what in religion might actually correspond to some understanding of ultimate reality.

From a scientific perspective, however, there is no a priori reason to privilege one tradition over another. We have three logical options with regard to the truth of religion. The first option is that all religions are grossly mistaken and contain no insights into ultimate reality, as witnessed by their inability to integrate the scientific worldview and critical thinking. This is the position advocated by the New Atheists. The second option is that there is one true religion and the others are inferior and mistaken. Science and comparative religion are largely irrelevant in this second case because this approach tends toward solipsistic rationalities. To the extent that science is considered, it will tend to be used selectively for apologetics. This is the position advocated by all proselytizing religious believers of different faiths. The third option is that all religions are partly true. In this understanding, religious stories and doctrines evolved in culturally and historically specific ways, but in ways that nevertheless enable them to transcend their specificity and establish universal profundities. If there were no mapping of religion onto some kind of truths in the universe and in the human person, then it would be difficult to understand why and how religions persist and why they evoke such fierce commitments and debates. Religions, in this third view, are then tested and filtered through centuries of human experience and must now be retested and reinterpreted in light of scientific realities. This approach also allows us to differentiate between traditions and different aspects of these traditions because religions need not be seen as equally true, good, and useful. Some may be deemed better or worse than others based on their correspondence to certain truths or their pragmatic impact in the contemporary global environment or past situations. The third option is my point of departure and a distinctively minority position in the world. I will argue that religions are all partly true and that they actually correspond to something profound and real in the universe. I seek to establish this by way of this long detour and a lot of detective work from the *outside in* and the *bottom up*.

Nonreductive functionalism, therefore, leaves open the possibility that religions are in some sense also true, perhaps true about the most profound and important existential issues that humans face, but this approach requires that I work circuitously before presuming to understand the central core. Revealed traditions address this ultimate reality by many names: as Allah, and Mohammed is his Prophet (PBUH [Peace be upon him]); as Jesus Christ, my Lord and Savior; as the God of Abraham, Isaac, Jacob, and the Hebrew prophets; as the avatars of Brahma; as the Buddha nature in all things; and as Ch'i, the Dao, Shang Ti, and Li in the Chinese traditions. The approach taken in this book gets us perhaps as far as the concept of *God-by-whatever-name*, but not so far as a *God-by-a-specific-name*. I consider many different religions because I do not intend to privilege any particular religious tradition, though certainly my own cultural biases, intellectual finitude, and contextual limitations will leave their marks on this inquiry. After considering various sciences of religion and a religious interpretation of science, all of us will have a fuller and richer understanding of the phenomena. Having taken this journey, we will be better able to address the many truth claims of religions.

Are religions one, or are they many? Are some religions "better" than others? Are religions mutually exclusive? These are tough questions, which in the end may only be satisfactorily addressed inside a particular tradition, much as people speak one particular human language at a time. Working scientifically from the outside in and the bottom up, I will end at a place I call *particularist universalism*. I will have closed the gap between religion in general and science in general, but I will not get as far as establishing the validity of any particular religion. New constraints will be introduced on the interpretation of religion as well as on the interpretation of science.

This book is an exploration. We will cover an impossibly broad territory, many sciences, and many religions, the latter including many different scriptures, histories, languages, and cultures. As already noted, science works best when it does not contain a strong ideological project. Religion, on the other hand, works best when it is motivated by a deep commitment. This journey requires that we suspend our prejudices and commitments, if only for a time. Let's leave our biases behind, pro or con, and try to understand the phenomena on their own terms, in new and unexpected ways, without flattening manifest and multilevel complexities. I promise to return my religiously inclined readers safely to their church, synagogue, mosque, or temple, though different for the journey and with many new tools for thinking about ancient verities and universal truths. And I promise to return my scientifically inclined readers safely to their study, laboratory, or classroom with a new and humble appreciation of science and the incredible complexity of the human phenomenon.

An Apostate's Journey

My interest in religion is not simply academic. I have my own existential doubts and worries, my own family of origins and societal context, and my own philosophical and ideological commitments. In exploring these new sciences of religion, I am also seeking something. Let's call it wisdom based on credible beliefs. I am a seeker of transcendent meaning and purpose in life, which also entails transcendent meaning and purpose in death. As you will soon discover, I am a student of all religions, an expert in none, and respectfully heterodox in my approach. This book, as are all scholarly undertakings, is partly an autobiographical journey.

For me, as with all of us, the challenge of religion and spirituality began in my youth, in my family, in a particular social location and time. The sociology of religion suggests that one's family of birth is the biggest determinant of whether and how one will be religious. As adolescents and young adults, people today often become disillusioned with their family's religious orientation; but as they grow older, particularly when they themselves have children, they tend to drift back to the religion of their family of origin. Sometimes the disillusionment is more severe, resulting in a deep alienation from religion and family, but generally with a very specific content informed by childhood and adolescent experiences in a particular religious milieu. Conversion to a different tradition turns out to be very unusual—not many Jews become Buddhist, not many Christians become Muslim, not many Hindus become Christian, and not many "scientists" become religious. I am a convert of the latter sort, an apostate of a different kind, a scientist-by-birth, if such a thing were truly possible, who became fascinated with religion as an adult.

Scientists, of course, are not born; they are trained in a discipline over many years. Today, I make the distinction between science and scientism, the latter being my family's "religious" orientation. I grew up in Wilmington, Delaware, in the 1960s and early 1970s. My parents had moved to Wilmington from Canada to work in the growing chemical industry. My father studied chemistry at the University of British Columbia and McGill. He was the first in his family to go to college, let alone receive a doctorate, and was hired out of graduate school to be a research scientist at the Hercules Chemical Corporation. I was the fifth of six children. We attended a Unitarian-Universalist church as children with my mother. This particular congregation at that particular time was secular humanist. The G-word would never be mentioned in the minister's sermons. The hymns sung, while often traditional, had been rewritten in keeping with the secular ethos of the congregation, which was composed mostly of other research scientists' families from Hercules, DuPont, and the other chemical and pharmaceutical corporations located in Wilmington. In Sunday School classes, we did "situation ethics."

Though we never really discussed religion much as a family, or for that matter at church, somehow I came to believe that religion was "a crutch" used by people who could not deal with reality. Belief in God was for stupid and weak people. The dominant religion, Christianity, was held out for particular disdain, Catholics and Pentecostals most of all. Science was worthy of our confidence and effort. We had faith in science and were expected to grow up and become scientists. Science was understood to be the antithesis of religion. We believed that all religions were the same, so we valued none of them equally. This is unfair to Unitarian-Universalists in general, but it was true of my particular congregation and my particular family in that place and time. Today, in jest, I call myself "a recovering Unitarian-Universalist."

The story of my growing interest in religion is a tall tale I shall leave for another occasion. Suffice it to say that I increasingly found myself like a character in Edwin Abbott's 1884 novel *Flatland,* and the dimensions in my world expanded from two to three to four.[4] The geometry of my intellect would soon be plotted on curved surfaces. The fundamental axioms and assumptions of my childish scientific worldview were neither adequate nor real. I had experienced what Alfred North Whitehead called "the fallacy of misplaced concreteness."[5]

There were other crises in my youth that caused me to question the atheism and scientism I had absorbed as a child. These were existential and moral crises, related to the tumultuous events of 1968, my father's death in 1969, the first Earth Day in 1970, experimentation with drugs in high school, romantic loves won and lost, and my hitchhiking through Europe, Canada, and the United States in the 1970s. Suffice it to say that by the time I got to college, I was no longer interested in becoming a scientist, though a certain aptitude and fascination for science remained.

Fast forward through my undergraduate studies at Middlebury College, a voyeuristic year studying religion and politics in Jerusalem, ten years of working with religiously based peace-and-reconciliation organizations, marriage and children, graduate school, a dissertation on science and religion, and university teaching to the founding of the Metanexus Institute on Religion and Science.[6] The curious term *metanexus* was created by taking the Greek prefix *meta-,* meaning "transcending or transforming," and combining it with the Latin noun, *nexus*, meaning "connection or core." Philologists say that one should never combine Greek and Latin.[7] Similarly, it seems the terms *science* and *religion* should not be in too close proximity in our culture. Metanexus literally means "transcending and transformational networks." The world needs bridges between different academic disciplines, different institutional forms, and different religious and cultural traditions that will help us transcend and transform our thinking and doing in wholesome and creative ways. That remains the rather large ambition of a very humble organization with which I have been privileged to work and learn.

This book is the product of that journey. It is a journey that took me around the world—Cambodia, Canada, China, Colombia, England, France, Germany (East and West), Greece, India, Indonesia, Iran, Israel, Italy, Lebanon, Mexico, Nepal, Palestine, Poland, Spain, Scotland, the Soviet Union (but not yet Russia), Sri Lanka, Switzerland, Thailand, Turkey, Yugoslavia (the former and the divided). It is also a journey that afforded me the opportunity to meet with many of the world's greatest scientists and religious thinkers. For much of the learning, I am especially in debt to the twelve years in which I worked with Metanexus, work that was supported in large part by the John Templeton Foundation. In this capacity, I ran or attended dozens of international conferences on topics covered in this book. I also managed numerous requests for proposals, distributing many millions of dollars in research funding to hundreds of scientific studies on religious and spiritual phenomena. This book, indeed the need for this book, is a result of these studies, conversations, and travels.

The Map Is Not the Territory

How will this exploration proceed? The argument is presented in two parts, nine chapters, and a conclusion. Part 1 examines the new sciences of religion, specifically economic, evolutionary, neuroscientific, and medical models of religion. Here I work from the *outside in* to try to understand how religions work for individuals and groups. Part 2 is an attempt to ground religious truths from the *bottom up*, working tentatively from the new naturalistic worldview without privileging a received tradition or a revealed text. This is the new religion of science, but not in the sense of scientism, which has aspired since the Enlightenment to somehow replace religion with science. My goal in part 2 is to delineate how some of the core truth claims of religion might be grounded in the contemporary scientific worldview.

In the first chapter, I explore the problem of classifying and defining religion and spirituality. The very diversity of the phenomena will be the central problem. I consider the insider/outsider challenge in the study of religion and argue through an analogy to linguistics that it is possible to decode a universal "grammar" of religion that transcends the diversity of beliefs and practices. Indeed, I argue that there is more functional diversity within any major tradition than there is functional diversity between major traditions.

In chapter two, I examine the "old" sciences of religion by focusing on the thoughts of Auguste Comte, an eccentric French genius who profoundly influenced Karl Marx, Sigmund Freud, Émile Durkheim, and other early theorists of religion. This discussion will lay out some of the different theoretical approaches to the scientific study of religion. I then develop the concept of nonreductive functionalism, the basic analytic orientation of this book. Readers who are familiar with the challenges of comparative religion and the Enlightenment intellectuals may choose to skim these preliminary chapters.

In chapter three, I begin with the new sciences of religion by considering the impact of religions on economic development, as well as economic models for understanding religions. I offer a brief case study of economic development and Islam. Economic terminology, such as "utility function," "opportunity costs," "social capital," and "rational choice," will be employed to understand the dynamics of religion as a variable in economics. I consider also how social values, often encoded in religious context, are a part of the formula for economic development. The chapter works toward considering both religion and economics as symbolic systems of value that radically change the material world.

In chapter four, I turn to evolutionary theories of religion, offering an understanding of religious beliefs and behavior through the lens of survival and reproduction. Three competing evolutionary accounts of religion will be considered. Two of these approaches argue that religions are a dysfunctional by-product of human cognitive evolution. The other approach argues that religions are evolutionary adaptations that served to promote group survival and reproduction. I offer a fourth possible interpretation that takes a bit from each, but sees also the profound ways in which humans have increasingly transcended biology.

In chapter five, I turn to the cognitive neurosciences to try to understand religious experience inside the brain. I look at a number of different models, including disease and injury-based models, brain-imaging studies, pharmaceutical studies, and developmental studies, ending by considering a number of scientific and philosophical problems with this approach. Along the way, I will also develop a much more detailed typology of religious experience.

In next chapter, I take on the medicine of religion. There is a growing interest in spirituality and health, and much interesting research has been conducted in the field. I discuss the problem of measurement, research design, and research results, including double-blinded, controlled, randomized trials of spiritual interventions. I consider complementary and alternative medicine as part of the spirituality-and-health marketplace. The growing fields of psychoneuroimmunology and psychoneuroendocrinology now provide plausible "top-down" causal pathways inside the mind-brain-body to account for the efficaciousness of spiritual attitudes, rituals, and interventions. I argue for a new appreciation of placebos in all medical therapies in what I call "the deep semiotics of health."

Part 2 begins with chapter seven, on the narratives of religion. I return to the question of whether and how religions may be true by first considering the status of revealed scriptures in a bottom-up approach. Even as the natural sciences challenge the plausibility of religious cosmologies, the historical sciences challenge most people's understanding of sacred scriptures as revealed texts. Instead, serious scholars understand scriptures to be human-authored and politically redacted texts that arose in specific historical and cultural contexts. As a case in point, I examine current scholarship on the New Testament and then posit new ways of interpreting sacred text as profound stories and humans as profoundly storied creatures. The latter insight begins a larger discussion of the narrative nature of human nature. In this postmodern moment, there is an apparent inability to adjudicate between solipsistic religious rationalities and other self-referential worldviews, because the narratives employed structure how we think and even what counts as relevant evidence. I develop a new hermeneutic for thinking about the many entangled and conflicting narratives in our global civilization. I argue for a limited field of plausible interpretations based on a critical-realist understanding of science, but do so in a way that distinguishes between science and the interpretation of science. Nor is it the case that the scientific approach is capable of describing the entire complexity of the universe and human experience.

In chapter eight, I use religious categories to develop a new metaphysics of science. I argue that the natural and human sciences lend themselves to a new religious worldview. This new "religion of science" is not necessarily antithetical to traditional religions; indeed, it offers insights that may lead to the recovery of neglected, perhaps more authentic, interpretations of sacred scriptures. Here I work from the bottom up toward a robust concept of transcendence through science. To do so requires a short tutorial in the philosophy of science and an argument for critical realism in science based on what I call symbolic realism. Along the way, I offer a new composite definition of science.

Finally, in chapter nine, I move in a more theological direction, developing the concept of God-by-whatever-name from the bottom up. I argue for a new understanding of God-talk in intellectual and religious discourse. The many languages of God, much like human languages, share a common "grammatical" structure as well as a common "semantic" reference in the lived experiences of humans in diverse contexts. I close by affirming the diversity of religions, much like the diversity in human languages, in what I call *particularist universalism.*

The short conclusion then brings this all back together in five propositions.

Caveat Emptor

The juxtaposition of the concepts "science" and "religion" in our civilization is a kind of Rorschach test for all kinds of deeply held prejudices and beliefs. The terms are often thought of almost as antonyms and reflect a profound cultural ambivalence in our postmodern, global civilization. This book has a big ambition in trying to close this gap between the domains of science and religion. The approach is to develop a network of transcending and transformational connections—a metanexus—between diverse sciences and religious traditions. While I write primarily for scholars of religion and the social scientists who study religion, as well as for their students, I will attempt to present the findings in a manner useful to those educated lay readers who are willing to slog through some technical vocabulary. I write for both the scientifically inclined and the religiously motivated, though not necessarily in the same person.

Writing for an interdisciplinary audience is particularly challenging, as I cannot assume a common foundation of information upon which to build. Some parts of this book will seem introductory and obvious to experts in a particular field. There are many books and authors referenced herein that might be a better guide to some particular area of expertise. I am simplifying and reducing huge areas of scholarship into short chapters and make no claim to be an expert in any or all the fields under consideration. What is different about this book and unique about my approach is that it is informed by training in comparative religion, the philosophy of science, and the philosophy of interpretation. What is also different about this book is the large sweep of disciplines that I try to bring to bear upon its central questions. Its strength will no doubt also be its weakness.

Specialization rules today in academics and with good reason. Humans have made enormous progress through specialization and the division of labor. Yet we miss out on many important and crucial insights if all we do is specialize. An overly specialized and compartmentalized mind is also an impoverished mind. It will lack the tools for appropriate generalizations and creative synthesis, tending to mistake a particular map for real life. An overly compartmentalized civilization is a fragmented civilization easily torn apart by sectarian forces. In overspecialization, we will not understand the varieties of knowledge, their limitations, their uses and abuses. If we misunderstand the unity and value of knowledge, then we will fail at building civil, democratic, scientific, humane, and healthy societies and at being productive citizens of such societies.

In writing a book that aims at such a wide-ranging synthesis, I risk making a fool of myself. Many specialists will be quick to criticize the inadequacies of my scholarship and the deficiencies in my analysis. In 1943, Edwin Schrödinger, the Nobel Prize–winning physicist, gave a series of lectures in Dublin, which became the book *What is Life?* (1944). Schrödinger was an expert in quantum mechanics. He was not trained in biology, geology, paleontology, not even really in astronomy; but he risked undertaking one of the first truly modern syntheses of science, sensing that science was putting together in bits and pieces a new, unified evolutionary cosmology. He acknowledges the dangers involved at the outset of his book:

> We have inherited from our forefathers the keen longing for unified, all-embracing knowledge. The very name given to the highest institutions of learning remind us, that from antiquity and throughout many centuries, the universal aspect has been the only one to be given full credit. But the spread, both in width and depth, of the multifarious branches of knowledge during the last hundred odd years has confronted us with a queer dilemma. We feel clearly that we are only now beginning to require reliable material for welding together the sum total of all that is known into a whole; but, on the other hand, it has become next to impossible for a single mind to fully command more than a small specialized portion of it. I can see no other escape from this dilemma (lest our true aim be lost for ever) than that some of us should venture to embark on a synthesis of facts and theories, albeit with second-hand and incomplete knowledge of some of them—and at the risk of making fools of ourselves. So much for my apology.[8]

I am no Edwin Schrödinger, but I will use his apology as my own. This book is a synthesis of "second-hand and incomplete knowledge." There is no other way that such a book could be written. My attempt and intention are to piece together a larger puzzle by reading widely, seeking everywhere, and keeping an open mind.

This book will be easier if the reader retains the concept of nonreductive functionalism, an approach that we will keep coming back to with many examples and applications. Nonreductive functionalisms means that (1) religions can be both functional and dysfunctional depending on the context and (2) there is no single analytic framework sufficient to understanding this multileveled and multivariable phenomenon. This is part 1 of the book, in which we work from the outside in. Implied in nonreductive functionalism are two additional corollaries: (3) religions may in some sense be profound, indeed profoundly true, and (4) the adjudication of such truth requires a thoroughgoing reinterpretation of religion in dialogue with contemporary science and history. This is part 2 of the book, in which we work from the bottom up.

The sciences of religion are devilishly complex. The people who do social-scientific research on religion often lack an understanding and appreciation of the multileveled complexity and diversity of the phenomena they purport to study and explain. As I detail in the chapters that follow, they draw conclusions that may not be generalizable. They sometimes infer causation from correlations. They regularly assume a metaphysics and interpretation that need not be so and, indeed, may not be justified. They often import ideological and apologetic biases. They can be remarkably arrogant and confused. They study the trees but miss the forest.

By taking a broad overview of the new sciences of religion, I hope to offer a better appreciation of religion and spirituality, whatever the terms may actually mean, and, therefore, also a more rounded and wholesome understanding of the human phenomenon. If I succeed, we will see the whole forest but also a lot of different trees and a good deal of the details in the complex religious ecosystems that we all inhabit, even those who call themselves atheists.

Far from turning us all into atheists, the new sciences of religion should turn us back to religion, but in new ways. Yes, mythological literalism in religions will be undermined, but the enduring questions and perspectives raised by religions will be revalorized in society and in intellectual life. The new sciences of religion will lead us to a more authentic and more wholesome understanding of religion in our individual and collective lives at an extraordinary moment in the cultural evolution of our species and the natural history of our planet. At least, that is my hope. That is what I have discovered along the way and hope to share with the reader in these pages. In the end, you will be the judge of whether I have succeeded to your edification and satisfaction.

PART 1

Religion from the Outside In

CHAPTER ONE

The Challenge of Comparative Religion

There are some preliminaries that need to be addressed. We think we know what religion is and what religions are at first consideration. There is Christianity, with its Catholic, Protestant, and Orthodox varieties. There is Judaism, which now comes in the flavors of Reform, Reconstructionist, Conservative, and Orthodox, as well as its Ashkenazi and Sephardic ethnic variations. There is Islam, which comes in the form of Sunni, Shiite, and Sufi, the latter being a somewhat mixed category. There is Hinduism, which comes with a huge pantheon of gods, philosophies, and practices—too many to list. Buddhism, on the other hand, is neatly divided into two streams—Theravada and Mahayana—although this turns out to be quite misleading. In China, we find a synchronistic mix of Taoism and Confucianism, which also picked up a lot of Buddhism along the way. To this survey, we might add a few smaller but significant sects, including Sikhism, Jainism, and Zoroastrianism from South Asia, as well as innumerable primal religions from surviving indigenous peoples all around the world. Shintoism in Japan and other ancestor-worship cults might be best understood as surviving primal religions. The absence of Baha'i from this list will disturb some, but then I did not include Yoruba religions either. This is the basic typology of the standard "Introduction to World Religions" course offered to undergraduates at colleges and universities all over the United States.

If we wanted to be more comprehensive, we would need to add extinct religions to the list. Two thousand years ago, the Greek and Roman religious synthesis would have been the world's largest religion. Today, we study the mythology, history, and archeology of this era, but we do not find people actually worshipping Zeus, Athena, Dionysus, and the rest. Similarly, the ancient Egyptian pantheon—Amun, Isis, Ma'at, Osiris, Ra, and others—was the dominant religion of the Nile Valley civilizations beginning about 3000 B.C.E. Elsewhere we also discover extinct cultures and extinct religions—Olmec, Mayan, Aztec, Inca, Babylon, Celtic, Germanic, Norse, and Slavic, to list but a few. "Extinct" is perhaps too strong a word, as these religions have evolved and in many ways have profoundly influenced our contemporary civilizations. Recollect for a moment that Christmas trees and Easter eggs are pre-Christian pagan practices that became major features of Christian holidays. We are also witnessing neopagan revival movements that try to recreate some of these religions from the past in our contemporary world.

In terms of numbers, Christianity is the largest religion in the world today, consisting of some 2.1 billion adherents, or 33 percent of the world's population. Islam is next, consisting of some 1.5 billion people or 21 percent of the world's population. Hinduism accounts for some 900 million people, or 14 percent of the world's population. Buddhism accounts for 376 million people, or 6 percent of the world's population. Chinese traditional religions, which includes many Buddhists, account for another 394 million people or 6 percent of the world's population.[1]

By some counts, "nonreligious" comes in third after Christianity and Islam, beating out Hinduism, which is left in fourth place. "Nonreligious" accounts for some 1.1 billion people or 16 percent of the world's population, but this term turns out to be difficult to define and to measure. The nonreligious category includes agnostics, atheists, and secular humanists, as we might expect; but it also includes people who have conventional and unconventional religious beliefs but who do not belong to and practice within a conventional religious institution. In other words, many of these are people who might describe themselves as "spiritual, but not religious." We will come back to that curious phrase. Note that the largest numbers of "nonreligious" are in Russia and China, which had formally antireligious governments until quite recently. Today in China, the Communist Party is promoting a revival of traditional religions for sociological, economic, and ideological reasons, so these numbers might be very different in a decade or two. All these statistics are suspect, given changing demographics, changing beliefs, and the inherent difficulty of estimating these numbers, not to mention the motivations of those for whom such "soul counting" matter.

Given the diversity of beliefs and practices inside these major traditions, this typology of "great" religions may not be all that useful. Think for a moment about the great variety of Christian denominations, beliefs, and practices. Is this really one religious movement or many? Sociologists estimate that there are some 4,200 distinct subcategories of "religion" in the world today, but this list does not include other kinds of "primary identity subcultures and movements," which we might better classify as "religions."[2] These might include Communist groups, objectivist libertarians, vegetarian/animal-rights activists, feminist movements, evangelical environmentalists, racial supremacists, science-fiction cults, occult practitioners, sport-and-fitness fanatics, political parties, ethnic separatist movements, Alcoholics Anonymous and other twelve-step movements, drug subculture, goth and rave subcultures, technophiles, and a whole slew of other possibilities for "primary identity subcultures and movements."

What is your "primary-identity subculture"? For many reading this book, science will be that identity, so we will have to ask if and how it is appropriate to apply this type of sociological analysis to understanding the phenomena of scientists doing science, in this case doing the sciences of religion.

Elusive Definitions

If we want to talk about the new sciences of religion, then we are going to need to talk about definitions. Given the complexity and diversity involved, I prefer to use the phrase "the sciences of religious and spiritual phenomena." The words themselves—*religion* and *spirituality*—beg for rigorous definitions, but this will prove elusive. The term *religion* is derived from the Latin verb *religare*, which means "to tie together, to bind fast." In the original understanding, "religion" was about expressing proper piety, that is, binding oneself to God. Later, the term would also be used to designate a bounded belief systems and set of practices, as in the religions of the Greeks, Romans, Jews, Muslims, Hindus, Chinese, and others.

Today, in the United States and elsewhere, it is quite common for people to say that they are "spiritual, not religious." The definition of *spiritual* is also elusive. The term derives from the Latin *spiritus*. The Latin verb root is *spirare*, literally, "to breathe." The connotation is that we are surrounded by a divine reality as pervasive, intimate, necessary, and invisible as the air we breathe. Similar concepts can be found in the Hindu word *prana*. The Chinese concept of *chi* energy may be analogous. Jewish mystics noted that the sacred name of God in Hebrew, YHWH, a name written in the Bible but never pronounced aloud by pious Jews, might itself be understood as the sound of human breath—an inhalation "YH" and an exhalation "WH." Thus, every time a person breathes, she is actually saying the name of God. Muslim mystics make similar claims about the aspiration of the name *Al-lah*. To talk of spirituality, then, is to affirm that there is an all-encompassing realm, an invisible reality that somehow transcends and sustains human life, consciousness, and values, indeed the entire universe.

In the contemporary context, the phrase "spiritual, not religious" is used to disassociate oneself from the institutional and historical manifestations of religions. One wants the "goods" without the long histories of failures and hypocrisy. Religions are organized groups. Spirituality is something an individual can have without being implicated in the ambivalent complexity of human societies and institutions. In this sense, "spiritual, not religious" can be seen as a modern manifestation of a historical, sociological cycle of trying to recapture the imagined authentic, unmediated, and uncorrupted origins of religion. This pattern of recurrent reformations turns out to be a theme in many revitalization movements in diverse traditions—an attempt to return to an imagined original, pure connection with a foundational moment, a mystical experience, or the teachings of a charismatic leader.[3] Humans, of course, are a social and political species, so it is only a matter of time before "spirituality" also gets messy. Indeed, the notion "spiritual, not religious" is itself the product of a culture that emphasizes individualism and consumerism.

I prefer the term *religion* precisely because it invites us to look at and, more importantly, take responsibility for the entire complexity of the phenomena—the good, the bad, and the ambivalent—which is not to say that I do not also seek to breathe and take direct personal inspiration from an invisible spiritual reality that is all around me, everywhere, all the time. I just do not trust myself or anyone else to be an unbiased and uncorrupted pure vessel for that everywhere-present Presence, whatever it might be.

The term *religion* does not simply translate into other cultures and languages. In Sanskrit, the Hindu term used to indicate religion is *dharma*, which means "teaching" or "practice"; but this is hardly a parallel concept, and much that is not *dharma* would count as religion in Hinduism. In Chinese, the term *Zongjiao* was coined in the modern era to mean religion. The etymology of the term reflects a Confucian understanding of the teaching of lineage.[4] In Judaism, the Hebrew word *dat*, meaning law, is used, reflecting a Jewish preoccupation with religious laws and justice. In Arabic, the term *religion* is translated as *din*, meaning simply "the path" or "the way." Regardless of how it is translated, the modern European concept of religion has now traveled the world and reached humans everywhere in our global civilization's struggle to understand how religions stand apart from and perhaps transcend other dimensions of human culture.

Religion from the Inside

Most people in the past and today study religion from the *inside*, as a believer and practitioner of a particular tradition. A Jew studies Judaism; a Buddhist studies Buddhism; a Muslim studies Islam. This book is mostly about studying religion from the *outside* as a nonbeliever and nonpractitioner, but it is important to note that a serious study of a religion from the *inside* is complicated and engaging work. The subject matter—"my religion"—deals with *self, society,* and *cosmos*. Religion from the *inside* has a lot to say about what it means to be a fully realized individual human, living in a social context with other humans in a universe imbued with power, purpose, and significance.

The subject matter—my religion—is *diverse, particular,* and *universal.* Any serious study of one's own religion from the inside will show that there is heterogeneity within any major tradition. The tradition as a whole and in its diversity relates to particular histories, languages, and cultures. In spite of this diversity and particularism, every religion also makes universal truth claims that apply to all humans everywhere at all times—indeed, truth claims about the fundamental character of the universe as a whole. One of the major preoccupations of the study of religion from the inside is this diversity. Until recently, most religious arguments were inside the tradition, trying to establish a normative understanding of the tradition in opposition to "heretical" understandings of that same tradition—Sunni Muslims versus Shiite Muslims, Theravada Buddhists versus Mahayana Buddhists, Protestant Christians versus Catholic Christians, Evangelical Protestants versus other Protestants, liberal interpretations versus conservative interpretations, charismatic-mystical approaches versus rational-textual approaches, and so forth.

For instance, there are hundreds of different sects within Christianity. Recently, I had the opportunity to visit with Maronite Christians in Lebanon. They speak Arabic in their homes and use the ancient language of Syriac-Aramaic in their liturgies. Their priests marry, but the Maronite Church is affiliated with the Roman Catholic Church, which forbids priests to marry. It would take a lot of history to explain this interesting situation. In spite of these idiosyncrasies, their understanding of Christianity—of sin, sacrifice, sanctification, and salvation—is taken to be universally true for all people, not just Lebanese Maronites. We could fill this book and many libraries with other examples from around the world of a tradition's diversity, particularity, and universality.

It turns out that a serious study of religion from the inside requires a lot of work. One needs to study the tradition, its sacred scriptures, the original languages in which scriptures were written, the translations and interpretations of those scriptures, the histories of the tradition, the legal codes and case law within that tradition, the liturgical practices, the saints and sages, the tradition's teachings about the everyday, mundane life—and all this while paying attention to one's own personal

Figure 1.1   Studying Religion from the *Inside*.

experiences as a believer and practitioner within the tradition. Of course, studying the tradition—my religion—is supremely about some concept of the sacred, the divine, a notion of transcendence, God-by-whatever-name (see Figure 1.1).

We will come back to the divine mystery, the God question at the center of all religious phenomena. I will argue throughout this book that it is inappropriate for the sciences of religion qua science to try to resolve the God question.[5] For now, note only how intimidating a serious study of religion from the inside would be. A scholar of Christianity, for instance, would need to know Latin, Greek, and Hebrew, just to begin with biblical interpretation. If he is a serious scholar, he is also going to study Aramaic and Syriac because these were the languages spoken in first-century Palestine by Jesus and the apostles. Then he is certainly going to need to know French, German, and English because so much of Christian history and thought was shaped inside these European languages and cultures. And that is just the language-study part of the curriculum.

Believers and practitioners of a religion are always looking for a short-cut to the sacred that will bypass all this hard work—and understandably so. It is just too much homework, and life is short. Hence, the contemporary phenomenon of "spiritual, not religious" is a recurrent theme as old as humanity itself. Religions would be pretty useless if everyone were required to do all this hard work. There exists a division of labor in the domains of religion with a class of religious professionals, who can be playfully and cynically referred to as "the second oldest profession." There is also the hope and the promise of having "authentic" experience and "unmediated" inspiration of the spiritual origins that motivate the religious quest. In the Christian idiom, we might call such an experience being "born again." The ecstasy of St. Paul at the crossroads is preferred to the agony of Jesus on the Cross and the graduate student writing a dissertation. The gospel of health, wealth, and eternal bliss is an easier sell than "pick up your cross and follow me." Spiritual inspiration is just so much easier than strenuous scholarship or sacrificial service. A lifetime devoted to the serious study of religion from the inside, particularly in the contemporary world, is not likely to be a very remunerative career choice, although for some it turns out to be extremely profitable and we wonder how and why.

Of course, some believers take their faith very seriously and devote themselves to the daily study of ancient scriptures. They attend religious services regularly. Some people know their "book" backward and forward and can quote with precision chapter and verse. Some significant few do undertake sacrificial service based on their deeply held convictions. We find such people working with the homeless in our cities, in the refugee camps around the world, adopting AIDS orphans in Africa, and much more. In all walks of life, there are serious insiders who orient their entire lives around the reading and interpretation of some sacred text and tradition. For such persons, "spiritual *and* religious" would be the better description.

Outside In

Today, we are also all confronted with the challenge of studying religion from the *outside* because we live in a world where we are confronted with diverse beliefs and practices. The German poet, scientist, and philosopher Johann Wolfgang von Goethe said that "he who knows one, knows none." Goethe was talking about human languages. If we only know our *Muttersprache*, the language we were raised speaking, then we do not understand the magic of language at all. Precisely by learning a foreign language with some facility and felicity one understands the grammatical, semantic, and semiotic structure of language in general, including of one's own native tongue.

Is Goethe's aphorism about human languages applicable to human religions? When studying a human language, after a lot of hard work and practice, one can hope to experience a remarkable and progressive gestalt shift in which *outside* knowing becomes *inside* knowing. When fluency is acquired, the student begins to think, feel, and dream inside that foreign language, no longer translating as she goes, but living within that language. Can one have the same experience of a foreign religion? Can one be fully Muslim and Buddhist, at the same time, switching back and forth, as if between English and French? Can one be Christian, Jewish, and Hindu at the same time, especially when we understand that the traditions themselves sometimes talk of exclusive truth claims available only to the initiated member? It may not be possible, but one of the useful insights from the analogy to human languages is that we should not think it easy to obtain multiple "fluencies" in comparative religions. Comparative religion may be no easier to approach than, say, learning Mandarin or Tamil as an outsider.

Yet, in spite of the challenges of comparative religion, we recognize today that we are all members of the same species. We share the same biology, the same DNA, and the same blood. Humans share the same basic physiological trajectory and psychological repertoire throughout the world. We are conceived in passion, born in pain, and have a long period of childhood dependency. If we are lucky, we grow older and are initiated into adulthood with its pleasures and pains and a growing mastery of skills and ideas, always with the necessity of crafting our lives and identities in networks—familial, social, economic, cultural, and ecological. We may have children. If we are lucky, we grow old, perhaps wiser. We all anticipate and someday confront the terror and the mystery of death.

It matters not with respect to our biology whether we are Muslim, Hindu, Christian, Buddhist, Jew, Atheist, or Stoic. It matters not what ethnic or racial background we belong to. We can all interbreed, that is, we are one biological species, and we are all confronted with similar psychological, social, and biological challenges by virtue of being *Homo sapiens*. The anthropologist Donald Brown has compiled a list of 300 human universals that appear in every human culture.[6] The question now becomes how to account for the variation in human cultures and religions and how significant are these variations in the sciences of religion.

Every leaf on an oak tree is technically unique, but we can safely ignore these differences in the taxonomy of oak trees. Is comparative religion like comparing leaves on a single tree? Or is it more like comparing different species of trees, in which case our "dendrology" of different religions will have some significant differences as well as many compelling similarities? What if religions are more akin to different families, phyla, and kingdoms in nature, so that comparing them is like comparing trees, reptiles, birds, mammals, and insects? In this case, we are going to have a much less compelling case for a science of religion; there can be only sciences of particular religions. The differences that matter, or not, turn out to be an important and highly charged issue in comparative religion and the scientific study thereof.

In the last decades, the academic study of religion has rebelled against grand comparative theories of religion and instead has focused on differences, described with increasing detail and nuance. It is too simplistic and certainly counterfactual to say simply that all religions are the same. The academic rebellion is partly in opposition to Mircea Eliade (1907–1986) and others, who purported to have a grand unified theory of religion, theories that were obscurantist in their leaps to overgeneralize and often lacking in empirical evidence.[7] Other religious universalist theorists, like C. G. Jung (1875–1961), tended themselves to be morphed by their intellectual descendants into their own sectarian creeds and cults.[8] The fashion today in the guild of the American Academy of Religion is to distrust religious universalism, grand theories, and triumphant syntheses, even as the new sciences of religion aspire to achieve this God's-eye analytic vantage point on the phenomenon of religion.

Religions themselves tend to be uncomfortable with the label "religion," suggesting that they are merely one among many. "Authentic" Christianity, for instance, invites its followers to have a personal relationship with Jesus Christ, the Lord and Savior, and "by no other name" shall salvation be achieved (Acts 4:12). It makes an exclusivist claim, although we could point to other scriptural sources and interpretations that would argue within the Christian idiom against this very exclusivity.[9]

There is simply no such thing as "generic religion," which puts a damper on the proposed scientific study of religion. The twentieth-century Harvard philosopher and atheist George Santayana (1863–1952) notes:

All religion is positive and particular. Any attempt to speak without speaking any particular language is not more hopeless than the attempt to have a religion that shall be no religion in particular....Every living and healthy religion has a marked idiosyncrasy. Its power consists in its special and surprising message and the bias, which that revelation gives to life. The vistas it opens and the mysteries it propounds are another world to live in: and another world to live in—whether we expect ever to pass wholly over into it or no—is what we mean by having a religion.[10]

An Analogy to Linguistics

Let's turn Santayana's analogy between particular religions and particular human languages upside down, recalling also our discussion of Goethe's aphorism. Instead of supporting his extreme particularist conclusion about religions as incommensurate, the analogy to human languages actually provides a new way to think in universal categories about diverse religions.

While all human languages are idiosyncratic, there is, nevertheless, the field of linguistics that allows us to talk about the common grammatical structures of different human languages. True, one cannot practice linguistics without using a specific human language to discuss the philosophy and structure of language. English linguists speak in English as they compare Chinese and Russian. French linguists speak in French as they compare Hindi and Arabic. Chinese-, Russian-, Hindi-, and Arabic-speaking linguists are happy to return the favor in comparing English and French. All of them use the same concepts and terminology—nouns, verbs, tense, phonemes, semantic meanings, semiotic codes, and so on—and apply these concepts universally to deciphering the universal regularities of particular human languages.

Nor are these particular living human languages ever really isolated islands unto themselves. Languages evolve over time, and this often involves significant borrowing from other languages. Furthermore, while something is surely lost in translation, every living language can be translated. The term for "dog" or "god" in various languages is particular, seemingly arbitrary, but the objects that they universally reference are real, explicitly in the case of the dog and perhaps implicitly in the case of the god. The diversity of human languages is surely idiosyncratically evolved, but it would be strange to declare chauvinistically that the only valid way one can order a cup of coffee is in German. *Eine Tasse Kaffee, bitte!* The implication here is that there is a universal "grammar" of religions, that they are not fundamentally incommensurate, and that we can go beyond the peculiarities to decode common patterns, structures, and functions.

Religions in this view are minimally systems, like human languages, that systematically code and transmit information. The British philosopher John Bowker also uses this definition: "At their most basic level, religions can best be understood as systems organized (in very different ways) for the coding, protection and transmission of information (some of it verbal, but a great deal of it, in the religious case, non-verbal)." This seems to me an accurate and purely descriptive account of religion, but Bowker goes on to suggest that religions are "discoveries of human competence," "proved to be of worth," and "tested through many generations."[11] This positive assessment of religion will be explicitly challenged by many of the theorists and scientists we encounter in the following chapters, who will claim that religions are inventions of human incompetence of little worth and now proven to be fundamentally wrong in detail.

The analogy to human languages is also illuminating on another level because it can account for the variety of religions in the world today. The idea of creating a universal human language, Esperanto, is and was a misconceived idea because it would necessarily become merely one new particular language among the many. So too is a religion of all religions, which would simply be a new particular religion, as in the case of the Baha'i faith. A science of all religions, not unlike linguistics, may be a possibility, though we might be forced to employ a particular religious idiom (and practice) in order to plum the deeper semantics of the phenomena. As Ferdinand de Saussure (1857–1913), the founder of modern linguistics, successfully proposed, we can separate the regular structure of a language—*langue*—from the meaningful uses of the language in everyday situations—*parole*. This distinction between the semiotics of language and the semantic reference of language can be only a temporary move, however, because we cannot understand how languages arise and evolve over time without understanding their semantic uses in living cultures.[12] Here, then, is our analogy between the semiotics-structure of religion and the semantics-meanings of religion. An adequate science of religion can only temporarily ignore the questions of meaning and reference, if we are to understand fully the phenomenon, its origins, uses, and evolution.

This brings us to the idea of *particularist universalism* in religion, a concept that I will return to at the end of this book. The idea is again by analogy to human languages and linguistics. The ultimate truth of religion will best be explored inside a particular religious idiom, much as we live, love, learn, work, and dream within one particular human language at a time. And while it is possible to be bilingual and multilingual, it is not possible to speak two languages simultaneously. This discussion of particular idiosyncrasies and universal truths of religion, however, must be postponed, until we complete the first stage of this phenomenological inquiry.

The Universal Grammar of Religions

I will now make a bold assertion, which many will find implausible. There is more functional diversity within a great tradition than between great traditions. By way of example, I am asserting that there is more functional diversity of beliefs and practices among Christians than between Christians in general and Buddhists in general. Of course, Christians and Buddhists do not share the same foundational stories and scriptures, so they disagree about dogma and doctrines. If, on the other hand, we undertake a phenomenological and functional analysis of religions, we will discover many commonalities in the range of actual practices and the "structures" of actual beliefs.

Western appropriations of Buddhism tend to focus on meditative practices and supposed lack of belief in supernatural deities, but this completely obscures the actual practices of the vast majority of Buddhist around the world. By far the largest branch of Buddhism is known as Pure Land Buddhism, in which believers devote themselves to a particular bodhisattva in hope of sitting out eternity in a hedonistic heaven through the grace and supernatural intervention of the bodhisattva. It turns out that the god-like bodhisattva has made a Jesus-like sacrifice on our behalf. During my recent stay in Sri Lanka, I witnessed many of these "Mahayana" practices at Buddhist temples and homes in an ostensible orthodox Theravada country. Technically, the bodhisattva is not a Theravada concept, but in practice, lay Buddhists in Sri Lanka, with the support of the monks, make offerings and recite prayers in the hope of superhuman assistance in their daily lives and future incarnations. This feature seems to me to be functionally equivalent to Pentecostal Christianity, Bhakti Hinduism, and devotional Islam, and everywhere throughout the world ends up being the most popular form of religiosity.

Similarly, scholars of religion and apologists for specific religions have tended to draw a sharp divide between the monotheism of the Abrahamic faiths, the "Western religions," and the polytheism and nontheism of "Eastern religions." Here, too, I think we miss the point. In practice, the monotheistic traditions often elevate Satan to a force independent of God, thus reverting to what is technically a heresy and turning themselves into something more akin to Zoroastrianism, with its concept of the dueling deities of Light and Darkness. Furthermore, the monotheistic faiths include a whole apparatus of angels, archangels, and saints, which further blurs the lines with polytheism. In his book *God: A Biography*, Jack Miles offers a psychohistorical reading of the Hebrew Bible and concludes that we have traded many gods with many personalities for a single God with multiple personality disorder.[13] Hinduism, in theory, is more accepting of this ambiguity, even as it affirms its own kind of transcendent unity in the notion of Brahma. "The Truth is one, but the wise man calls it by many names" is the classic verse from the ancient Rig Veda (1.164.46).

The diversity of world religions is perhaps analogous to what we now know about ethnic diversity and genetics. If we trace the genetic diversity of humans through our mitochondrial DNA, which is transmitted only on the female side, it turns out that we may have more in common genetically with someone of another race than with someone in our own race. It turns out that most of the phenotypic differences between different races—skin color, eye color and shape, hair color, and so on—have been only recently been acquired in the evolution of humanity. As recently as seventy thousand years ago, humanity may have experienced sudden catastrophic climate change due to the eruption of Mt. Toba in Indonesia, which reduced the human population to as little as ten thousand breeding pairs. We are all descendants of these survivors. Most of our racial and genetic diversity as a species is thought to have developed after this earth-shattering event.[14]

I am arguing again that the new sciences of religion should be understood as something akin to the field of linguistics; they are seeking the "grammatical" structures of religion in general based on a careful analysis of particular religions. We can also study the evolution of particular religions and their family trees, just as we study the evolution of languages. Only then can we engage in philosophical speculation about the nature of religion as such and whatever universals might be deduced or implied. Based on the biological and anthropological commonality, there is a lot of exciting work to be done, but this must also embrace textual, theological, and philosophical analyses. It is time for the intellectual pendulum to swing forward toward a study of the universality of religions, though in doing so, we cannot ignore the differences and the concrete particulars.

The New Sciences of Religion

First, we must note that the new sciences of religion, to which we now turn, include all the old disciplines—sociology of religion, psychology of religion, and anthropology of religion. The old masters in these fields need to be studied and debated anew, the new empirical research critically considered and absorbed. These disciplines are also more mature than they were in the past. There is now a self-critical history of the fields that is appropriately taught, studied, and debated, and this leads to some appropriate humility and critical introspection about the disciplines themselves and mistakes that have been made in the past.

The new sciences of religion also include many new approaches—economic models of religion, cognitive neuroscientific theories of religion, behavioral genomics patterns of religion, medical epidemiology of religion, physiology of religion, evolutionary psychological explanations of religion, and game-theory simulations of religion. The new sciences of religion include human history and quickly drift into evolution, cosmology, and metaphysics. The approaches are represented schematically in Figure 1.2.

Studying religious and spiritual phenomena from the outside can fruitfully involve all these disciplines, but what it cannot do is ignore the details and complexity of the phenomena inside the circle. One cannot be an effective scientist of religion without also being a humanistic scholar of religion. The details inside the circle still matter—history, tradition, authorities, scriptures, languages, interpretations, legal systems, saints and sages, rituals, liturgies, practices, daily life, and subjective experience are all part of the data set for any responsible scientific study of religion.

Nor should we assume that religious and spiritual phenomena can be exhaustively described, understood, or explained by any single scientific

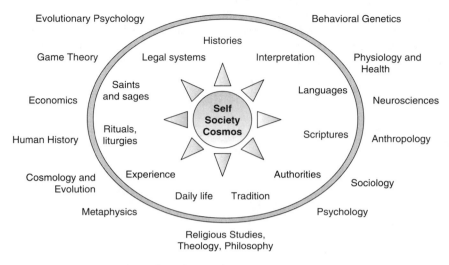

Figure 1.2 Studying Religion from the *Outside*.

paradigm on the outside. The scholar-scientist might be enamored by rational-choice theory in economics and use it to understand religion, or by the role of neurotransmitters in specific religious experiences inside the brain; but these cannot be a complete description of the phenomena, which involve the self, society, and cosmos, and which are heterogeneous, particular, and universal. If the scientist uses a single analytic framework to understand religion, the phenomenon will surely tend to conform to the theory because the theory acts as a filter for what we see or fail to see. A single scientific paradigm induces empirical myopia in this undertaking. This is one of the reasons I advocate multiple methodologies and a nonreductive functionalist approach to the scientific study of religion.

The new disciplines being applied to the scientific study of religious and spiritual phenomena are exciting and promising, but they are not yet mature, in comparison with the more established fields of psychology, sociology, and anthropology of religion. As we will see in the following chapters, the new disciplinary protagonists often display a lack of familiarity with the history of these endeavors and the complexity of the phenomena they purport to study scientifically. Too often, they are motivated by nonscientific ideological concerns of displacing and abolishing religion from the world. We will consider this Enlightenment project in the next chapter, before embarking on a review of the economics of religion, the evolution of religion, the neurosciences of religion, and the medicine of religion. This survey will then serve as the foundation in part 2 for a consideration of the truth of religion, when I examine the narratives of religion, religious interpretations of science, and a theology of God-by-whatever-name that makes no reference to ancient revelations but works bottom up from contemporary science toward a naturalistic interpretation of transcendence and divinity.

CHAPTER TWO

The Old Sciences of Religion

Before we examine the new sciences of religion, we need to take a quick survey of the old sciences of religion that arose in the nineteenth and early twentieth centuries. By doing so, we will come to recognize the challenges of creating any kind of science of religion. Along the way, we will discover certain patterns of thought and concepts that persist in our contemporary approaches to explaining and understanding religious and spiritual phenomena.

With few exceptions, nineteenth- and early twentieth-century theorists saw religion in negative terms, as a set of beliefs and practices that were immature, backward, superstitious, irrational, and regressive. There is a significant basis for these negative assessments of religion, but this is also a selective reading of history. Most assumed that science would somehow replace religion as the Enlightenment progressed. Positioning science as the antonym of religion, then, turns science into simply another religion.

I begin this survey with the eclectic French philosopher Auguste Comte because many of these ideas originated with him. Comte is less known than other early theorists of religion but turns out to be very influential in this intellectual history. Yet for reasons we will discover below, he does not figure prominently in Anglo-American philosophy and intellectual history; nor does he receive the credit he deserves in the story generally told of the old sciences of religion.

The High Priest of Positivism

Isidore Auguste Marie François Comte (1798–1857) was one of the more original modern theorists of religion. Comte directly and indirectly influenced a number of other thinkers, including Ludwig Feuerbach, Karl Marx, Charles Darwin, Sigmund Freud, and especially Émile Durkheim. Comte coined the term *positivism* to identify science, and the term stuck in what became the Positivist school in the philosophy of science, later synonymous with the Vienna Circle. Positivism, or what should more precisely be called neopositivism or logical positivism, persisted as an active research project in the philosophy of science into the 1950s, at which point it was widely rejected as impractical and unrealistic, though a number of naive holdouts remain.[1]

Comte is also credited with coining the word *sociology* to identify a new science of society. He argued that the application of scientific and mathematical principles to the study and management of society promised enormous benefits to humanity. He understood sociology to be the last and most important development in the hierarchical ordering of six fundamental disciplines—mathematics, astronomy, physics, chemistry, biology, and sociology—in turn. The classification was hierarchical and emergent. Mathematics was required to do astronomy, but astronomy could not be reduced to mere mathematics. Physics was necessary for chemistry to emerge, but chemistry could not be reduced to mere physics. Biology was necessary for humanity to exist, but sociology could not be reduced to mere biology. Different methods of inquiry were required for different types of science. Comte's classification of the sciences accounts for their diversity, as well as the overall unity of the scientific enterprise. We can think of Comte as one of the first modern philosophers of science.[2]

Comte was also given to excess, so many of his contemporaries and many recent scholars prefer to ignore him or selectively acknowledge him, much as we honor Isaac Newton today for his scientific genius and ignore his obsessive fascination with Unitarian theology, Kabbalah, and the occult. Comte probably suffered from what we today call bipolar disorder or manic depression. He was twice hospitalized for mental illness. He was given to grandiosity, so we get a grand theory of religion, history, and society. Toward the end of his career, he went off the deep end in his attempt to create a new religion for humanity based on science, in which scientists would function much like clerics in the Roman Catholic Church; he considered himself to be the pope of this new church. The motto of this movement was "Love as a principle and order as the basis; progress as the goal." He called it the Church of the Great Being, in which the Great Being was humanity, not God. In 1889, followers of Comte in the newly formed Republic of Brazil would add his *Ordem e Progresso* to the newly design Brazilian flag.

Rather than seeing Comte's new religion of humanity as disconnected from his earlier work, we should understand it as the logical conclusion of his insights. Humanity faces a great dilemma in Comte's analysis. The inherited religions can no longer be considered true (as David Hume before him had argued). Science had replaced religion in matters of truth. The problem is that religion is vital to the proper functioning of society. Religions provide the psychological and social glue for a harmonious, peaceful, and productive society, even though they are not literally true. Religion promotes morality and curtails anarchistic tendencies in people. Comte believed that humanity would not progress unless it could institute some new religion to fulfill these vital social and psychological functions. Religion is dead; long live religion!

The Three Stages of Cultural Evolution

Comte proposed and developed a theory of cultural history as an evolutionary process of staged developments, what he called "a natural law regulating the progress of civilization,"[3] one of the first temporal, evolutionary paradigms used to understand history, religion, and society. According to this formulation, there are three stages in the evolution of religion and society—the theological or fictional, the metaphysical or abstract, and the scientific or positive.[4] Even today in France, every school child learns this formulation.

The theological stage of human evolution corresponded to feudalism, medieval Catholicism, and everything that preceded these in human history, all the way back to when humans were "barely superior to that of a society of great apes."[5] The theological stage was broken down in three substages—fetishism, polytheism, and monotheism. Fetishism is the naïve anthropomorphization of the natural environment, what would later be called animism. At this stage, even inanimate objects in nature are attributed with humanlike personality and will.

The supernaturalism of the theological stage in human evolution is seen as a manifestation of an instinctive scientific impulse. Humans have an innate drive to observe, explain, understand, and control the universe in which we live. "With all its imperfections," writes Comte, "this [supernaturalism] forms the only mode of connecting facts possible at that epoch," in which direct observation is enhanced by imagination.[6] Anticipating Freud and developmental psychology, Comte draws a parallel between the anthropomorphic and animistic tendencies in early human civilization and our individual development from childhood into adults. Thus, the maturation of civilization runs parallel to the maturation of individual humans in the course of their lives:

> [T]he earliest advances of the human intellect could not be effected in any other way than the theological method, the only one susceptible of spontaneous development. It alone possessed the important property of presenting from the outset a provisional theory, vague and arbitrary, it is true, but direct and easy, which immediately grouped the primary facts and, by cultivating our faculties of observation, prepared the advent of a positive philosophy.[7]

Fetishism (basically animism) slowly gives way to polytheism, which requires more-developed theoretical constructs to account for the observations. Sensing thunder and lightning and noticing the seasonal patterns in weather and stars in themselves are not knowledge. Only when humans attributed these natural phenomena to the personalities of gods or spirits did they have knowledge (albeit false knowledge). For Comte, this correlation of observations and theory is what constitutes knowledge.

Note that the evolution of humanity through the theological stage is also a scientific evolution. "The great revolution that carried men on from fetishism to polytheism," writes Comte, "is due to the same mental causes, though they may not be so conspicuous, that now produce all scientific revolutions,—which always arise out of a discordance between facts and principles."[8]

Polytheism then gives way to monotheism as a response to these discordant facts and principles. Monotheism is a further simplification and rationalization of the supernatural or theological stage in human evolution. Comte calls monotheism "an admirable simplification of theological philosophy." Like polytheism before it, monotheism

> reduced the action of the chief supernatural power, in each special case, to a certain general direction, the character of which was unavoidably vague. Thus the human mind was authorised, and even strongly impelled, to study the physical laws of each class of phenomena regarded as a mode of action of this power.[9]

As humans progressively leave supernatural explanations behind, humanity moves into the metaphysical stage, in which we discover that the natural order is governed by regular and impersonal laws. In entering the metaphysical stage, humans progressively dispense with supernatural explanations and attribute natural phenomena to abstract, impersonal, and law-like processes. We see this in the progress made in mathematics and astronomy in the early modern period, in which the laws of physics were mathematical in form and able to describe the motions of the planets and other phenomena with great precision. We also see this in the advent of abstract metaphysical concepts such as individual human rights, which Comte opposed in favor of a more communitarian ethics of society as a kind of superorganism. The individual was merely a part of this large whole. Comte understood the metaphysical stage to correspond with the period of European history beginning with the Protestant Reformation through the French Revolution, a period of war and anarchy.

A Functional Account of Religion

It is important to understand what distinguishes Comte from his predecessor, the English philosopher David Hume (1711–1776). Both agreed that in light of science and philosophy, religion must now be thought of as untrue. Comte, however, argued that religion was a necessary stage in the development of science, so he has some appreciation of the evolutionary role played by religion as a protoscience. Unlike Hume, Comte also argued that religion played a necessary role in the evolution of civilization by providing social harmony. Religion might become intellectually obsolete, but the social and psychological functions of religion in society were as vital as ever to the future well-being of any successful society:

> [N]o real and coherent society can form and maintain itself except under the influence of some system of ideas, fitted to surmount the opposition of individualising tendencies, always so strong at the outset, and to make these concur in maintaining a settled order."[10]

One trajectory of Comte's analysis leads to Hume's explanation of religion as pseudoscience, now superseded by real science. The other trajectory leads to the conclusion that the psychological and social functions of religion need to be carried on in some new way in the future. Theological philosophy, even though it is factually wrong, nevertheless plays an important social role. "To it [theological philosophy]," Comte writes, "we must naturally ascribe the original establishment of all social organization."[11]

Comte was enthusiastic about the potential for science to improve human life, to take control of nature, including our human nature. Through a "positive" science, we could bend nature toward our will to improve the human condition. However, he also perceived a great threat to progress in the rising individualism, self-centeredness, and anarchistic tendencies of humanity throughout the metaphysical stage into his own time:

> [T]he existing disorder is abundantly accounted for by the existence, all at once, of three incompatible philosophies—the theological, the metaphysical, and the positive. Any one of these might alone secure some sort of social order; but while the three co-exist, it is impossible for us to understand one another upon any essential point whatever.[12]

He might as well be describing the current world of globalization, clashing civilizations, and culture wars. Social harmony requires a unifying worldview and internalized moral motivations in which "the parts ... converge towards the general order from which they always tend naturally to deviate." Society can allocate rewards and punishments to promote social harmony, but without the moral means to regulate the opinions and will of individuals, centrifugal tendencies will tear society apart. Civilization requires a "continuous state of sacrifice" in which each person must experience "a certain degree of sacrifice without which it could not maintain itself, having regard to the opposition of individual tendencies, which is, in some degree, absolutely inevitable."[13] Here, too, Comte anticipates Freud in noting that the repression of sexual passions is a necessary sacrifice for enjoying the benefits of civilization.[14]

Religions function throughout human evolution to unite societies. Comte writes critically of his own time and perhaps prophetically about our own:

> Minds, no longer united by any real bond, diverge on all essential points, with that license which unregulated individualism must produce. Hence the entire absence of public morality; the universal spread of egotism; the preponderance of considerations purely material; and, as a last inevitable consequence, corruption erected into a system of government, as being the only kind of order applicable to a population become deaf to all appeals made in the name of a general ideal and alive only to the voice of private interest.[15]

Born in 1798, Comte was a child of postrevolutionary France. The anarchy unleashed by the metaphysical stage in the evolution of European history was part of the problem he sought to solve in his program of positivism. For Comte, the metaphysical stage in human history lacked a constructive social potential. It was necessarily anarchistic and destructive, albeit more true than the earlier theological stages in human history. The metaphysical stage is perhaps best represented in the rallying cry of the French Revolution—*Liberté*, *Egalité*, and *Fraternité*. Note that these abstract concepts embraced by the masses were seen by Comte as leading to the Reign of Terror and the Napoleonic Wars.

The New Religion of Science

Late in his life, Comte published a four-volume work entitled *System of Positive Polity* (1851–54). The subtitle is "Treatise on Sociology: Instituting the Religion of Humanity." The project of creating a new religion based on science, a religion of and for humanity, prefigures much of the ideological antipathy toward religion and fervor for science that intellectuals displayed in the ensuing century. In Comte's view, humanity needs to heal the fissure between our cognitive lives, informed by modern science, and our affective lives, informed by our loves and passions. "The Order based on reality was unable to satisfy the emotions so well as the Order based on fictions."[16] The answer lies in attaching our affections to humanity as the "Great Being." A belief in progress and humanism can replace what was believed to be an antiquated belief in God as the unifying social ideal, all the more so because the new sciences and technology promised a stream of continued discovery and technological improvements in our lives.

The Church of the Great Being was modeled after Roman Catholicism albeit without Christ. In Comte's church, humanity, progress, and science were to be worshiped and celebrated. We needed to link our emotional affections to our cognitive insights. Comte was a utopian thinker, not only in his project of creating a new religion from science but also in a deeper sense. He understood the human perception of time to be order past > future > present, because it is our understanding and experience of the past and our expectations and exertions toward the future that give rise to our transitory present circumstances. The present, Comte argued, "a vague and fleeting span which fills the interval between two immensities of duration, and binds them together..., can only be properly conceived with the aid of the two extremes which it unites and separates."[17]

A New Calendar for a New Age

One of Comte's more fanciful proposals was the creation of a new calendar for the new age of positivism (1848), which he developed in great detail. We need to put this in historical context, remembering that the world was still divided on whether to use the Julian calendar or the Gregorian calendar. Postrevolutionary France had also adopted a new calendar, the French Revolutionary Calendar, which the government used from 1793 through 1805 and briefly revised in 1871. Comte's Positivist Calendar at least had the advantage of using a simpler and more logical structure and later became the model for the "International Fixed Calendar" promoted in the early twentieth century.

The Positivist Calendar has thirteen months of twenty-eight days' duration. Each month has four seven-day weeks beginning with Monday, so the days of the month always fall on the same weekday. Thus, Friday would always be the fifth, twelfth, nineteenth, or twenty-sixth day of the month. There would never be a Friday the thirteenth, because the thirteenth day would always fall on a Saturday. An intercalary day was included at the end of each year and another at the end of each leap year. The Positivist Calendar is a perennial calendar; it is the same every year. Like the French Revolutionary Calendar, it began counting years in 1789, the year of the Revolution. So the year 2009 is the year 220 in the Positivist Calendar.

All fine and well, except that there were no "Mondays" and no "Fridays" in the Positivist Calendar, as the days of the week changed with each week of each month. What made Comte's Positivist Calendar bizarre was that he named the thirteen months after heroes in human history, each month dedicated to a theme and each day of the month dedicated to an exemplar of that theme. Inspired by the many holidays in the Roman Catholic liturgical calendar dedicated to saints, Comte created a new liturgical calendar dedicated to the heroes of human progress taken from all nations and ages.

The first month is Moses. The thematic focus is the initial theocracy. The twenty-eight days of the month of Moses are Prometheus, Hercules, Orpheus, Ulysses, Lycurgus, Romulus, Numa, Belus, Seostris, Menu, Cyrus, Zoroaster, the Druids, Buddha, Fo-Hi, Lao-Tsu, Meng-Tseu, Theocracts of Tibet, Theocrats of Japan, Mano-Capac, Confucius, Abraham,

Samuel, Solomon, Isaiah, St. John the Baptist, Haroun al-Raschid, and Muhammad. The Sabbath festival days of the month of Moses would, thus, celebrate Numa (the mythic king of early Rome), Buddha, Confucius, and Muhammad.

The second month is the month of Homer, dedicated to ancient poetry. The major festival days were dedicated to Aeschylus, Phidias, Aristophanes, and Virgil. The third is the month of Aristotle and is dedicated to the heroes of ancient philosophy. The fourth month is Archimedes, its theme ancient science. The fifth month is Caesar, with the theme military civilization. The sixth month is Saint Paul, dedicated to Catholicism. The seventh month is Charlemagne, and the theme is feudal civilization. The eighth month is Dante, the theme being modern epic poetry. The ninth month is Gutenberg, the theme modern industry. The tenth month is Shakespeare (modern drama), the eleventh Descartes (modern philosophy), and the twelfth Frederick (modern polity). And the thirteen month, dedicated to modern science, the culmination of civilization's advance, is named Bichat after the French physician Marie François Xavier Bichat (1771–1802). Major festivals were to be held on the seventh, fourteenth, twenty-first, and twenty-eighth days of the month of Bichat in honor of Galileo Galilei, Isaac Newton, Antoine Lavoisier, and Franz Joseph Gall. In all, thirteen major and 365 minor heroes of human civilization are honored, mostly men, with some minor saints thrown in for leap years.[18]

The purpose of the Positivist Calendar, as in the Church of the Great Being, is to promote "sound training in positive thought" and to awaken "perpetual feelings of veneration and gratitude" and "enthusiastic admiration of the Great Being, who is the Author of all these conquests, be they in thought, or be they in Action."[19]

We in the twenty-first century also seek to venerate the great heroes of science and civilization: witness the recent celebrations of Charles Darwin, the iconic image of Albert Einstein, or the aura surrounding winners of the Nobel Prize. Science needs its exemplars no less than religion needs its saints.

Comte's Long Shadow

Many of his contemporaries and many modern-day scholars draw a sharp distinction between Comte's early and late works, the "good" Comte and the "bad" Comte. They recognize originality and brilliance in his early works and criticize the late Comte, rejecting the grandiosity and absurdity of his efforts to create a new religion of and for humanity. The English philosopher John Stuart Mill (1806–1873) made this argument explicit in his book *Auguste Comte and Positivism* (1865).[20]

I choose to introduce the old sciences of religion by reviewing the work of Comte in part because of this grandiosity. Any science of religion is a grand proposition. Comte has provided a theory of religion from which others borrowed mightily. By briefly examining Comte, we encounter most of the themes that would dominate nineteenth- and early twentieth-century approaches to the scientific study of religion.

First, we note an evolutionary theory of religion and society developing in stages, moving from animism to polytheism to monotheism to secularism. As civilization developed, especially through science and technology, people would come to recognize religion as superstition. In basic outline, this staged evolutionary account of religion would be adopted by the British anthropologists E. B. Tylor (1832–1917) and James George Frazer (1854–1941), among many others.[21]

Second, we note in Comte a dynamic relationship between cultural ideas and cultural structures, for instance between the religion and the political economy of a society. The ideas and structure of a society evolve together in patterned ways. In basic outline, we now have pieces of the accounts of religion offered by both Karl Marx (1818–1883) and Max Weber (1864–1920). We will return to these two thinkers shortly.

Third, we have discovered in Comte a theory of religion that draws parallels between the historical development of civilizations and the psychological maturation of individual humans. Early human societies are thought of as childlike with their magical thinking, while contemporary scientific civilization is thought of as adultlike with its mature realism. This, of course, prefigures some of the ideas about religion and psychology offered by Sigmund Freud (1856–1939) and repeated by some evolutionary psychologists today.[22] We will come back to Freud later in this chapter.

Fourth, we discover in Comte the kernel of a substantive definition of religion. Religion was understood to be supernaturalism, that is, the belief in supernatural beings or powers. Religion was set up as an imaginative protoscience, an early attempt to explain natural phenomena. As science progresses, it necessarily challenges religious myths. This definition of religion as "supernaturalism" dominates the old sciences of religion. We find it explicitly articulated by Tylor and Frazer but also assumed by Marx, Freud, and many others.

Fifth, Comte introduced the concept of anthropomorphization of gods and God as a kind of alienation from our true human potential. We attribute to imagined divinities superhuman powers and qualities when it is, in fact, humans who possess these superior powers and superior qualities, if only we would apply ourselves. This, of course, anticipates the theory of religion as alienation articulated by Ludwig Feuerbach (1804–1872) and adopted whole cloth by Marx.[23]

Sixth, Comte developed a hierarchical and emergent understanding of the scientific disciplines. He classified the six fundamental sciences as mathematics, astronomy, physics, chemistry, biology, and sociology. At the top of this hierarchy was sociology because it dealt with the most recent and most complex natural phenomena—humans and their societies. Comte understood there to be a dynamic relationship between the adjacent levels in this hierarchy, but he was not arguing for a thoroughgoing reductionism. He did, however, argue that mathematics was important throughout the sciences and imagined the possibilities of quantitative studies in the human sciences. He also developed a nuanced understanding of the relationship between observation and theory. So, in Comte, we find the early articulation of a comprehensive philosophy of science, a program that would concern philosophers and scientists right up until today. Note that the primary preoccupation of the philosophy of science is defining the boundaries of what counts as science and what is not science (e.g., religion).[24] We will return to these issues in chapter nine.

Seventh, Comte gives us a functional account of religion. Religions arose and persisted in human civilization because they helped bind together the parts (individual humans) and the whole (the functional society). Take away religion, and the centrifugal tendencies of our selfish and sensuous egos would result in anarchy, chaos, and collapse.[25] Religions were not true, according to Comte, but they were useful. They served to internalize the mores of a society in individuals, promoting moral restraints on behavior and harmonious cooperation within society. This leads us directly to the theory of religion articulated by Émile Durkheim (1858–1917), who saw religion as "a unified system of beliefs and practices... which united into one single moral community called a Church, all those who adhere to them."[26] Comte also anticipates Freud by identifying society's need to repress individual sexual passions if civilization is to thrive

With this insight about the secular utility of religion comes a great dilemma for the Enlightenment project, a dilemma that Comte recognized and addressed. If religion is useful and necessary for society, then somehow it would need to be reinvented in the modern age of science. Comte's functional account of religion leads to a broadening of our definition and the recognition that beliefs and practices that we might not normally think of as religion can serve "religious functions" in society. Here, Comte anticipates the theoretical work of the American anthropologist Clifford Geertz (1926–2006), who argued, for instance, that Communism functioned like a religion in the former Soviet Union.[27] We will return to Geertz in the section "Pragmatism and the Study of Religion," later in this chapter.

The ninth innovation we can find in Comte is the germs of what would later be called secularization theory. Civilization evolves through stages. As science, economic, and educational levels around the world increase, it was predicted that societies would increasingly dispense with the old-time religions. Academics throughout much of the twentieth century believed in secularization theory, although, as we can see, religion is back with a vengeance at outset of the twenty-first century.

Finally, we encounter in Comte a utopian program of progressive humanism and progressive science. Comte makes explicit what has often been assumed. Science supersedes religion, not just in matters of truth but also in matters of faith. Many in the nineteenth and twentieth centuries adopted faith in science as a kind of secular salvation story.[28] Science has certainly extended and enhanced human life; science has certainly extended and enhanced our understanding of the universe and ourselves. The kinds of technologies that science has bestowed on humanity today would have been unimaginable to Comte and his contemporaries 200 years ago. Today, we fly around in airplanes at 35,000 feet, complaining about bad food and uncomfortable seats, when the whole concept would have been unbelievable in the nineteenth century. Tools that we take for granted, like the Internet and cell phones, would have appeared to our ancestors as magic.

Of course, science and technology have also brought new dangers such as nuclear war, antibiotic-resistant diseases, environmental carcinogens, and anthropogenic climate change. And while we may be more powerful than our ancestors, it is not clear in the killing fields of the twentieth century that we have become better people in any moral sense. In Comte's progressive science-based humanism we see prefigured the utopian transformation of society envisioned by Marx and others. Of course, one of the reasons we today are less optimistic is that Communism and other utopian movements have failed to transform human nature. Indeed, the very utopian drive helped to create many of the great tragedies of the twentieth century. Perhaps other Promethean tragedies lie before us, enabled by science and our frail humanity. Science may have given us powers we would have better lived without, so our faith in science will have been misplaced. On the whole, though, from my own limited vantage point, I would enthusiastically endorse Comte's notion of progress through science, at least some kinds of progress. Comte can be seen as one of the early prophets of our age. His philosophy became the default ideology of elite European and American universities in the twentieth century with the disestablishment of the Protestant establishments in most of those same universities.[29]

Reductionism in the Science of Religion

One of the things that distinguishes Comte from those who followed is the role of reductionism in their theories of religion. Comte was not a strict reductionist, whereas others, in particular Marx and Freud, proposed reductionistic accounts of religion. Let us briefly examine each in turn.

Karl Marx argued that the economic system was foundational in understanding human society. If the economic system changed, then everything about society—the legal system, the educational system, the family system, and also religious beliefs and institutions—would all change with the economy. Marx used the metaphor of a house with its *foundation* and the *superstructure* built on top of this *base*. Economics was privileged in Marx's view because, through the economic system, humans got the necessities of survival. Change the economic base, that is, the modes of production, and everything in the superstructure would have to change as well.

Medieval economy was based on feudal estates owned by nobility and agricultural labor provided by peasants. In Marx's understanding, this feudal economic system gave rise to the institution and beliefs of the Catholic Church. With the rise of middle-class merchants, guilds, and industrialization in early capitalism, Catholicism progressively gave way to Protestantism. Marx developed the idea of alienation and false consciousness. Belief in God was a fantasy, akin to children's believing in Santa Claus, and resulted in humans being alienated from their true potential to become creative laborers. Marx famously referred to religion as "the opium of the masses" because it promoted docility among terribly oppressed workers in the growing industrial cities in Europe. Thus, religion was reduced to an expression of economics. To the extent that Marx was on to something true about religions, we would expect profound changes in religions in the twenty-first century based on the current globalized economic system of production.

Sigmund Freud was also a reductionist, believing that religion was an unhealthy illusion, but he rejected Marx's theories as overly optimistic about human capacities to lead moral lives in harmonious cooperation with others. For Freud, the base or foundation of human society is the instincts and structures of the human psyche; the human brain is shaped by millennia of evolution and the necessity of survival and reproduction. Note that Freud shares with Marx a materialist understanding of psychosocial causation and that Freud is influenced by Charles Darwin in emphasizing survival and reproduction as the biological backdrop imprinted in the structures of our brain. Freud understood there to be an eternal struggle between our individual instincts for sex, food, and aggression and the needs of society to control our instincts. Fulfilling our instinctual desires makes us content but renders life short and brutish, full of deadly competition. Denying our instinctual desires, as required by civilization, makes us miserable but renders life orderly and luxurious. Freud understood religion to be one of the ways that society programmed the "superego"—the internalized "should"—with the guilt that regulates the instinctual "id." He understood belief in God to be a form of "infantile regression." Humanity creates God in our own image (not the reverse) to have an imaginary protective parent-figure in our psyche to comfort and control us in adult life.

Deconstructing the Base-Superstructure

Early social theorists on religion all used some version of Marx's base-superstructure model of causation, though they may not have used the exact terms. Some natural or material factor that determines the beliefs and behaviors of individuals—economics for Marx, the human psyche for

Freud, society for Durkheim—is foundational. Religion is created and determined by other forces; it is not itself a cause. When the foundation changes, so too changes what is built on top—in this case, religion. The early Freud was more optimistic about the Enlightenment project. He believed that if we could understand the origins of religion in human history, we might better take control over it; hence his book *Totems and Taboos* (1918). Without necessarily crediting Comte, all adopted a progressive view of increased secularization as a good that resulted from economic and scientific development. The later Freud was less optimistic. He had lived through World War I and saw the clouds of another great conflict building at the end of his life in exile from Austria because of the Nazis. He did not really think that the foundation, the human psyche, to be all that mutable. So Freud leaves us simply stuck with the dilemma described in his book *Civilization and Its Discontents* (1930) and its dark premonition about the violent chaos about to be unleashed in Enlightenment Europe.[30]

The German sociologist Max Weber wrote *The Protestant Ethic and the Spirit of Capitalism* (1905) partly as a rebuttal to Marx. The point was to reverse Marx's causal relationship between base and superstructure, to take religion out of the realm of the superstructure and put it into that of the foundation as a driver of economic change. Weber argued that the values of worldly asceticism, independence, and self-discipline nurtured by Protestant Christianity, particularly Calvinism, played a central, albeit unintended, role in the development of European capitalism. He contrasted this with the influence of Catholicism. In other writings, Weber argued that the religions of China, India, and the Muslim world were antithetical to the rationalities and sensibilities of modern capitalism.[31]

Today, most social theorists would reject the base-superstructure model as too simplistic, although there remains a natural tendency toward the self-importance ascribed to one's own pet theory. It is not clear anymore what is foundational and what is the causally dependent variable since everything reciprocally affects everything else. Religions, like humans, are complex and dynamic.

Today, most informed social theorists are also forced to reject secularization theory. Religions are on the rise throughout the world, in spite of dramatic economic growth and scientific advance. It is hard to deny the fact, even if one wishes it were not so.

The Anathema of the University

What is important to note at this stage of our discussion is that the social sciences—psychology, sociology, and anthropology—were largely founded by thinkers who took for granted that there was no truth content or value to religions, that religions were irrational, superstitious, regressive, and dysfunctional. They all bought into Comte's vision that the natural trajectory of human civilization was toward secularization and away from religion. As societies became more economically and scientifically developed, they would forsake these "childish" beliefs and adopt scientific attitudes and worldviews. To use psychological terminology, the social sciences were founded with a lot of animus toward religion, so it is little wonder that the faith factor is the forgotten variable in much of the social sciences in the decades that followed, as these sciences and their respective guilds within the university developed, expanded, and evolved.

It is not an overstatement to say that the modern research universities were founded with an explicit agenda of getting rid of religion. Andrew Dickson White, the founding president of Cornell University, expressed this sentiment in his 1896 book *A History of the Warfare of Science with Theology in Christendom*.[32] The religious virtue of spiritual enlightenment was turned upside down by the Enlightenment. Perhaps we can laugh about this as a backhanded proof of Freud's Oedipal complex. In this case, the "father to be killed" was the religious institution that created the modern university in the first place, that is, the medieval church and its Protestant offspring. Freud met a similar fate as the "father of psychology" and is largely denied and displaced within his own guild.

In any case, there is a lot of ideological and emotional baggage here. Science, most would agree, needs to be first descriptive, not prescriptive. Because of the ideological baggage of scientism, disciplines such as sociology, psychology, and anthropology have largely not developed an adequate descriptive phenomenology of religion and spirituality. Instead, the founders of these disciplines and their intellectual descendants have dismissively sought to put religion neatly into an intellectual box, a single, simplistic paradigm by which it could be dismissed.

Pragmatism in the Study of Religion

One important exception in the antireligious trend among social scientists was the American psychologist William James (1842–1910). James is regarded as a pioneer in the philosophical movement known as pragmatism and the psychological movement known as functionalism, the latter owed in part to Auguste Comte. James argued that the truth of a belief or practice is established a posteriori by its practical, functional consequences in someone's life. If belief in God leads to a healthy and constructive life, then it could be understood as true for all practical purposes. The individual's experiences and the lived consequences of those experiences are proof enough of the "truth" of religion. In *Varieties of Religious Experience* (1902), James developed a phenomenological approach to religion, taking first-person accounts of religious experiences of numerous historical persons at face value, adopting an attitude of positive agnosticism toward the larger truth claims, and looking toward the functional and practical consequences of those beliefs, practices, and experiences in the individual's life.[33]

Another more recent advocate of a pragmatic and functionalist approach to the study of religion was Clifford Geertz, who helped complete the story of the old sciences of religion by more fully laying out the dissenting approach already articulated by Durkheim and James.

Geertz did extensive fieldwork in Indonesia and North Africa. Much like a detective uncovering some hidden and complicated truth, he sought to understand how religious beliefs, practices, and relationships function within a society. He called his method "thick description." In his 1973 classic *The Interpretation of Culture*, Geertz offers a stunning definition of religion:

> Religion is: (1) a system of symbols which acts to (2) establish power-ful, pervasive, and long-lasting moods and motivations in people by (3) formulating conceptions of a general order of existence and (4) clothing these conceptions with such an aura of factuality that (5) the moods and motivations seem uniquely realistic.[34]

Try this definition out the next time you go to church or synagogue, to temple or mosque. This is not how one normally thinks of religion, especially not one's own. An adequate definition of religion, however, needs to embrace a great variety of beliefs and practices, most of them quite foreign to you in the taken-for-granted comfort of your own "primary subculture." Geertz gives us a phenomenological definition of religion. It talks about "systems of symbols" and "moods and motivations," but it does not try to prejudge the content of the beliefs, practices, and values. Theistic, polytheistic, pantheistic, animistic, and nontheistic religions are all included. There is no hierarchical ranking of religions nor any progressive evolutionary development of religions implied in the definition.

Geertz's definition does not use the word *supernatural*. The typical move in the social sciences is to define religion as some belief in or relationship with "supernatural agents." Tylor, one of the founders of cultural anthropology, defines religion as belief in "spiritual beings."[35] The Swiss-German anthropologist Walter Burkert defines religion as a "tradition of serious communication with powers that cannot be seen."[36] The anthropologist Scott Atran defines religion as belief in "supernatural agents,"[37] while the anthropologist Pascal Boyer says that religion "is about the existence and causal powers of nonobservable entities and agencies" and later "supernatural matters."[38] These can all be referred to as substantive definitions of religion. The use of the concept "supernatural" imports many metaphysical assumptions at the outset and precludes by definition the possibilities that religions may intuit and infer, discern and discover, something empirically real and ontologically profound about the universe as a whole and human life within the universe. I am happy to grant that most religious stories are "supernatural" and that these cannot be understood as anything but imaginative myths. These mythologies, however, may point toward a deeper insight about the human condition and a transcendent reality that are empirically and philosophically justified. In this view, "God" is real and works only through "natural" processes.[39] Religions of the world would, then, represent millennia of empirical research about this ultimate reality, and the findings of this research have been well tested and winnowed in the received traditions—Judaism, Christianity, Islam, Hinduism, Buddhism, Confucianism, Taoism, and so forth. Today, the received traditions need to be retested and reinterpreted in dialogue with contemporary science, but there is no reason to suppose that they will be refuted and rejected whole cloth, no reason to throw "God" and the baby out with the bathwater. This, at least, is a hypothesis that we should not rule out by importing a metaphysical dichotomy at the outset between "naturalism" and "supernaturalism" in our very definitions of science and religion. This will be the topic of part 2 of this book, when I take a bottom-up approach, working from contemporary science toward religious truth claims.

Rather than beginning with a substantive definition of religion, I will side with the phenomenological approach articulated by Geertz so as to temporarily avoid a complicated discussion of the philosophy of science and possible metaphysics derived therefrom. I realize that we cannot avoid this discussion if we are to entertain seriously the possibility that religions are in some sense true, profoundly true, as they themselves all claim to be.

Important for our discussion also is that Geertz's definition includes things that we do not normally think of as religions. For instance, there is an entire chapter in his book about how Communism functioned in the Soviet Union as a form of religion. The inclusiveness of Geertz's definition of religion, however, is also considered to be its weakness. Nothing is excluded. Baseball, football, and other sporting obsessions can take on the characteristics of a religion, which is not a surprise to most baseball fanatics. Political movements and parties take on some of the same characteristics. Western Europe no longer seems so secular if environmentalism and other political causes can also function like a religion for many of their followers. With Geertz's definition, my daughter's Suzuki violin classes start looking like a strange cult.

And as already noted, when some enthusiasts of science see science as a substitute for religion, science is turned into scientism, that is, another faith among many with its own "systems of symbols" and "moods and motivations." Indeed, scientism can be seen to offer its own secular apocalyptic-prophetic narratives, as well as its own secular salvation story. We see this, for instance, in the apocalyptic fears of climate change or the utopian promises of transhumanism.[40] We see this also in the extremism of the New Atheists—Dawkins, Dennett, Harris, Hitchens, and others—who mirror the fundamentalism of religious extremists in their righteous anger and narrow analysis.[41]

Remember that this phenomenological approach to the study of religion is, at the outset, primarily concerned not with the truth claims of religions (or scientism) but with accurate descriptions and analyses of how beliefs and practices function for individuals and groups and what pragmatic benefits ensue or not in what contexts. It can be illuminating to see "religion" in some of the least expected places. Indeed, if religion is a human universal, then we should expect to see it everywhere, reinvented and repackaged in secular guises all around us. This renders the scientific study of "religion" more difficult but also much more compelling.

CHAPTER THREE

The Economics of Religion

Typically, when we juxtapose the terms *religion* and *economics*, people immediately begin to think about morality and ethics. Religions have a lot to say about economic pursuits, and most of it is critical. Perhaps there is something called "Christian Economics," "Buddhist Economics," and "Islamic Economics." All major religions teach about the dangers of "materialism" and promote some concept of spiritual investment in eternal verities and otherworldly realities. More and more, religions also have a lot to say about environmental degradation and the obligations of responsible stewardship of the planet. In all the major religions, we find some formulation of the Golden Rule, that is, do unto others as you would have others do unto you. We might ask, as many have, what an economic system based on the utility function of the Golden Rule would actually look like and note that such systems have never been realized on any grand scale.

These are all examples of a normative approach to religion and economics, taking a religious perspective and applying it critically to understanding the world of production and exchange, wealth, and poverty. This is not the purpose of this chapter. Instead of asking what religions have to say about economics, we want to first ask what economics has to say about religion. We begin by asking two questions about religion as social scientists: (1) How do religions impact economics in various social and historical situations around the world? (2) Can we apply economic models to understanding religious behavior in what is increasingly a global marketplace for religious ideas and practices?

Religions, we will discover along the way, are always both dependent variables and independent variables in economic development. Religions do make a difference to economic activity, but it is very hard to specify what in religion makes the difference. Whatever it is will be subtler than detailing the doctrinal and dogmatic differences between the great religious traditions. In different times and different circumstances, the great religious traditions have all thrived and all failed in myriad ways in different economic systems. And while economic models can be used to illuminate religious behavior, these can also distort our understanding of the phenomenon. Finally, we will use religious categories to reconceptualize economics itself as a kind of "religious" way of seeing the world.

The New Economics

We begin as economists, sociologists, political scientists, and historians, not as priests, rabbis, imams, gurus, and pundits. For now, we are not interested in questions of ultimate reality, the existence and nature of God, or the meaning and purpose of life.

Let's begin by briefly reframing human history in economic terms. Human economic activity is complex, dynamic, and adaptive. It is accelerating. In the last 250 years, the world gross national product (GNP) per person has increased thirty-seven-fold even as human population has soared.[1] The miracle of economics is that 6.7 billion people today participate in a $69 trillion global economy.[2] No one oversees it. No one designed it. No one can control it. Economic complexity emerges from the bottom up. How has this marvelous self-organized system evolved? What is economic growth, and how is it created? What is the origin of wealth, and how can individuals, business, and societies get more of it? Why, in spite of this incredible new wealth, are so many still impoverished? How and why do economic systems and civilizations sometimes also collapse?

The world we live in today is vastly different from the world of our ancestors in ancient India and Greece, in first-century Palestine, or in seventh-century Arabia. Today, we enjoy a huge variety of foods, products, services, entertainment, education, communication, and travel that would boggle the imaginations of our ancestors of even a hundred years ago, let alone two or three thousand years ago. How was this new "stuff" created in such remarkable variety and abundance?

To understand this dynamic economic history, many theorists are turning to evolution, complexity theory, and other disciplines. Wealth depends on two kinds of technologies, what we can call *physical technologies* and *social technologies*.[3] We see new physical technologies all around us. The domesticated plants and animals that we eat every day are perhaps the most significant physical technologies in human history, along with the controlled use of fire. The agricultural revolution began about ten thousand years ago and marked the beginning of a great transformation. Certainly, the ability to harness fossil fuels, as well as other new sources of energy, is a critical component of the last century's economic boom. Today, physical technologies also include the many wonders of scientific invention, like the mobile phone in my hand or the computer on my lap.

Social technologies often get short shrift in the academic study of economics, but it is here that we will discover an important role for religion. In the history of economics, social-technological innovations include the division of labor, trust and reputation, the use of money, property rights, double-entry accounting, limited-liability joint-stock corporations, the rule of law, effective banking systems, economic transparency, lack of corruption, family networks, mutual support, and something that economists now more broadly call "social capital." All these play a profound role in determining economic outcomes in communities and nations. Social technologies, as well as physical technologies, are necessary for unleashing the non-zero-sum dynamics by which new and exponentially more wealth is created.[4]

Let me put my cards on the table, because I am not a cultural relativist when it comes to human progress. It is pretty much universally the case that people everywhere prefer health over sickness, freedom over slavery, prosperity over poverty, education over ignorance, empowerment over powerlessness, pleasure over pain, justice over injustice, and living over dying. Missing from the list are three other universal preferences; humans prefer belonging over isolation, meaning over meaninglessness, and certainty over uncertainty. We might well expand this list. We may disagree about the degree and interpretation of these terms, but not about the basic principles. How much is enough? When is enough too much? And, critically, how do we decide when these universal preferences conflict with each other in actual life as they necessarily do? In economic terminology, we can refer to these values as "utility functions." The problem is that these various goods invariably conflict with each other. We cannot maximize all goods simultaneously. Religion turns out to intersect with all these utility functions and weighs in on the trade-offs among them that necessarily arise as we try to negotiate the satisfaction of our conflicting aspirations and desires.

I am convinced that our material needs, as well as our spiritual aspirations, are best served by limited forms of government that protect individual liberties. Individuals should have the freedom to produce and consume, negotiate and exchange, and worship and express themselves according to their own preferences and abilities. The role of government is critical in protecting private-property rights and individual liberties in such a free society and free economy. Limited government can also regulate commerce, communication, and other services in an effort to increase efficiencies, including goods and services such as education, transportation, and environmental protection. Limited government can also promote forms of social insurance. In the latter categories are police and national defense, but also health care and services for the poor. Taxes are the price of civilization. It is reasonable that those who benefit most from civilization pay a larger share of the costs. These convictions place me ambiguously somewhere between libertarianism and democratic socialism. What I have just articulated is now a mainstream consensus among political scientists and economists, though not universally so.

Note that these convictions are not really matters of religious doctrine. This is largely a secular argument, although the position I have articulated can be supported or rebutted with various religious arguments. There is sufficient theological and philosophical plasticity in any major religious tradition to adapt to this worldview or to resist it. We could have an endless and fascinating debate about when and how Christianity, Islam, Hinduism, or any other religion promotes or inhibits this understanding of human nature and political economy.[5] Note that this understanding of limited government, individual liberties, and market economics is also quite new in human history. The contemporary moment is thus quite unique. We should not expect ancient scriptures to map neatly onto this contemporary world and worldview. What is interesting is to see how religious thinkers interpret their traditions in support of or in opposition to our rapidly changing global economy, what evidence they muster, and what impact this agitation has within the marketplace of ideas and actions.

The Impact of Religion on Economics

Religions can be understood as part of the *social technologies* that humans invent and reinvent[6] to advance these universal values and economic objectives. Social scientists now recognize the importance of what is alternately referred to as "human capital," "social capital," and "cultural capital" in economic activities.[7] The concept of human capital recognizes that individual, groups, and cultural resources, as well as relationships, family, and friends, can have a profound effect on economic opportunity, successes, and failures. Human capital includes a number of intangible factors such as education, skills, and values. By equating these elusive human-relational qualities with the concept of "capital," we come to see these as "resources" that are also "invested" in the world of production, services, and exchange. Economists, sociologists, political scientists, and psychologists have developed multiple models, measures, and theories about how human capital and social capital impact economic development in diverse individual, microeconomic, and macroeconomic contexts.

In evaluating sources of human capital, it is clear that religion and spirituality, however they are understood, play a significant role in their development. We can call this spiritual capital.[8] The question is how social scientists can refine the study of human capital to focus specifically on how religions and spiritualities impact economic development in diverse contexts.[9] Academic guilds now exist that study these questions with the tools of economics, political science, sociology, and psychology. In particular, I call your attention to the Society for the Scientific Study of Religion (SSSR) and the recently formed Association for the Study of Religion, Economics, and Culture (ASREC).[10]

In thinking about the economics of religion, we should resist wanting to define, constrain, or distinguish the concept too narrowly. There are macroeconomic issues about religion, culture, and economic performance that need to be considered. There are microeconomic issues about particular industries or companies. And there are individual issues about discrete persons, entrepreneurs, and families. For instance, how would one measure the positive economic impact of a spiritually motivated person such as Mohandas Gandhi or Martin Luther King Jr. or, for that matter, the negative economic impact of religious fanatics? Are some people also "spiritual entrepreneurs"? And does what they help create also have economic value?

The Spirit of Capitalism

A little over one hundred years ago, the German sociologist Max Weber wrote *The Protestant Ethic and the Spirit of Capitalism.*[11] Weber argued that the values of Protestant Christianity, particularly Calvinism, played a central role in the development of European capitalism. He argued that the worldly asceticism, independence, and self-discipline nurtured by Protestant Christianity helped fuel capital formation and new industry in the early years of the Industrial Revolution. Note that Weber understood this to be an unintended consequence of Protestant Christianity— people did not convert to Protestantism to become successful capitalists. He contrasted this with Catholicism, which he assumed to be more sensuous, communal, interdependent, and spiritually lenient. It is worth remembering that Weber did not express a preference for Protestantism over Catholicism. He saw his political science as an "iron cage" of objectivity in a demystified world. Unbridled economic rationality, he warned, is also corrupting, as it substitutes the impersonal rule of bureaucracies for the moral obligations of kinship. By making this argument, he was not advocating Protestantism, Christianity, or religion in general.

However intriguing Weber's theoretical argument, it is not grounded in actual history. Most economic historians would credit the fourteenth- and fifteenth-century Northern Italian city-states with the creation of modern capitalism.[12] Venice, Genoa, Florence, Pisa, and Milan were all Catholic and pre-Reformation centers of commerce and banking. Indeed, the Italians were the bankers for all of Europe and engaged in all manner of production and trade throughout the Mediterranean and northern Europe.

As noted in the previous chapter, Weber's argument was partly a rebuttal to Karl Marx. Religion was not merely a consequence of the economic system, as Marx argued, but could also be a causally significant independent variable in transforming the economic system. In other writings, Weber argued that the religions of China, India, and the Muslim world were antithetical to the sensibilities of modern capitalism. Some of these societies, however, have done quite well in the interim, though with different cultural strengths and weaknesses. South and Southeast Asian societies, for instance, often lack an independent legal system capable of enforcing business contracts, something that Weber thought was essential to capitalism's success. Instead, these Asian societies rely on extended family ties and honor-bound networks of friends to cement trust, a necessary catalyst in economic exchange. The Chinese refer to this social solidarity as *guanxi*. Japan, Korea, Taiwan, and now mainland China have done quite well in adapting to modern, global capitalism. Chinese immigrants also play an important role in the economies of Indonesia, Thailand, Malaysia, Singapore, and the United States.

Social scientists in the last century, also reflecting Weber's antipathy toward religion, predicted that religion would fade away with the rise of capitalism, increased levels of education, and democratic cultures. This was referred to as the secularization theory, which we briefly considered in the last chapter. It turns out to be wrong, as we have witnessed a resurgence of Islam in Muslim countries, the rise of Hindu nationalism in India, the growth of congregational Buddhism in Southeast Asia, the renewal of Eastern Orthodox Christianity in the countries of the former Soviet Union, and the penetration of Christian Pentecostalism in Latin America, Africa, and Asia. The sociologist Peter Berger predicts that the twenty-first century will be the most religious century in 500 years.[13] How this global religious revival will impact economic and political life is perhaps one of the most important questions of the twenty-first century, perhaps even more important than developments in science and technology.

Culture matters in economic development around the world in different contexts because cultures can either lubricate economic activities or add friction and inefficiencies. These effects often fall in the domain of values, beliefs, and norms and, thus, are difficult to measure and quantify. Without some level of honesty and trust, however, people will not risk trade. Fatalism is not conducive to entrepreneurship. Frugality, delayed gratification, literacy, and the role of women are other factors that profoundly influence economic development and are all variables influenced by local religious cultures. Religion can be thought of as the DNA of culture, as a mechanism for programming certain values and norms into a distributed social network. Religion, however, much like gene expression in developmental biology, is also extremely variable in changing circumstances.

Francis Fukuyama provides a useful model for thinking about the different ways that social norms are constituted and propagated in societies and individuals, shown in Figure 3.1. He sets up a model with two axes and four related quadrants. There is a "rational" and an "a-rational" axis; and there is a "hierarchically generated" and a "spontaneously generated" axis. Between these intersecting lines, we now have four quadrants: values that are a-rational and spontaneous, values that are a-rational and hierarchical, values that are rational and spontaneous, and finally, values that are rational and hierarchical. In the a-rational and spontaneous

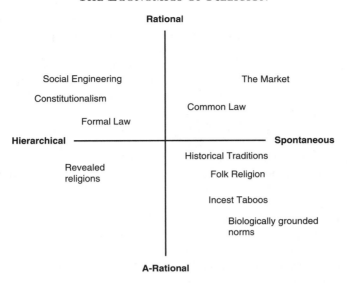

Figure 3.1   Sources of social norms and values.

quadrant, we have biologically grounded norms, like the incest taboo, as well as folk religions and historical traditions. These are emergent morals and values. In the hierarchical and a-rational quadrant, we find revealed religions and authoritarian societies. Here, morals and values are imposed from the top down by fiat. In the spontaneous and rational quadrant, we find common law and economic markets. These are emergent values, but ones that are tested by the rationality of the market. And in the hierarchical and rational quadrant, we find formal law, constitutions, and social engineering. Here, morals and values are imposed from the top down, but with rational justification.[14]

Note that religion can and does play a role in each of these axes and all four of the quadrants. Religiously motivated norms can be rational or a-rational in their justification. Religions can also be generated hierarchically from the priesthood down or spontaneously from the masses up. The distinctions further blur when we consider the possibilities of rationalizing what began a-rationally, in the activities of theology and philosophy, for instance. The opposite is also the case when rationalized religions move in the direction of fideism. What begins hierarchically can morph into a spontaneous societal norm and what begins spontaneously can be reified through hierarchical legal institutions.

This complex understanding of the religious basis of societal norms is further complicated by the variability of religions in different historical contexts. Is Confucianism particularly conducive to capitalism and progress, as some argue today? This is not what Sun Yat-sen and the other Chinese revolutionaries thought when they overthrew the last emperor in 1911. Now, suddenly, Confucian sensibilities are credited by some with the economic success of Singapore, Taiwan, and the People's Republic of China.

In *The Victory of Reason*, Rodney Stark argues that there is a necessary correlation between Christianity and "Freedom, Capitalism, and Western Success".[15] I am doubtful about the possibility of telling such a "big story" about a strong ideological correlation between any particular religion and any particular historical development. There are simply too many historically contingent variables and too many counterexamples that preclude this kind of sectarian triumphalism and cultural chauvinism. One can speculate that Protestant Christianity is good for economic development and that Taoism is bad for economic development, but it is an impossible proposition to prove. Each religious ideology is extremely plastic. Religions change and are reciprocally changed in specific historical and economic situations. We cannot isolate the impact of religion from other historical and geographic contingencies. It will not do to resurrect a simplistic base-superstructure model, in which we now valorize religion as the foundation and economic history as merely a consequence of a particular religious orientation.

The Case of Economics and Islam

Islam presents an interesting case study for the economics of religion, though as we will see, the connections are not necessarily directly linked to the teachings of Islam as such but often to unintended consequences and contingent historical developments. In this section, I will draw heavily on the work of Timur Kuran, a Turkish-American professor of political science, now at Duke University.[16]

In the golden age of Islamic civilization from the seventh to the fifteenth century, Islamic countries enjoyed some of the most successful economies of the world. These countries extended from Spain and North Africa, across the Middle East and Central and South Asia, all the way to Southeast Asia with corresponding long-distance trade routes by land and sea. It was a mercantile and market economy based on a stable currency in the form of gold and silver. A number of innovations in the social technologies of wealth creation originated in Islamic civilization, including the Hindu-Arabic number system, bills of exchange, limited partnerships, checks, promissory notes, and trusts.

How, then, did one of the world's greatest market economies fall on such hard times in recent centuries? Consider the recent UN Arab Development Reports, written by and for Arabs.[17] These studies look at twenty-two Arab countries, totaling 280 million people, countries that are overwhelmingly Muslim. They look at all dimensions of development— economic, social, civil, political, and cultural. They detail some progress, for instance, in increased life expectancy, but economic development is in decline in these Arab countries. Poverty is increasing in the Arab world; under- and unemployment is severe. The gross domestic product (GDP) in all twenty-two Arab countries stood at $531 billion in 1999 (less than Spain's, at $595 billion). Remember that these figures also include the enormous oil wealth controlled by a few of these Arab countries.

Of course, one approach is to blame this all on the legacy of European colonialism, but that begs the question of how the Islamic world became so weak, such that the Europeans could colonize their countries in the first place.[18] Others suggest that the discovery of oil in the Middle East was actually not a boon but a curse. It turns out that oil may not be such a good thing for economic development. Known as "the resource curse," there appears to be a negative relationship between extractive industries and economic development. Oil-rich countries have generally experienced poor economic performance in the last fifty years, especially when compared to developing countries with few natural resources.[19] Not included in the UN Arab Development Reports are Iran, Afghanistan, Pakistan, the Central Asia republics, Bangladesh, Malaysia, and Indonesia. Some of the analysis of the economic failures of the Arab countries might well apply to these non-Arab, predominantly Muslim countries as well. Many non-Muslim countries may also suffer from the "resource curse," quite independent of their religious and cultural assets and liabilities.

How did the Middle East go from being one of the strongest economies in the world to one of the weakest? In response to this humiliation and frustration, the twentieth century saw first the rise of anticolonial movements, followed by a pan-Arab nationalist movement, and later a pan-Islamic religious movement. Part of the impetus for the latter arose not in the Arab world but on the Indian subcontinent. The anticolonial struggle in India led to the partition of India and Pakistan in 1948. The creation of Pakistan required a new kind of religious ideology to legitimate its identity as an explicitly Muslim state. In constructing itself as a Muslim nation-by-design, rather than by default, Pakistan had to build an ideological justification for its violent birth to distinguish and separate itself from India. The spread of this invented religious ideology would later be financed by Saudi Arabian elites in the 1970s, who needed to legitimate their own private accumulation of oil wealth by paying off local religious leaders in Saudi Arabia. This then empowered fundamentalist Muslim missionary work around the world. Note that Christianity and other religions also experienced a similar revival of neo-orthodox and fundamentalist ideologies in the same time period, so there is also a global dimension to this phenomenon.

One aspect of this ferment was the reframing of Islam as a complete way of life. The concepts of "Islamic science" and "Islamic economics" were invented and legitimated in this postcolonial period. In both cases, the goal was not so much to promote science or economics but to promote a certain version of Islam. There is no such thing as Islamic physics or chemistry, nor is there a distinctly Islamic way to build a car or a cell phone, but that has not deterred Muslim intellectuals from advocating vague commitments to creating new disciplines of "Islamic science" and "Islamic economics."

An important intellectual in this history is Savyid Abul Ala Mawdudi (1903–1979), a Pakistani who developed many of these new ideas. "True Muslims merge their personalities and existences into Islam," writes Mawdudi. "They subordinate all their roles to the one role of being Muslims. As fathers, sons, husbands or wives, businessmen, landlords, labourers, employers, they live as Muslims."[20] Mawdudi helped give rise to the field of known as Islamic Economics. Today, there are academic research centers and journals on Islamic Economics throughout the Muslim world. Many of these ideas have now been institutionalized and mandated by governments in Pakistan, Saudi Arabia, Iran, Malaysia, and Sudan.

Islamic economics begins with the Qur'anic prohibition against charging interest (*riba*), as well as prohibitions against participating in forbidden activities like gambling or consumption of alcohol (*haram*), and the obligation of Muslims to contribute to charities (*zakat*). Let's look at how each of these has been interpreted and implemented.

Riba was a pre-Islamic practice in which a debt doubled if the debtor defaulted. If he defaulted a second time, the debt doubled again. The Qur'an refers to this directly, admonishing, "Those who believe do not eat up *Riba* doubled and redoubled" (3:130). In this context, the Qur'anic prohibition against *riba* can be seen as something like modern bankruptcy law, that is, as a form of debt relief. It was not a ban on interest per se. Throughout most of Islamic history, some form of interest was commonly used in actual practice. Modern banking, as in the pooling of financial resources of thousands of depositors and the lending of those resources to thousands of others, did not really enter the Middle East until the early twentieth century. And distinctly Islamic banks did not appear until the 1970s. In these Islamic banks, *riba* is interpreted as the charging of *any* interest. One can deposit money in a bank risk-free but will receive no interest. One can deposit money in a bank and receive a profit only if one shares a risk of capital loss in some "partnership" enterprise. In borrowing money from a bank, say, to buy a house, there are two options. The borrower repays the money at cost plus some predetermined fee, or the borrower and the bank form a "partnership." The partnership technically owns the house, and the borrower pays rent to the partnership until the lease is paid off. These rents can be fixed or variable depending on how they are structured. In setting these fees and rents for such loans, Islamic banks, in fact, index the time-value of money as interest added, adjust for inflation, and then repackage the loan terms under the nomenclature of "Islamic banking." It turns out to be more of a marketing ploy than a truly alternative form of banking. There is nothing wrong with offering investors and lenders the choice of participating in such institutions, but today this form of banking is mandated by law in Pakistan, Iran, Saudi Arabia, Malaysia, and Sudan. Some have argued that theses "Islamic" regulations create risk–adverse investors and entrepreneurs and promote deception in the reporting of actual profits and losses, assets, and liabilities.[21]

Note that Judaism and Christianity also explicitly forbade usury, but that these prohibitions were reinterpreted and rejected already in medieval times. In 1989, Muhammad Sayyid Tantawi, the grand mufti of Egypt, the highest religious authority in Sunni Islam, issued a fatwa allowing interest-based banking instruments, as long as they can reasonably be expected to benefit everyone, including third parties. No matter. Islamic banking practices have become more entrenched in the Islamic world in the last two decades.[22]

Haram are practices forbidden by the Qur'an. These include the consumption of alcohol and pork, eating and drinking during the days of Ramadan, engaging in gambling or prostitution, and immodesty in dress for men and particularly women. For instance, one does not find Muslim pig farmers. When Muslims live in proximity with people from other cultures, however, as we all do today in a global civilization, they cannot help but be exposed to different cultural values and practices that they consider *haram*. Exposure to these other cultures threatens the religious identities of Muslims (and others). The response is often withdrawal and self-imposed isolation, typically justified through a chauvinistic reading of tradition as superior to that of Other, who are imagined to be immoral or ignorant. This reaction to outsiders can lead to economically destructive conflicts, such as terrorist attacks on tourists and violent prohibitionist movements. Remember that fundamentalisms, both in their religious and secular manifestations, have a stake in perpetuating and heightening the perceptions of insurmountable divisions with "evil" outsiders. We will return to this dynamic in the next chapter as well as in chapter seven.

Zakat, the giving of charity, is mandated in the Qur'an and is considered one of the Five Pillars of Islam. The Qur'anic guidelines are based on the major sources of wealth in seventh-century Arabia—livestock, agricultural products, and precious metals. The prescribed rates of *zakat* vary from 2.5 percent (on crops) to 20 percent (on mining). The prescribed beneficiaries of *zakat* include the poor, the handicapped, orphans, widows, the dependents of prisoners, slaves (and the freeing thereof), *Zakat* collectors, and those who promote Islam. Note that this tax is on wealth and not simply on income. And while *zakat* is potentially an important tool for promoting public welfare, its effects are often paradoxically regressive, especially in cases where national governments have mandated *zakat* through the implementation of some version of government-enacted Sharia law.

Most forms of modern income and wealth are no longer agricultural, so the most important sources of income and wealth are often excluded from this tax. There are also loopholes by which individuals avoid paying *zakat* or otherwise hide their assets and income. A number of studies suggest (1) that the rates of *zakat* collection in Muslim societies can be as low as 0.01 percent of GDP, (2) that the agricultural sector, that is, the poorest sector of society, pays a disproportionately high percentage of *zakat*, and (3) that the poor receive the lowest percentage of charity from *zakat* while the promoters of Islamic causes and the *zakat* collectors receive the lion's share of the money accrued. Whatever *zakat* was originally intended to be, in actual practice today it tends to be a regressive tax that primarily supports the propagation of conservative Islam, not the redistribution of wealth in support of the poor.[23] When it comes to religion and economics, we need to be sensitive to unintended outcomes and paradoxical effects.

One historical outgrowth of *zakat* is the development of the *waqf* system.[24] *Waqfs* are unincorporated trusts established under Islamic law by an individual owner to provide a charitable service in perpetuity. Services provided by *waqfs* include building and maintaining mosques, schools, orphanages, bridges, hospitals, and lighthouses. The provisioning of public goods through private *waqfs* tended to retard the development of effective municipal governments in the Islamic world. By the eighteenth century, *waqfs* owned a quarter to half of the real estate in the Ottoman Empire. *Waqfs* were also popular as a "tax" shelter for private property, which was not otherwise protected from Islamic inheritance laws and from seizure by autocratic rulers. The founder of a *waqf* could appoint himself as its trustee for life, set his own salary, make appointments, and designate successors. The endowed assets of a *waqf* circumvented liquidation of estates under Islamic inheritance laws. While there were many benefits to *waqfs*, they were economically stagnant organizations, unlike self-governing corporations. Thus, the *waqf* did not cultivate strong civil societies in the Islamic world. And because civil society organizations were weak in the Middle East, these societies could not resist the formation of autocratic governments in the twentieth century.

Here we have some examples of how religion can negatively impact economic development, albeit largely through unintended consequences. It seems that bad things can happen for good reasons and good things can happen for bad reasons. Why, then, do Muslims today choose to pursue economic strategies that seem to contribute to their continued underdevelopment and impoverishment, especially when there are proven alternatives consonant with Islamic theology and actual history? One reason is that Islamist subeconomies and networks provide a vehicle for circumventing otherwise corrupt governments and class-stratified societies. These subeconomies protect against being cheated in commerce by creating a trusted cohort with whom one can conduct exchange and seek mutual aid. Supporting Islamist causes also provides those who do participate in corruption an opportunity to expiate their guilt. Islamic health clinics, clubs, schools, and camps provide valuable services to disadvantaged groups, albeit at the price of conforming to strict Islamic interpretations. Furthermore, by promoting a puritanical lifestyle, Islamist movements turn poverty into a virtue for frustrated youth with few job prospects. Finally, Islamic organizations are often the only organization within these autocratic societies where oppositional politics can be waged against corrupt regimes. Is it any wonder that Islamism is thriving and that governments seek to legitimate themselves by co-opting these very movements? Note that major political and economic reforms are most likely to originate within these very Islamic organizations, as was the case with the overthrow of the Suharto regime in Indonesia in 1998. If the energies and discipline of Islamism were diverted to education, self-improvement, and development, instead of fighting outsiders, then the movement might actually be an engine for economic progress and meaningful political reform. The industrialization of Japan in the late nineteenth and early twentieth centuries provides an interesting analogy and possible role model for the Muslim world.[25] All this should alert us to the fact that what appears dysfunctional on one level may actually be highly functional on another. Context matters in our nonreductive functionalist approach to religion.

One of the main utility functions of Islamism, as with any religion, is identity and belonging. This is not a concept that computes with most economic theorists, but clearly people will suffer material losses to shore up a threatened sense of cultural or group identity. Call it irrational-choice theory, if you like, but, clearly, man does not live by bread alone. In some profound way that economists cannot quite grasp, people desire and need a strong sense of group identity. Throughout the world today, we can see examples of religious and nationalist movements—Christian, Jewish, Muslim, Hindu, Buddhist, and so on—wherein people sacrifice their material well-being and freedoms for a stable sense of identity in a rapidly changing world.

I want to emphasize that Islam has a positive attitude toward commerce and industry, which we certainly see in the golden age of Islamic civilization. Islamic theology and institutions are not inherently static. Reflect for a moment on the recent innovations in microfinance, for which the Grameen Bank founder, Muhammad Yunus, a Muslim, received the Nobel Peace Prize in 2006. Nevertheless, there is an important relationship between Islam and economic development, and it needs further exploration by economists, historians, and Islamic scholars, particularly as we look forward to what we hope will be a more positive future for these countries and the world.

In this case study, as in others, there is often a gap between what a religion teaches and how it actually behaves in the world. The economic consequences of religious culture and institutions are often unintended and not directly related to their beliefs and practices. The interactions of religion, economics, and society are also incredibly complicated and historically contingent. For instance, the socioeconomic status of Muslim immigrants to the United States is quite high in contrast to the socioeconomic status of African American converts to Islam.[26] The difference is not about Islam as such, but other factors such as educational attainment, the legacy of racism, and the strength of family networks.

Religious Norms and Capitalist Virtues

In thinking about the economics of religion in other contexts around the world, we see an obvious link between religion and social values and norms, vices and virtues. Weber has already called our attention to thrift and the work ethic in the formation of investment capital and productivity in European capitalism, but we might also include concern for waste, the role of charity, truth-telling, and a sense of fairness as important, often religiously motivated values essential for healthy economies and functional societies. The understanding of family versus societal obligations is an important example. In the West, publicly held corporations and government offices define nepotism as a crime, whereas in other cultures, the employment of family members might be considered a moral obligation and normal. Similarly, the West understands bribery to be corrupt and illegal, whereas the payment of baksheesh is a normal part of "greasing the wheels" of business in many Muslim and non-Muslim countries. This gift-giving plays an important role in many primal societies and has been extensively studied by anthropologists around the world.

Some argue that Christian ethics, for instance, as presented by Jesus in the Sermon on the Mount, is fundamentally incompatible with capitalism, while others argue that Christianity cultivates capitalist "bourgeois virtues," that is, hope, faith, love, justice, courage, temperance, and prudence.[27] Let's contrast Jesus and Adam Smith. In *The Wealth of Nations*, Smith understood capitalism to be about individuals rationally maximizing their economic self-interest and thereby promoting the good of all. In the Gospel of Matthew, Jesus tells us,

> [D]o not worry about your life, what you will eat or what you will drink, or about your body, what you will wear.... Look at the birds of the air; they neither sow nor reap nor gather into barns, and yet your heavenly Father feeds them.... Consider the lilies of the field, how they grow; they neither toil nor spin, yet I tell you, even Solomon in all his glory was not clothed like one of these. But if God so clothes the grass of the field... will he not much more clothe you—you of little faith? Therefore do not worry, saying, "What will we eat?" or "What will we drink?" or "What will we wear?" (Matt. 6:25–31)

This does not sound like the description of an energetic entrepreneur trying selfishly to maximize his self-interest or the rest of us simply trying to pay our monthly bills. Jesus goes on to say that "it is easier for a camel to go through the eye of a needle than for a rich man to enter the kingdom of God" (Matt. 19:24). It is a wonder that anyone calls himself a Christian and a capitalist.

"Lay not up for yourselves treasures upon earth," warns Jesus. "You cannot serve both God and Mammon" (Matt. 6:19, 24). Mammon is the personification of greed, a false god. In the Spanish Bible, the word is simply translated as *dinero*, that is, money. The Ten Commandments warn "not [to] covet...anything that belongs to your neighbor" (Ex. 20:17). Of course, the whole advertising industry is about promoting just such desires and envy, not that we would necessarily notice by looking at our Christian neighbors or ourselves. In the New Testament, Paul warns of the spiritual dangers inherent in the love of money, "the root of all kinds of evil" (1 Tim. 6:9–10).

Scriptures talk about the injustices of poverty and the obligations of the wealthy to provide charity for widows, orphans, strangers, the sick, and the poor (Deut. 15:7–12; Qur'an 2:177). Jesus calls the poor "blessed." He says, "[J]ust as you did it to one of the least of these, who are members of my family, you did it to me" (Matt. 25:40).

I am not going to try to do an exegesis on the Bible. Like other sacred texts, the Bible is a subtle, sometimes paradoxical text. It is enough merely to point out that there is a lot of debate about whether and how capitalism can be reconciled with the values of Christianity. There are similar debates within Buddhism, Hinduism, Islam, and other religions. The point is that religion matters in how individuals and societies engage in manufacturing and commerce. Religions also have perceived and deeply held "utility functions" for their "consumers."

It is useful to remember that Adam Smith's first book was on moral philosophy, not economics. In *The Theory of Moral Sentiments* (1759), Smith argued that people have natural moral sympathies with their neighbors. There are "evidently some principles in [man's] nature," he wrote, "which interest him in the fortune of others, and render their happiness necessary to him, though he derives nothing from it except the pleasure of seeing it." He celebrates virtues and values like "humanity, justice, generosity, and public spirit," but especially "prudence."[28] By the time he published *The Wealth of Nations* (1776), Smith sees a different side of human nature:

> It is not from the benevolence of the butcher, the brewer or the baker that we expect our dinner, but from their regard of their own interest. We address ourselves not to their humanity, but to their self-love, and never talk to them of our necessities, but of their advantage.[29]

Altruism and greed are apparently in conflict in these two classic texts by the same author. It may be, however, that these two very different books by the great theorist of laissez-faire economics are closely related, that without a society guided by moral sentiments, the centrifugal forces of capitalism would tear a society apart. Religion, as one of the primary conveyors of our natural moral sentiments, is, thus, a necessary part of a successful capitalist society. In this view, the very tension between religious morality and capitalist greed is a necessary condition for the success of capitalism.

A balanced study of religion and economics must consider the positive and negative aspects of both with reference to particular goods accrued or foregone in different business situations and different cultural contexts. The economic implications of religion are not necessarily all positive, as we saw in our case study on Islamic economics. Religions are often used to support exclusivist ideologies and promote violent conflicts. Religiously motivated conflicts destroy not only human life but also economic productivity. Is it possible to isolate and measure religion's contributions to war or, for that matter, the prevention and resolution of societal conflicts?

Are there downsides to investing time and resources in religion? Can we think about investments in religion and spirituality as a kind of "opportunity cost"? How would we calculate cost–benefit comparisons of investing in building a new church versus some other economic activities? What are the many utility functions of religion, perceived and real? How do these utility functions differ for individuals and groups? Of course, the priest, the imam, the guru, and the rabbi in any organized religion also have a utility function in the promotion of their religion, which is why the priesthood is sometimes playfully and cynically referred to as "the second-oldest profession." We will not be able to answer any of these questions definitively, but posing the questions in this manner turns out to be quite edifying.

Shifting the Bell Curve

The best way to illustrate the impact of religion on economics is to think of probability distributions in statistics, for instance, in relation to the physical characteristics of a species, where we discover a universal pattern known as the bell curve. If we plot the distribution of the height of a large group of people on Cartesian coordinates—the horizontal for height and the vertical for number of individuals—we discover that there are very few short people and very few tall people, while the vast majority will occur somewhere in the middle. It is called a bell curve because it looks a lot like the profile of a bell, with a flange at the bottom of a tall, rounded shape. We can assume, and social scientists have tried to measure, that many other human traits have a similar distribution, whether we are talking about musical and artistic creativity, mathematical intelligence, athletic abilities, or moral character and economic virtues. If we could measure it, the population distribution of goodness and virtue would look very much like a bell curve. There would be very few psychopaths and laggards in any society. There would also be very few exceptionally morally virtuous and economically superproductive people. Most of us would fall somewhere in the middle. External circumstances involving culture, religion, education, and political structures can shift the distribution of goodness and virtue in one direction or another, but the basic distribution pattern will remain the same. Perhaps in extreme situations, the bell curve can become distorted, but this will be the exception, not the rule.

Good religion will have an effect similar to good governance. Good religion is about creating a value structure and a decency system that limit the destructive sides of human nature and accentuate the positive. Good religion can help internalize values that help the vast majority of us in the middle choose to do the right thing, in part by shaming vices and in part by celebrating virtues. When religions, cultures, and governments are dysfunctional, otherwise good people can be compelled to do very evil things in extreme circumstances. And when religions, cultures, and governments are functional and wholesome, otherwise bad people can be encouraged to be productive and functional members of society, given a "sacred canopy" of constraints and incentives suspended in a web of transcendent hope for the future.[30]

Economic Models of Religion

Our second major question in this chapter is how to apply economic models to understanding religion itself. One of the first to advance such a theory was Karl Marx, who argued that religions were a product of the economic system. In Marx's analysis, feudalism created Catholicism, and capitalism created Protestantism. Religion belongs to the superstructure, a reflection of the economic base. This theory of religion is too simplistic, most would agree today. To reverse Marx's metaphor, religions can also be part of the base, the foundation that shapes the economic structure of a society. The directions of causation run both ways. Religion is both a dependent and independent variable in economic development.

To the extent that economic structures influence religiosity, however, we should be expecting and are witnessing dramatic changes in religion in the era of global capitalism. We are seeing the rise of consumer-driven religion in the world. Instead of investing all their spiritual resources in a single tradition, people are developing "diversified religious portfolios." Part of the "spiritual, not religious" phenomenon is a new interest in "shopping around" for religious ideas and practices from a variety of traditions. Certainly, more people practice hatha yoga today in the United States than do so in India, but this yoga is largely disconnected from its Hindu spiritual roots. Evangelical Christians now teach Christian "yoga," as in "Stretching for Jesus." The Sufi mystic poet Jalāl ad-Dīn Muḥammad Rūmī, as translated by Coleman Barks, is now the most popular poet in the United States, but few of his readers could tell you what the Five Pillars of Islam are. Kabbalah, the Jewish mystical tradition, has attracted non-Jewish celebrity disciples, including the rock star Madonna. New Age conferences and publications are a virtual Walmart of different esoteric practices taken from here, there, and everywhere.

Paradoxically, fundamentalism is also a response to religion in an era of global capitalism. In a time of rapid change and uncertainty, it may be more spiritually, psychologically, and sociologically comforting to have a single and rigorously defined belief system and group identity. As we will learn in the next chapter, there are advantages to belonging to a defined group, religion being one of the markers of group identity. And the stricter the group, the greater the benefits of membership tend to be. Economists use the language of "irreversible investments" to describe certain types of "religious investments." In fact, the fastest-growing religions in the world today are Islam, Pentecostal Christianity, and amorphous New Age–type syntheses. The first two are "irreversible investments," while the latter can be thought of as a "diversified portfolio."

We can now talk about a global marketplace for religions. The University of Chicago economist Gary Becker has developed competitive models of religious markets. Not unlike corporations, religions seek monopolistic control over their religious markets. Adam Smith addresses this phenomenon in *The Wealth of Nations* and clearly favors the idea of religious competition, although he himself is not particularly religious. State religions in Europe are examples of religious monopolies, often established centuries ago. Other examples might include Islam in Iran and Saudi Arabia or perhaps Buddhism in Thailand and Sri Lanka. Becker argues that competition is good for religious markets. In those countries where there are religious monopolies, religiosity ultimately declines, as in the case of Western Europe.[31] In those countries where there is healthy religious competition, such as the United States, religiosity thrives and grows.[32] Historical studies in the nineteenth and early twentieth centuries also suggest that, in those countries where Catholic and Protestant missionaries competed with each other, the religious groups provided better schools and hospitals, whereas in those countries where they had monopolies, the services provided were inferior.[33] In this analysis, religious competition is a good thing, and the world needs more of it. We must make sure, however, that this competition between faiths does not turn into violence, in which case all of us will be losers. Certainly, the complex mixture of churches and temples in local communities is an increasingly global phenomenon, one that we need to manage carefully and nurture in order to prevent destructive religious competition, as witnessed so often in the past.

Rational Choice Theory in Religion

Another version of the economic modeling of religion uses rational-choice theory, as promoted by Rodney Stark and others. In this view, people are making rational choices about the utility functions of religion. As with other investments or purchases, the benefits are largely a matter of perception once we get beyond the maintenance of basic biological needs. The utility function of adopting a particular religion can be eternal or merely temporal. Stark uses these insights to explain the rapid rise of Christianity in the Roman Empire.[34]

Now, there are a lot of problems with rational-choice theory in classical economics. It turns out to be a gross distortion of real human economic activity. Traditional economic models assume "incredibly smart people in unbelievably simple situations," while the real world involves "believably simple people [coping] with incredibly complex situations."[35] How would one actually be an informed consumer of religion in a global market-place? What would it mean to select "the best" religion, and how would one go about doing this? Most people are simply born into and raised in a tradition. If they become disillusioned with that tradition, they do not necessarily convert to another tradition. Sociologically, they tend to drift back to their tradition when they begin to raise children. In many cases, there are severe penalties for conversion, including social ostracism or even death in the case of strict Islamic law. So the economics of religion is not really a free market.

As already noted, we are increasingly encountering what might be called "supermarket spirituality," in which people mix and match a little bit of this and that—yoga on Monday, AA on Tuesday, Zen on Wednesday, hedonism on Thursday, Sufism on Friday, Kabbalah on Saturday, and Unity Church on Sunday. While some of this approach may be crass and superficial, the history of all religions has involved lots of cross-fertiliza-tion, borrowing, and outright plagiarism. It is just that now the pace of this cross-fertilization is accelerating in our globalized world. Religious movements now use radio, television, and the Internet to promote them-selves with the marketing acumen of Madison Avenue.

Rational-choice theory is about perceived benefits, so it need not be "rational" at all, but then neither are everyday economic choices necessar-ily rationally self-interested. The theory, as applied to religions, however, does lead to some interesting hypotheses about the decisions of individuals and the behavior of religious movements. For instance:

Hypothesis: "In making religious choices, people will attempt to conserve their religious capital."

Hypothesis: "The greater their religious capital, the less likely people are to either reaffiliate or convert to a new religion. When people reaffiliate or convert to a new religion, they will tend to select an option that maximizes their conservation of religious capital."

Hypothesis: "To the extent that religious groups provide individu-als with religious capital that is inimitable (cannot be imitated), the religious capital will retain members."

Hypothesis: "When religious groups offer inimitable core teach-ings, which protect existing religious capital, the chance of a schism is reduced."

Hypothesis: "To the extent that religious groups are able to ease entry into the group by accepting existing religious capital and are still able to offer distinctive capital that prevents defection, they will hold a competitive advantage."[36]

There are also often perceived material benefits to conversion. For instance, in moving to a new community, people will seek to join the

"right" church or synagogue to gain access to social elites or other networks. Economic and educational opportunities may have a lot to do
with explaining why Roman Catholic seminaries in India today are filled
with young men studying for the priesthood, while Roman Catholic
seminaries in the United States are largely empty. Increasingly, educated
English-speaking Buddhist monks have opportunities to travel and teach
in the United States, Canada, and Europe. Though these monks may be
sincere and serious Buddhists, the visa and the plane ticket are still nice
perks. Perhaps also some of the appeal of Pentecostalism in Africa, Asia,
and Latin America today is linked to hoped-for material benefits in this
life, more so than in the next. The gospel of health and wealth is often
preached at Pentecostal churches. Certainly, conversions to Christianity
during the colonial period often involved subtle and not-so-subtle forms
of economic coercion. In all cases, membership has its privileges.

In a related development, some use evolutionary models to study religion. In *Darwin's Cathedral*, the evolutionary biologist David Sloan Wilson
uses group-selection theory to argue that religions function to promote
in-group altruism and, therefore, promote group survival in competition
with other groups. The willingness of some to sacrifice for the group is
necessary for the survival of any society. With that also comes a dangerous side of religion in promoting intergroup competition.[37] This will be
the subject of my next chapter, but note that there is an explicit economic
dimension of this approach.

The Economics of Religious Minorities

In many situations around the world, minority religious groups within a
larger society are often quite successful with regard to the dominant culture. We might call this the "successful minority syndrome," and there
is almost always an ethnic and religious dimension of this phenomenon.
Whether we are talking about Chinese descendants in Southeast Asia,
Parsis in India, Jews in Europe and North America, Tamils in Sri Lanka,
or recent Asian and African immigrants in the United States, within a
generation or two, these groups are often very successful in socioeconomic
terms. The reasons for their success have a lot to do with the sociology of
being a minority group within a larger society and the perceived need to
stick together through mutual aid, hard work, and educational advance-
ment in reaction to real and perceived insecurities from the dominant
society. Minorities often become "middle men" in economic production
and exchange, so ethnic minorities are often well placed to take off in
capitalist societies. Religion may be part of the glue that holds the group
together and prevents assimilation. Tragically in these situations, envy,
resentment, and scapegoating by the dominant group often lead to communal violence, as happened in the 1998 riots in Indonesia, when Chinese
Indonesian shops were burned and thousands killed in mob violence.

I need to emphasize, however, that minorities are not always successful, as in the case of African Americans in the United States or Muslims in India, for many complex and vexing historical reasons. The power of the state and the dominant culture can also be manipulated to discriminate against minorities. Our discussion of religion and economics can help us understand the circumstances in which religiously motivated violence is likely to increase. When there is a link between religion and ethnicity, there is an increased risk of religiously motivated violence. When political movements are based on a religious agenda, there is an increased risk of religiously motivated violence. When state power is used to favor a particular religion, there is a danger of religious violence. And when political, social, and economic power is distributed based on religious identity, there is an increase in religiously motivated violence. Religion is one of the markers of group identity and majority and minority status within any society and between societies. So, religion can have positive and negative repercussions for the group and the society as a whole. The need to mitigate religiously motivated violence is one of the reasons that I am bullish about limited government and individual liberties in the modern world. The alternative looks like endless violent conflicts, as I have witnessed while living and studying in Israel-Palestine and Sri Lanka.

Economics as a Religion

This chapter has surveyed some of the interesting theories and research being undertaken under the rubric of the economics of religion.[38] We have asked what impact religions have on economics in different situations around the world. We have also asked how economic models can be used to understand religious commitments and behaviors. The results are inconclusive and complex but extremely interesting.

It should be clear now why I advocate a nonreductive functionalist account of religion. In our consideration of the economics of religion, we have already encountered many different theoretical approaches and historically contingent interpretations. Religion turns out to be both a dependent and independent variable in economic history. Because religion is functional, it can also be dysfunctional, but the adjudication thereof requires a careful consideration of specific macro- and microeconomic situations and an appreciation of unintended consequences and paradoxical effects. None of this discussion as yet has any direct bearing on the truth claims of different religions, but all this can help religions in the hermeneutics and practices of becoming more wholesome and more effective in promoting material and perhaps also spiritual well-being.

Global capitalism is a dynamic, creative, and powerful force reshaping the world as we speak. While we have witnessed enormous progress and prosperity in the last century, we should also be aware that almost half of the world's population lives on less than two dollars per day and is confronted with life-threatening poverty. Capitalism is also inherently unstable, as we are witnessing in the recent global economic collapse. All of us have a responsibility to look beyond mere supply and demand, profits and losses, and the fluctuation of stocks and bonds to address the needs of the poor as well as threats to the environment. Here, too, religion and economics overlap.

Economics can also function as a religion for some, if we take the broad definition of religion that I am advocating. Economics as a "religion" manifests itself not just in the sometimes destructive pursuit of easy wealth by individuals and nations but in many of the guiding and unexamined assumptions embedded in the academic discipline of economics.[39] It is not necessarily the case that exponential economic growth and excessive wealth lead to happier and healthier lives. Nor is exponential economic growth necessarily sustainable vis-à-vis a finite planet with limited energy and material resources.

Every day we use a "system of symbols"—money—that comes with its own "moods and motivations," to reference Clifford Geertz's broad definition of religion in the last chapter. Money, after all, is merely a symbolic system of value. Money is not "real." I cannot literally eat a dollar bill, nor would it literally be much use in providing shelter or clothing. The symbols of economics only have relative values; they have no ultimate value. Money only has power when we invest it with exchange value for things that are really useful, like food and shelter, goods and services. The miracle is that this "mere" symbol system dramatically changes our material lives in profound ways that are both intimate and global.

It is now well established in economics that the psychology of the market matters. Distributed psychological attitudes are a significant factor in how economies perform. We are warned of the dangers of "irrational exuberance," which leads to economic bubbles bursting and fortunes real and virtual being lost. So too, a market that is "cynically cautious" depresses economic exchange and investment, leading to negative outcomes. We would all hope to be "considered optimists," investing wisely in the hopes of a positive return through activities that are well managed with sound finances and wealth-creating innovations. Some days, the best that I can muster is "hopeful pessimism." In all these cases, the psychology of the market is partially a self-fulfilling prophecy. This we know about economic markets.

Religions are minimally also symbolic systems of values. Again, we can bracket for the time being their truth claims, adopting instead a phenomenological, functional, and pragmatic approach to religions. In the marketplace of religious ideas, we can also invoke similar concepts used to describe economic markets. Irrational exuberance on the part of religions can result in very dangerous and destructive outcomes for societies. Cynical caution can also be toxic for individuals and societies. Considered optimism is hypothetically optimal for religion, as it is in the market. In their prophetic roles, religions should minimally promote hopeful pessimists, a hope against all odds, carefully and soberly reckoned. As it is with economics, so too is it with religions. All these attitudes are partially self-fulfilling prophecies, both for individuals and for societies.

Religions, broadly defined, are part of the distributed systems of values that shape human thought and behavior. Economic markets are in a profound sense also "moral markets," insofar as they represent a kind of aggregation of human virtues and vices. Moral values can alternately lubricate economic development or add friction. We need to talk about these moral markets—the economics of values—that undergird healthy economic activity, remembering that these values are also transformed as economies evolve.

Economic markets are complex distributed systems with their own logics and rationalities that we cannot fully understand, predict, or manage. Religions are also complex distributed systems, but religions point beyond themselves to questions of ultimate meaning and values. In closing, we might recall the words of Socrates: "Wealth does not bring goodness, but goodness brings wealth and every other blessing both to the individual and the state."[40]

CHAPTER FOUR

The Evolution of Religion

We now turn to new evolutionary accounts of religion. As before, I invite you to look at the world and religion with new eyes, to suspend for a moment whatever religious or philosophical commitments you bring to this discussion. For the time being, we bracket the truth claims of religions and seek to understand only how religions function in human societies. To begin this review of the evolution of religion, we need to think in terms of human history and prehistory.

Explaining Religions

The rise of global maritime travel in the fifteenth century and, with it, the European colonial expansion marked the beginning of what might be called the third or fourth great migration of humans around the world (the other great migrations occurring before the invention of agriculture). And with this migration, Europeans and other peoples of the world were confronted with the great variety of languages, cultures, and religious beliefs and practices. Not only did great civilizations now interact across great distances, but innumerable smaller populations in isolated areas such as Australia, the Amazon, Africa, and the South Pacific islands also came into contact with Europeans and, with these contacts, encountered the challenge of understanding, translating, and comprehending diverse cultural and religious practices.[1] These other civilizations and primal cultures seemed strange to the European scientists and explorers, many of whom were also starting to question their own religious tradition. Other cultures were faced with a similar disorientation in this global encounter.

Why this diversity of religious beliefs and practices? Indeed, why religion at all? Remember, we are thinking about all religions, not just the one that you are familiar with from the inside. Not all gods are the same. Not all views of the one God even within the same tradition are the same. Supernatural agents can be very different. Some spirits are stupid and can be tricked by clever humans. Some gods die. Some religions are exclusive; others are inclusive and synchronistic. The official religion of theologians, pundits, and philosophers is generally not the religion practiced on the streets. Some religions emphasize orthodoxy; others emphasize orthopraxis, that is, it is not what you believe that counts, but what you do that matters. Indeed, many religions do not even have the concept of "religion."

How are we to account for this wild world of different faiths and practices? There are four traditional responses in the social sciences to explaining religion. These will be familiar to most of you.

First, it is thought that religions provide explanations for natural phenomena and existential concerns. Why the seasons of the year? Why the motions of the sun, moon, and stars? Why natural disasters like earthquakes, volcanoes, floods, and droughts? Why lightning and thunder? Why is there disease? Death? Why do the living vividly remember the dead? Why do we dream at night, and how should we understand these dreams? Why do some people have peak mystical experiences? Why do some people seem to have special charisma? Why are some people crazy? The great minds of diverse civilizations and isolated tribes reflected on these great questions and devised answers in stories of gods, spirits, and cosmologies. Religion, then, was akin to science in its purposes, but its answers are primitive, fantastic, and wrong.

The second line of thought in explaining religion is based on our psychological need for comfort in the face of existential terror before evil, suffering, death, and uncertainty. Because of our human self-consciousness, our species can anticipate its death, and this creates extreme anxiety. Furthermore, we witness and fear evil and suffering in the world. Religion, then, arises as compensation, as a way of relieving these anxieties with a hoped-for life after death or reincarnation. Furthermore, this future would provide heavenly recompense for the toil and suffering experienced in this life, as well as just punishment for those who caused evil and suffering to others in this life. Like Dante in the *Inferno*, we can take some comfort and perverse pleasure in the torment of those who torment us today and hope for eternal happiness in a hedonistic heaven as repayment for the pain and finitude that we experience in this life.

The third theory of religion proceeds from the needs of societies, not individuals. In order for small- or large-scale social groups to work, they need some mental-moral "glue" to bind individuals together in moral order and social harmony. Humans are otherwise thought to be too egotistical and self-centered to live well together. We have a proclivity to be lazy and lustful, to rape, murder, pillage, and steal. Though society may have rules, we also tend to bend and break the rules; we want to receive the benefits but not pay our dues. External compulsion to cooperate is extremely limited. Religions provide not only a means to articulate the rules for a society and a mechanism of enforcement but also a way to internalize the social norms of society in individuals and families through the repetition of stories and rituals. Religion is, therefore, functional, indeed necessary, for social order. When one religion is removed, it will have to be replaced by a new religion, or social chaos will ensue.

The fourth theory of religion argues that people are naturally superstitious and credulous. Whether because of wishful thinking or gullible stupidity, it seems you can coax people into believing and doing all kinds of ridiculous things. When these bizarre beliefs and practices are reinforced from childhood on by families, friends, and cultures, they become irresistible and taken for granted. It is not just in areas like the I-Ching, astrology, tarot cards, voodoo dolls, and alien abductions that we witness this credulity among our fellow humans; government-sponsored lotteries in the United States and elsewhere are best understood as a tax-on-stupidity. Even most educated people do not understand simple principles of probability, let alone scientific causality. As the saying goes, "There's a sucker born every minute."[2] Religions thrive on this credulity.

These are the old sciences of religion. Some of these ideas we already encountered in chapter two in our review of Auguste Comte and others. Now, for many intellectuals, and indeed in popular culture, these four views of religion have become widely accepted and commonplace. To reiterate, religions (1) provide explanations, (2) provide comfort, (3) provide for social order, and (4) are illusions. This makes my job as a scholar of comparative religion rather frustrating because now everyone is an expert in religion with a just-so story that he can insert whenever it suits him. With these "scientific" explanations of religion, there is also no longer a need to pay attention to the stuff on the inside—the scriptures, authorities, histories, interpretations, saints and sages, rituals, and so on.—because none of it is true. In modern academe, a great ignorance now exists about religion. So, I get neither respect nor authority in my chosen academic field. One does not get that response when discussing genetic transcription factors, the mass of neutrinos, or the possibilities of quantum computation.

Let us revisit the question of "why religion" by first rejecting these four explanations. While useful as far as they go, these modern accounts of religion are simply not satisfactory.[3] First, religious explanations can be extravagant and complex, not necessarily easy to understand on an intuitive or causal level. I think, for instance, of Hindu cosmology with its extraordinary complexity and layers of elaborations. While Hindu cosmology is fantastic in scope and imagination, much simpler and perhaps much more satisfying explanations could be devised, indeed have been scientifically discovered. Why do humans create these sometimes baroque explanations, and why do they persist—for instance, in the case of Young Earth Creationism in the United States—even after scientific explanations have been discovered that conclusively prove a long Earth history—around 4 billion years—and an even longer universe history—around 13.7 billion years? At least Hindu cosmology intuitively captures the enormous scale of the universe, if none of the actual scientific details. Why do we passionately hold on to these antiquated myths in opposition to factually and practically true scientific accounts?

Second, while religions can be seen as a source of comfort, they can also be sources of new dangers and holy terror. Many feel some anguish in the face of religious demands for their behavior and obligations. Religious belief does not necessarily bring ease of mind or ignorant bliss; it can also bring many new fears of devils, demons, witches, ghosts, jinns, and angels. God's goodness is ambivalent; just ask Job or those who survived the December 2004 tsunami. Far from seeking revelation, the prophets of the Hebrew scripture generally resisted God's call, suggesting that maybe He had called the wrong phone number and certainly the wrong person. When we add to this the prospects for an afterlife or reincarnations, we now need to be afraid not just about this life but also about our eternal souls or karma. Religions need not be a source of comfort; indeed, they are often quite the opposite. Again, we are compelled to revisit the question of "why religion"

Third, while religions can be seen as a functional force promoting social cohesion and moral harmony, they can also be oppressive and divisive forces within society and between societies. Why would people "buy into" a belief system that can also oppress them and enrich others? Why would people invest in religious institutions and hierarchies that promote violence against others, including using their resources and their bodies as "canon fodder" in religiously rationalized wars? And why would people give up so much of their hard-earned wealth to support extravagant construction projects and lazy clerics living in relative luxury? Certainly, as much strife as harmony has resulted from religions. Religions may be functional, but they can also be dysfunctional. Again, we are compelled to revisit the question of "why religion."

Finally, we are told that religions are illusions and that people are rather gullible, full of wishful thinking and credulous beliefs. It turns out that we are not equally credulous. There are many religious ideas that we reject out of hand as implausible. It seems there must be some hidden grammar and syntax to why we believe what we believe and that we are not equal-opportunity fools to just any old tall tale. Indeed, there are many fantastical stories—one example that comes to mind is the Harry Potter phenomenon—that we enjoy without ever thinking of these as true. Many cultures have fantastical stories that they tell their children— for instance, the story of Santa Claus—but no one of a certain age believes they are true. Why do we invest so heavily in religious stories, as opposed to other fantasies we happily entertain, but do not take seriously? Why these particular religious beliefs and practices, instead of the set of all possible illusory beliefs and practices?

The Evolutionary Paradigm

In this chapter, we are going to put on the spectacles and filters of evolutionary psychology to try to understand religious and spiritual phenomena.

How might the evolutionary sciences help us understand the origins and persistence of religion? This is a useful hypothesis. Indeed, many aspects of human behavior can be understood on the basis of our genetically evolved physiological, mental, and social capacities.[4] In spite of our many significant differences from other cultures, we are, nevertheless, evolved animals, members of a single mammalian species, capable of interbreeding, and sharing remarkable cognitive and social capacities across every ethnic and linguistic group the world round. Given this universal human biology and the hundreds of universal anthropological characteristics we exhibit,[5] why the diversity of religious belief and practice? Indeed, as social scientists, we must ask why religion exists at all. Let us begin with a brief review of evolutionary history and theory, before we see how this might apply to humans in general and specifically to understanding the diversity and forms of religion.

Humans and our most immediate hominid ancestors evolved as hunters and gatherers in small tribes and extended families. Paleoarcheologists date the rise of modern *Homo sapiens* to around 160,000 years ago in Africa. For now, we do not need to concern ourselves with the many immediate precursors of *Homo sapiens*. We take it for granted that life evolves from life in a process dating back 3.7 billion years ago on this planet. The transmutation of species is the foundation of modern biology, and nothing makes sense in biology without this as our point of departure. There is no serious debate that some version of evolution is the case, though we can entertain lots of debates about how this happens and what it means for human culture. There is no serious scientific disagreement about *what happened when*. The sciences of evolution are based on sound geology, paleontology, radioactive dating, morphological studies, developmental biology, and, significantly today, genetic analyses of the diverse species of life. Indeed, if we go back far enough, not only do all of us share common ancestry with early humans in Africa,[6] but we are also all descendants of the so-called primordial slime. The point, however, is not to denigrate humans. The point is to appreciate that the genetics of even simple bacterial forms of life is very much a part of the human genome today. Life is us, though for our purposes, we need only focus today on the last 200,000 years.

Humans existed as small hunter-gatherer tribes for over eight thousand generations before the advent of agriculture. Our ancestors adapted and lived successfully in diverse climates, starting in the savannas of Africa and then traveling to coastal regions, tropical rain forests, high mountains, and cold Arctic regions. Our ancestors survived a major global climatic catastrophe some seventy thousand years ago with the explosion of Mt. Toba in Sumatra. This supervolcanic eruption, estimated to be three thousand times greater than the 1980 eruption of Mt. Saint Helens, changed everything overnight. The volcanic ash released in the atmosphere reduced average global temperature by 5° Celsius for seven years and triggered a global ice age. The Indian subcontinent was covered with five meters of volcanic ash. Humanity was reduced to some one thousand to ten thousand breeding pairs. Yet we survived; and as the sky cleared and the ice slowly retreated over the millennia, we resumed our expansion, eventually migrating to every continent except Antarctica. This is a story also recorded in our mitochondrial DNA.[7]

We need to know this story because, from an evolutionary point of view, 99 percent of human history occurred prior to the advent of agriculture, great civilizations, the printing press, and the Internet. If we want to talk about the biology of religion, we need to understand that we all still possess the genes, physiology, brains, and sociality of hunter-gatherers, albeit living in a very different environment today. To be sure, much has changed dramatically in the last centuries, but we are physiologically and psychologically more or less identical with these early humans. Conceived in pleasure, born in pain, we have a long period of childhood dependency before we are initiated as adults with the contingencies of survival and reproduction in small groups. Successful hunting and gathering required enormous skills and cooperation, communal knowledge of flora and fauna, seasons and geography, predators and prey, the making of tools and shelter, methods for maintaining group cohesion, and mutual support. Many of these skills were acquired in specific and diverse ecosystems, so we needed to pass on essential survival skills to the next generation through some form of non-genetic transmission, that is, education. It could not have been all in our genes. Humans are general-purpose adapters, the first large mammal successfully to inhabit all corners on the globe. This past, with all its diversity and flexibility, is encoded in our genes and the very structure of our brains. While we have differentially coevolved with our tools and our domesticated plants and animals in the last ten thousand years, in ways that have also changed our genetic make-up,[8] these genetic changes of the last ten thousand years are generally not deemed to be all that significant in terms of innate behavioral and psychological dispositions of modern humans.

The acquisition and development of language are certainly important parts of this story, but it is hard to know when and how language evolved, given that all we have are fossil remains and stone tools. Paleoarcheologists talk about a "Great Leap Forward" that occurred some sixty thousand years ago, characterized by more sophisticated stone tools. For instance, the bow and arrow appears somewhere in Africa or Eurasia some thirty thousand years ago but, by the dawn of agriculture, had spread to every corner of the world except Australia. Perhaps this "Great Leap" was correlated with some advance in human language, perhaps the advent of new grammar and complex conditional thoughts. In any case, by twenty-five thousand years ago, we see the emergence of symbolic culture—the cave paintings in Lascaux, France, and elsewhere; the Venus of Willendorf and other fertility statuary; the ritualized burials of dead humans—all suggestive of what we would have to call religious, symbolic culture, though we can only speculate on what the humans of those times actually were thinking and why they did these things.

The Principles of Evolutionary Psychology

We return to our guiding question: how does evolutionary psychology explain religion? To answer that question, we must briefly review the theory of evolution. That there is common descent and the transmutation of species over long periods of time is taken for granted in biology today. The evidence is overwhelming and conclusive. There is some debate within biology on *how* this evolution happens. We will revisit this question in chapter eight, but for now let us stick with the theory of natural selection as the account for the process by which evolution occurs. Charles Darwin's formulation of this is certainly the easiest to understand in its simplicity. Stated as a series of observations and propositions, the theory of natural selection goes like this:

1. Offspring of the same parents are similar, but not identical. There are variations among offspring.
2. All species are capable of reproducing at an exponential rate of increase.[9]
3. This reproductive drive to overpopulate leads to a universal struggle for survival, as resources are scarce and competition becomes extreme.
4. Those variations among offspring that tend to promote survival and reproduction will tend to be passed on, while those that do not will tend to die out. This is where the "natural selection" occurs, through disease, starvation, predation, and death, as well as in sexual competition to reproduce.
5. The accumulation of all these natural selections over long periods of time, including variations in ecologies and geographical isolation, leads to the transmutation of species

In Darwin's own words,

Owing to this struggle for life, any variation, however slight and from whatever cause proceeding, if it be in any degree profitable to an individual of any species, in its infinitely complex relations to other organic beings and to external nature, will tend to the preservation of that individual, and will generally be inherited by its offspring. The offspring, also, will thus have a better chance of surviving, for, of the many individuals of any species which are periodically born, but a small number can survive. I have called this principle, by which each slight variation, if useful, is preserved, by the term of Natural Selection, in order to mark its relation to man's power of selection. We have seen that man by selection can certainly produce great results, and can adapt organic beings to his own uses, through the accumulation of slight but useful variations, given to him by the hand of Nature. But Natural Selection, as we shall hereafter see, is a power incessantly ready for action, and is as immeasurably superior to man's feeble efforts, as the works of Nature are to those of Art.[10]

This is all fine and well for plants and animals, but what about humans? The earlier attempts to apply Darwin's theory to humans were referred to as Social Darwinism. Herbert Spencer coined the phrase "survival of the fittest," which Darwin incorporated into later editions of *Origins*. The phrase "survival of the fittest" would quickly become shorthand for natural selection, though the term is misleading. We might better say "survival of the fitting in," that is, fitting in to some particular ecological niche. Success is always context-dependent. In any case, Social Darwinism quickly became the all-purpose tool to support all kinds of ideological causes, from predatory capitalism to Communism, from racism to sexism, from European colonialism to Nazism, from eugenics to genocide. The application of Darwinian principles to human societies got a deservedly bad reputation. Historians suggest that the real impetus for the conservative religious reaction against Darwinism in the United States arose not from concern about the origins of species but from the perception that the theory of natural selection as applied to humans was inherently immoral.[11]

The ethical dilemma is that Darwinism understands only variation, survival, and reproduction. And survival only matters insofar as it serves the purposes of reproduction. There is no way something can persist in nature if it does not survive long enough to reproduce. The meaning and purpose of life, including human life, seem to be reduced to a rather primitive level.

There has been a revival in the use of evolutionary principles to understand human thought and behavior. In the 1970s, it was referred to as sociobiology,[12] but its advocates were criticized and denounced. Today, the discipline is referred to as evolutionary psychology, and its practitioners have been quietly studying human behavior, decoding the species-specific human nature that we have been endowed with due to our particular history as all-purpose hunter-gatherers. Evolutionary psychology is based on the study of adaptations, differentially selected, over hundreds of thousands of years. If it does not serve the needs of survival and reproduction, the characteristic would not and could not have persisted as a human trait for very long.

Probably you are not used to thinking like an evolutionary psychologist, so below are some insights without explanation of how problems of behavior and genetics are typically framed:

- intrasexual competition and the operational sex ratio (i.e., the ratio of males to females in different species as pertains to the competition for a mate)
- postcopulatory intrasexual competition (i.e., the competition between sperm from different males to impregnate the female egg in nonmonogamous breeding populations)

- sexual dimorphism in humans and other species (i.e., differences in size, strength, and features of male and female of a species, based on mating behaviors)
- criteria in human mate choice—male and female, cross-cultural universals (i.e., what do men find universally attractive in females and what do females find universally attractive in men in the selection of mates)
- encephalization quotients in hominid evolution and the female pelvis bottleneck (i.e., the size of our ancient ancestors' brains grew to such an extent that they often could not pass through the female pelvis at childbirth, so adaptations in female pelvis size ensued)
- gossip replacing grooming as form of maintaining social cohesion in humans (e.g., something like 40 percent of chimpanzee interaction is taken up by the act of grooming others in the tribe, understood to enhance social relations)
- comparative testis size in primate species and sperm competition (i.e., the correspondence between proportional sizes of primate male sex organs and the level of sexual competition that males face in impregnating a female)
- the puzzle of concealed ovulation in human females (i.e., it makes sex inefficient from a biological point of view, but perhaps helps promote male attachment, thus serving the needs of long-term child rearing).[13]

Needless to say, sex, that is, reproduction, plays a big role in the thinking of evolutionary psychology, but so do violence, cooperation, language, and morality. The last of these will serve as a bridge toward thinking about the evolution of religion.

The Puzzle of Altruism

With Darwin's theory of natural selection as our account of how evolution occurs, it is no longer difficult to explain why there is selfishness and evil in the world. These we can take for granted. The problem becomes how to explain the existence of morality, goodness, and other-regarding behavior. Darwin himself recognized this. The existence of other-benefiting traits in nature "would annihilate my theory, for such could not have been produced through natural selection."[14] Altruism, that is, benefiting another at one's own expense, is "a central theoretical issue" for sociobiology, notes E. O. Wilson.[15]

Why would a honeybee sacrifice its individual survival for the defense of the hive? Why would a soldier fight and die for his tribe, king, religion, or nation, when this sacrifice means that his genes will not be passed on to the next generation? Why, for that matter, would the Good Samaritan stop and help the injured stranger?[16] Darwin and most of the earlier evolutionists tried to explain altruism by invoking group-selection theory, but group selection fell increasingly out of favor with the rise of genetic analyses in biology. By the 1960s, group selection was out, and the age of the individual was upon us: indeed, soon biologists would be talking about "selfish genes" propagating themselves with no regard for the well-being of the individual phenotype.[17] The abandonment of group-selection theory made the challenge of explaining other-regarding behavior that much more difficult.

One noteworthy theory was advanced by William Hamilton, who developed the idea of "inclusive fitness." It makes perfectly good sense in a gene-centric view for a parent to sacrifice for his or her children, but how about for another closely related individual—a brother or sister, a cousin, a niece or nephew? Hamilton developed a simple mathematical equation combined with empirical data to show that individuals will sacrifice to propagate closely related genes; for example, the worker bees in the hive are all sisters of the queen, so their individual sacrifices do serve the purpose of indirectly passing on their own genes. This type of altruism is referred to as *inclusive fitness* or *kin selection*. Nepotism rules, but this is still not what we think of as compassionate acts of kindness to strangers, as, for instance, celebrated in our religious traditions.[18]

Another candidate to explain other-regarding behavior within an evolutionary paradigm is *reciprocal altruism*, the idea being that if I do something good for you, you will reciprocate in the future. This kind of reciprocation requires some way to keep track of individuals and an informal balance sheet of gifts given and received. Evolutionary psychologists are able to formalize reciprocal altruism in computer games. One simple example of this is the so-called Prisoners' Dilemma, different versions of which can be played. Indeed, the game need not involve prisoners at all. This is a subset of a new field of research called game theory. In all cases of game theory, the dynamic changes dramatically when the game is played in multiple iterations or with multiple players.

In the classic formulation of the Prisoners' Dilemma, two suspects in a robbery have been arrested by the police; but the police do not have enough evidence to convict them, so they put them in separate rooms for interrogation. If prisoner A betrays his accomplice, prisoner B, then A will go free, while B will go to jail for ten years. Prisoner B is offered the same choice: turn in your accomplice A and you walk, while A does hard time. Here is the catch, though: if neither of them confesses, then the state does not have enough evidence to convict them on the serious crime. Instead, they will each serve six months. If both "rat" on each other, then each will serve five years. Each prisoner has only two choices (see Table 4.1): (1) to cooperate with his accomplice (remaining silent) in hope of a lighter sentence (six months or ten years, depending on what the accomplice chooses) or (2) to defect and betray his accomplice in return for a lighter sentence (no time or five years depending on what the accomplice chooses). Both prisoners assume that their accomplice is rational and

Table 4.1 Prisoners' Dilemma

	Prisoner B stays silent	Prisoner B betrays A
Prisoner A stays silent	A serves 6 months B serves 6 months	B goes free; A goes to jail for ten years
Prisoner A betrays B	A goes free; B goes to jail for ten years	A goes to jail for five years B goes to jail for five years

self-interested. The logic of the game suggests that betrayal is the dominant strategy because one cannot know in advance what the accomplice will do. Betrayal minimizes risks and maximizes the possible gain. This is an example of a non–zero–sum game.[19]

The dynamic of the game changes dramatically when played over a number of iterations between two "prisoners" who remember the previous games. A 1959 paper on this scenario won Robert Aumann a Nobel Prize in Economics. Again, these games can be played with live humans in laboratory settings or modeled on computers. Greedy and self-interested strategies tend to do very poorly over multiple iterations, while more altruistic strategies do better in promoting the self-interest of the participants. The iterated Prisoners' Dilemma evolves quickly toward a strategy known as "tit for tat." One assumes that the opponent is a cooperator in the first round. If the opponent defects, then you retaliate in the second round, returning to cooperation in the next. Actually, the most successful strategy in playing this game is "tit for tat with forgiveness." The winning strategy in these computer games, and perhaps also in life, is to start by being nice toward the opponent. The logic of the game is that your self-interest will best be served by being a cooperator, rather than a defector. Always to cooperate, however, is a bad strategy, which will end up with your being exploited by others—one should retaliate when someone defects, but some element of forgiveness can help put an end to long runs of revenge and counter-revenge iterations. Finally, the winning strategy is nonenvious, that is, it does not strive to win more points than the opponent.

Forgetting that the original game scenario was set up as a compact between thieves, game theory suggests that moral principles can actually maximize self-interest in social interactions. The mathematics of game theory suggests symmetry with moral teachings. "Do unto others as you would have others do unto you" is a winning strategy in these games, at least within limits. The Golden Rule rules!

Indirect reciprocity is another variation on this theme. In this analysis, we introduce the idea of reputation, which people carry with them throughout the game of life. People act selflessly not because they are really selfless, which our evolutionists understand to be an impossibility, but because they gain reputation. Good reputation turns out to benefit players indirectly in the game of life. So people help little old ladies cross the road, give alms to the poor, and fight for their country because they collect lots of reputational capital, which they can cash in later in life.

What if there is a fake cooperator playing the game? A person could let on that he was a reliable partner, but when the stakes got really high, he could defect, cheating the others and laughing all the way to the bank, as it were. Of course, this happens in real life all too often: think, for instance, of how Bernie Madoff traded on his Jewish connections to bilk billions of dollars from his mostly Jewish clientele or how Jack Bennett preyed primarily on naive Evangelical Christians in his New Era Philanthropy Ponzi scheme. This fear of defection leads to all kinds of adaptations in human evolution. Humans are extremely sensitive to detecting insincerity, as reflected, for instance, in our mostly unconscious ability to "read" microfacial expressions.[20] We are vigilant in looking for hypocrites and fakes, people who say one thing in order to take advantage of us later on. This results in an evolutionary "arms race" between defectors and defector-detection devices. Indirect-reciprocity theory leads to "signaling theory," in which humans develop costly, hard-to-fake, and involuntary displays to assure others in the group that they are reliable cooperators. The shaved heads and robes of Buddhist monks are just such a costly, hard-to-fake display, but so too is the conservative dress of Muslim women or the yarmulke worn by observant Jews. Some groups have high costs for membership, but as we will see, these groups offer their members the greatest "benefits." If it were not for obedience and celibacy, I would immediately convert to Catholicism and become a Jesuit priest, as would many other academics. Costly signaling becomes a way to minimize freeloaders, who seek the benefits but do not want to pay the price of membership.

If every human behavior needs to serve the purposes of survival and reproduction in a competitive environment, then truly altruistic, self-sacrificial behavior is not a possibility because it would quickly breed itself out of the gene pool. At least, this is the conclusion of most evolutionary psychologists. Michael Ghiselin writes on behalf of the tribe of evolutionary psychologists: "No hint of genuine charity ameliorates our vision of society, once sentimentalism has been laid aside. What passes for cooperation turns out to be a mixture of opportunism and exploitation."[21] It seems that morality is just a front for nepotism, favoritism, and pretense. Human ethical behavior is viewed evolutionarily as "the circuitous technique by which human genetic material has been and will be kept intact; morality has no other demonstrable ultimate function."[22]

We need not buy into this extreme genetic reductionism, in which all human behavior is merely an expression of survival and reproduction of genes. We can still believe that morality exists somehow outside our genes, woven into the fabric of the universe or decreed on high by God. There is no necessary contradiction between moral realism and an evolved natural mechanism for morality in humans. Indeed, if morality is "real," then we would expect lots of evolved adaptations to moral behavior as part of our human nature. A moral realist can read evolutionary psychologists' accounts of morality and find hard evidence to support his or her interpretations without accepting the premise that morality serves only our selfish genes.

"It's good to be good," says Stephen Post, a bioethicist at Stony Brook University.[23] It is not just game theory and evolutionary psychology that validates this perspective. Many physiological, psychological, and epidemiological studies suggest that other-regarding behavior is a profoundly important component of our human nature, health, and happiness. We have been naturally selected to be cooperators. "It is better to give than receive" is also in our genes. This notion of natural moral law, independent of revealed moral law, was a common theological position among Jews, Christians, and Muslims in the medieval period. Love can be seen as a fulfillment of our human nature, rather than something imposed against natural selfishness.[24]

There is, however, a dark side to these moral dispositions, which we can also learn more about through game theory. When someone defects, the offended party tends to exhibit emotional outrage. We often seek to punish the offender, even if the cost of punishment to us is more than the actual offense. This irrational need to retaliate can also set up an escalating dynamic, even as it makes the threat of punishment for defection more credible. If we think we have been wronged, then wild passions can be let loose. The dark side of altruism, real, evolved or otherwise, is that our disposition to cooperate is generally within a known group of cooperators—our family, our tribe, our city, our race, our religion, our nation. This very disposition to cooperation and self-sacrifice can be harnessed to evil purposes by our propensity to demonize outsiders and to fight wars. Soldiers on both sides of a war exhibit the same self-sacrificial behavior, giving up their own reproductive fitness in biological terms for the perceived benefit of their group. This dark side of altruistic self-sacrifice, the immoral side of morality, may yet prove to be our species's evolutionary downfall.

Three Rival Theories

This discussion of morality from an evolutionary perspective gets us close but not all the way to our subject matter—how does evolutionary psychology explain the origins and function of religion? Evolution requires some kind of adaptive function; otherwise, why would it exist? If evolutionists have a hard time understanding altruism, they have an even harder time understanding religion. Daniel Dennett writes:

> Any phenomenon that apparently exceeds the functional cries out for explanation.... What benefits are presumed (rightly or wrongly) to accrue from this excess activity? From an evolutionary point of view, religion appears to be a ubiquitous penchant for somersaults of the most elaborate sort, and as such it cries out for explanation.[25]

Why, indeed, divert precious labor and resources to building cathedrals and pyramids, temples, and mosques? Why pay for a nonproductive class of priests, rabbis, imams, gurus, pundits, and monks? These are opportunity costs. The resources and labor might have been diverted to improving industry and agriculture, strengthening the national defense, improving education, and so forth. Why divert precious social resources away from the more pressing tasks of survival and reproduction into "somersaults of the most elaborate sort"?

I will explore three rival evolutionary theories of religion—memes, spandrels, and adaptations—and conclude by offering a fourth option.[26]

1. Religion as "memes"

The term *memes* was coined by Richard Dawkins in 1976, as a mental analogy to genes. Bits of information can be "copied," "transmitted," and "replicated" in the mental medium of human minds.[27] Examples of memes include jokes told at the local bar, popular songs that dominate the airwaves, advertisements that you cannot get out of your mind, ideologies that distort your mind, innovations that become ubiquitous, urban legends that have a life of their own, fashionable fads that create demands that never existed—hula-hoops and pet rocks, for instance. For Dawkins, religions are the quintessential meme because, just like his "selfish genes," religious memes replicate at the expense of human well-being.

The concept of memes means that humans have a "dual inheritance system." On the one hand, we are products of our genes; on the other, we are products of our memes. Once evolution creates a human mind with symbolic language and culture, there now exists a parallel form of evolution in the ideational space of brains, minds, and culture. The mental now transcends the biological; indeed, the mental evolution need no longer be biologically adaptive. "A mind," writes Susan Blackmore, "is just a meme's way of replicating itself."[28]

"If a meme is to dominate the attention of a human brain, it must do so at the expense of 'rival' memes," writes Dawkins. "Selection favours memes which exploit their cultural environment to their own advantage."[29] Maybe, maybe not. It is not clear that the mind is a zero-sum memory bank. Lots of different ideas can inhabit a human mind, though as I grow older I am increasingly aware of the finitude of my mind. I once learned and spoke German, Hebrew, Russian, Arabic, and Spanish. In high school, I excelled at advanced calculus. Only the German, my native English, and simple algebra remain in any proficiency. Languages and mathematics, however, are not really memes, at least not as I understand Dawkins. Rather, languages are the medium in which memes replicate, and now I am not sure whether memes are real—certainly not like genes are real—or rather just a misleading metaphor. The idea of memes has itself certainly been a successful meme, even if they are not real, which leaves me in an interesting cognitive bind. We will revisit this notion of dual inheritance below.

Dawkins is infamous for his hostility toward religion. He writes that "religion is a virus more destructive than smallpox, but more difficult to eradicate.... Science is the virus eradication software."[30] One can, however, adopt the meme metaphor without adopting Dawkins's harsh conclusions. Indeed, as evolutionary adaptationists, we might argue that religion, by virtue of its memetic and genetic successes, is viable and valuable, or it would not persist. If religions were as nonadaptive as Dawkins thinks, they would have tended to kill off their hosts, much like the deadly Ebola virus. Instead, religions replicate, adapt, and multiply.

2. Religion as a "spandrel"

Spandrel is a term from architecture that has become part of the terminology of evolutionary biology. The new usage began with a 1979 essay by Stephen Jay Gould and Richard Lewontin.[31] In architecture, a spandrel is the space between an arch and a rectangular enclosure. The arch is a functional innovation in construction, but the arch also creates these spandrel spaces, where now all kinds of artistic elaboration that serve no function except to decorate can occur. So, spandrels are by-products of something that is functional, although they themselves serve no structural function.

So too in evolution, argue Gould and Lewontin, in their critique of the adaptationist program in evolution. Not everything that exists in nature serves a purpose. Some things in nature are simply elaborations, by-products of functional adaptations, but not necessarily in the service of survival and reproduction.

For the anthropologist Pascal Boyer, religion is a spandrel by-product of the human brain-mind. Evolution gives us a mental toolbox, much like a Swiss-army knife, which tools served real adaptive purposes in our hunter-gatherer past; but then these mental tools are hijacked by religious elaborations that serve no function. Religions are mental fancies that take a free ride on these functional mental systems.

The human mind is modular in Boyer's understanding. Although we do not generally experience it as such, there is a division of labor within our brains. The mind consists of many evolved inference systems that allow us quickly to process data in our environment, determining what is relevant, how it should be classified, what it means, and how we should react to significant information. All these mental "inference systems" originated in our hunter-gatherer past.

Thus, we inherit lots of ontological categories and concepts. Agency detection, for instance, figures prominently in our big brains, even for babies as young as six months. We enter the world predisposed to intuitive psychology and intuitive physics. We have instinctive expectations, and when these expectations are violated, for instance, by counterintuitive events, this also impacts our mental recall. The story of Gautama Buddha is an example of a counterintuitive story that is, therefore, easy to remember. Most of us work hard and aspire to live the life of a wealthy prince in a palace with his beautiful wife and child. That Siddhartha Gautama walks away from all this immediately grabs our attention. It is counterintuitive, in the same way that the Moses, Jesus, and Mohammed stories are counterintuitive. When these stories are attached to other inference systems in our brain, then the alignment can produce the spandrel called religion.

It is important to remember that our mental templates are modular and universal. For instance, what counts as pollution varies from culture to culture, but the pollution template is very similar in all cultures, that is, it is a contagion template that activates the emotion of disgust. For some, the pollution contagion might be an encounter with a Hindu low-caste Dalit; for others, it might be a cockroach, a mouse, or pork; for others, it might be a menstruating woman or a homosexual.

Religions are not just any old wives' tale or superstitious practice, says Boyer; rather religions successfully harness multiple mental components in a powerful matrix:

> Some concepts happen to connect with inference systems in the brain in a way that makes recall and communication very easy. Some concepts happen to trigger our emotional programs in particular ways. Some concepts happen to connect to our social mind. Some of them are represented in such a way that they soon become plausible and direct behavior. The ones that do all this are the religious ones we actually observe in human societies. They are most successful because they combine features relevant to a variety of mental systems.[32]

Boyer's exploration of the evolved structure of the human mind and its many inference systems opens many new ways to think about religion. To say that the human mind is conducive to religion is no great insight; to show how the mind incorporates religious ideas and practices is helpful, indeed intriguing. This insight, in and of itself, however, provides no way of proving conclusively whether any particular religious belief is true or false or any particular religious practice functional or dysfunctional. God-by-whatever-name may be true, though the particular beliefs and practices of any tradition not necessarily wholly or holy true. Remember, Boyer's deconstruction of the religious brain is the same evolved human brain that is capable of doing advanced physics, inorganic chemistry, and physical anthropology. Shall we dismiss these too as mere spandrels, by-products of our mental architecture, that have serve no function and are not true?

Boyer's research program links evolutionary psychology with the cognitive neurosciences, the latter being interdisciplinary in nature, traversing the boundaries of anthropology, artificial intelligence, linguistics, medicine, neuroscience, philosophy, psychology, and sociology.[33] At the intersection of all of these disciplines are also religious and spiritual phenomena. In the next chapter, we will delve more deeply into the cognitive neurosciences.

3. Religion as Adaptation

Another evolutionary approach to explaining religion revives group-selection theory or, more properly, multilevel-selection theory. Selection works not just at the level of individual genes but also on networks of genes, individual phenotypes, groups of individuals, and even at the level of groups of species in ecosystems. The relevant level of analysis will be determined by the specific context.

Humans, like social insects, survive and reproduce in groups, so group selection makes sense. In this view, religions contribute to group survival and reproduction in diverse environments and in competition with other human groups. In particular, religions provide a way to promote group solidarity and cooperation, while minimizing the problem of freeloaders and defections.

One sees this in the frequent use of the body metaphor to describe the community. Plato invokes the metaphor of the body politic in *The Republic*. The Christian Church is referred to as the "Body of Christ." Many Buddhist monasteries in China and Japan are built in the shape of a human body. The *Ummah* can be thought of as the body of Islam.

David Sloan Wilson, trained in animal ethology, is leading this effort to revive group-selection theory, especially in its application to understanding religion. His book *Darwin's Cathedral* uses examples such as the Hutterites, John Calvin's (1509–1564) Geneva, the survival of Judaism in the Diaspora, and the Hindu Water Temple system in Bali.[34] Wilson argues that religions are not true, not in a factual sense, but they work in a practical sense. He is in awe of the practical power of religion as a group-level adaptation.

One of the insights derived from Wilson's approach is the dynamics of strict sects. The higher the price of admission to a religious group—in terms of the demands of observance, including strict rules and nonconformist dress and practices—the higher the benefits of membership and the greater the cost of defection or freeloading. Liberal religions, in this competitive market, tend to lose members and have more freeloaders. This is an insight we also discovered in our discussion about the economics of religion in the last chapter.

The dark side of the unifying spirit of religion is that it is often harnessed in violent conflict with outsiders. This troubles Wilson, as it should trouble all of us in contemplating the growing culture wars within and between our great civilizations. Objectively though, Wilson does not have high expectations of religions. He writes that "the failure of religion to achieve universal brotherhood is like the failure of birds to break the sound barrier."[35]

This distinction between factual realism and practical realism creates an interesting set of problems for Wilson and for us. "An atheist historian," writes Wilson, "who understood the real life of Jesus but whose own life was a mess as a result of his beliefs would be factually attached to and practically detached from reality." He continues:

> Much religious belief does not represent a form of mental weakness but rather the healthy functioning of the biologically and culturally well-adapted mind. *Rationality is not the gold standard against which all other forms of thought are to be judged. Adaptation is the gold standard against which rationality must be judged, along with all other forms of thought.* (italics added)[36]

This is a remarkable statement on two counts. First, it implies that the religious function, if not any particular religion, is necessary for any community or individual. A religion can be abolished, but it had better be replaced by another religion or the group will fail. Second, making rationality subservient to adaptation raises profound philosophical questions about the truth claims of both science and religion. Science might be factually true but practically false. Reflect for a moment on weapons of mass destruction, growing environmental problems, and alienated publics. Wilson suggests that "science might profit by becoming more religious along certain dimensions, as long as it remains nonreligious with respect to its stated goal of increasing factual knowledge."[37] Science as a community and institution also needs a unifying spirit. Yoking science and religion in a mutually constructive manner may hold the greatest promise for advancing both truth and goodness in the twenty-first century, a topic we will explore in part 2.

4. Lamarckian Cultural Evolution

I want to present a fourth evolutionary option to help us explain and understand religion. While the scenarios above are often presented as mutually exclusive, there is no reason that all these theories cannot be partially true, applicable in different circumstances, nuanced in different ways.

Our minds are surely shaped by evolution. We think and act through many innate and learned mental modules. Religion, like any human thought, including science itself, necessarily harnesses these inference systems. Much of religion may be spandrel-like elaborations that serve no profound truth about humans or the universe. Differences between religious practices may in large part be more like the differences between musical genres and human languages around the world. In other words, we can argue about correct Chinese grammar and our favorite jazz bands, but it makes little sense to argue about whether Chinese is better or worse than French or whether jazz is better or worse than classical Indian ragas.

Religions can also be seen as group adaptations, as well as individual-level adaptations that help promote successful communities and successful lives. Our pressing challenge in this context is to figure out how to make religions more functional and more adaptive in the context of the modern world. The warring minds of the hunter-gatherer may not thrive or survive twenty-first-century forms of chauvinistic tribalism, the emotional manipulations of modern mass media, and the growing availability of weapons of mass destruction.

The notion of memes also opens up other options, even if we reject the metaphor as a fiction. To the extent that we do have a dual-inheritance system—genetic and mental—then something altogether new is going on in evolution. Once evolution gave rise to our symbolic species with language, thought, tools, and culture, the Darwinian paradigm begins to take back seat to what we should now call the Lamarckian paradigm.[38] Humans have the capacity to pass on new innovations more or less directly to the next generation. Indeed, that is the whole purpose of education: to pass on and improve upon the discoveries, inventions, and wisdom of the ages. We do not need to reinvent the wheel or the microprocessor. We do not need to rewrite the Bible or the Bhagavad Gita. Once human symbolic evolution takes off, it proceeds rapidly; indeed, it is growing exponentially in the modern era. Humans engage in large-scale environmental engineering and are reshaping the earth. We are about to embark upon large-scale genetic engineering of other species and ourselves. Selection will continue to operate in the future, but the source of variation will be the intentional tinkering of humans, along with many unintended consequences. The future evolution of the planet will be increasingly dominated by human desires and values. Willy-nilly, we have stumbled into designer evolution, not that we completely understand what we are doing or can predict what the consequences will be. From the perspective of evolutionary history, it is perhaps not an exaggeration to say that nothing as significant as humans has occurred on the planet since the advent of photosynthesis some 2 billion years ago.

The point is that we humans increasingly transcend our biological origins. We are not slaves to our genes, nor need our morality be a slave to mere survival and reproduction. Humans are a transcendent species. On one level, we are simply another mammal; on another, we are more like a whole new phylum in the epic of evolution.

CHAPTER FIVE

The Neurosciences of Religion

In the last chapter, we learned how humans evolved as hunter-gatherers and how our genetic, mental, and behavioral nature was conditioned by and for this kind of life, even as we now live in a very different artificial environment created by agriculture, economic markets, and technology. We considered how evolution had shaped our predispositions for religion and what functions and dysfunctions religion might have played in our species's history. We were introduced to the idea that the human mind was modular, that there were *instinctive dispositions* that then developed in conjunction with social and environmental factors into various *inference systems* in our brains. Religion, we were told, could be understood as a potent combination of these different inference systems in our evolved brains—agency detection, ontological categories, intuitive physics, intuitive psychology, pollution-contagion templates, memory-recall patterns, and so forth, all assembled and accessed as independent mental modules.[1] This was one of several evolutionary approaches to understanding religion.

In this chapter, we are going to examine the human brain directly to see how the cognitive neurosciences try to understand and explain religious and spiritual experiences. There has been a tremendous amount of new research and new insights into the working of the human brain in the last few decades. Powerful new tools also allow us to examine the function of healthy human brains, and these tools have recently been used to study the brain functions of Buddhist monks, Catholic nuns, Pentecostals speaking in tongues, and others.

Inside the Brain

If you look inside the human brain, you do not actually see these mental modules previously referred to. There is no piece of the brain that one could label the "agency-detection module" or the "pollution-contagion module." In dissecting a human cadaver, we first see large-scale structures.

On the outside is the cerebral cortex, or neocortex, including areas labeled the frontal lobe, the parietal lobe, the occipital lobe, and the temporal lobe; and of course, these are divided into two hemispheres, right and left, with a broad band of nerve fibers known as the corpus callosum connecting the two halves. If we peel away the neocortex, we discover the mesocortex and subcortical structures in the limbic system, including the thalamus, the amygdala, the hippocampus, and the cerebellum, all connected to the brain stem and the spinal cord. This much you probably already know. Images of the human brain have become iconic in the modern world.

A lot of what we know about the specialized functions of different areas of the brain comes from observing survivors of traumatic brain injuries or stroke victims. In both cases, neuroscientists correlate the destruction of certain brain regions due to hemorrhaging or injury with the loss of particular mental functions, for instance, the loss of motor control, speech, or even particular parts of speech or sets of word concepts, the latter known as *aphasia*.

Curiously, memory seems to be distributed throughout the brain and is not located in any particular region. I recall a colleague at Oxford University, whom I visited in the hospital shortly after he had had a stroke. He could point to Paris or London on a map, but he could not say the word "Paris" or "London." Nor could he speak the names of any number of other common items and places, though he certainly knew what they were and could directly point to any of them. When I said "wallet," he reached into his back pocket, pulled out the wallet, but he just could not say the word. Our brains are strange indeed, though we take them for granted until something goes wrong. Fortunately, my friend was able to recover his speech fully but did so by training new regions of the brain to compensate for the loss of the one region destroyed by the stroke. This is an example of another curious characteristic of the brain called neuroplasticity, something that we progressively lose as we grow older. This neuroplasticity explains in part why young children can effortlessly learn foreign languages, while adults must struggle with the drudgery of repetition and memorization.

When we examine a brain under powerful microscopes, we see that it is made up of neurons. There are different types of neurons in the brain and throughout our central nervous system in the rest of the body, but they all share a basic structure. The cell body contains the nucleus and organelle. Extending out from the cell body are lots of dendrite "trees" and axon "arms." These connect to other neurons. This maze of connections ends in synapses, linking each neuron with hundreds or thousands of others. The neurons fire electrical charges in the form of chemical ions, which are mediated by a variety of neurochemicals produced endogenously by the brain. The chemicals produced and present in different areas of the brain are very important to how the brain functions.

There are a lot of neurons in the human brain, estimated at 10^{11} (100 billion). Each neuron has on average about 7×10^3 (seven thousand) synaptic connections. A three-year-old child has about 10^{16} synapses (10 quadrillion), but this happily decreases with age to a more manageable number between 10^{15} to 5×10^{15} synapses (1–5 quadrillion).[2]

Here are a few comparisons to help you remember these big numbers. The number of neurons in your brain is approximately the same as the number of stars in our Milky Way galaxy, which turns out to be conveniently also the number of galaxies in the observable universe, that is, 100 billion. Or if you prefer, there are more neurons in your brain than the number of hamburgers served at McDonalds, before they stopped counting. And it takes a lot of hamburgers, or other food, to keep our neurons firing. The 1.5 kilograms of your brain, give or take, represents only 2 percent of your body weight and yet it consumes 15 percent of your cardiac output, 20 percent of your body oxygen, and about 25 percent of your body's glucose consumption. Even when you're just sitting around, the brain needs about 0.1 calories per minute; with intellectual activity, this can increase to as high as 1.5 calories per minute. From a biophysical and evolutionary point of view, the human brain is an expensive item. In birth, the head's size makes it difficult for it to pass through the female pelvis, often resulting in the death of the infant or the mother. In life, it requires a lot of extra food and care.

The brain is best understood as a kind of Rube Goldberg machine. Goldberg was an American cartoonist who was famous for depicting complex devices that performed simple tasks in convoluted ways. One such cartoon depicts a man eating his soup. The spoon is attached to a string that flips a cracker to a parrot that then activates water pouring into bucket that pulls a string that activates a lighter that launches a rocket attached to a knife that cuts a string that turns on a clock with a pendulum that swings back and forth moving a napkin that now wipes clean the soup-eating man's mustache. The entire contraption is worn on the head of the mustached man as a kind of hat. Our brains are like this Rube Goldberg machine, except that the complex machine is worn inside our heads instead of outside. Neuroscientists today are developing algorithmic flow charts that map out neural processes. Something simple like engaging in meditation sets off an impossibly complex series of actions, reactions, and feedback loops.[3] We can be thankful that we do not need to be the least bit aware of any of these processes to have wonderfully functional brains allowing us to mindlessly perform lots of simple and complex mental activities every day. It is worth stopping a moment, however, to reflect that the most complicated object in the known universe is sitting right here between our ears.

The Explanatory Gap

It is hard to recognize ourselves—our subjective experiences, thoughts, emotions, and daily activities—in this neurological description of our brains. Normally, we have no conscious awareness of the cognitive modules and Rube Goldberg machines in our head. Cognitive neuroscientists and philosophers of mind refer to this as the "explanatory gap." Our physical descriptions of the way the brain works at the level of neurons, brain anatomy, and neurological processes bear no resemblance to our subjective experiences as people with brains having complex mental and emotional states. Nor is there any neurological definition of consciousness as such. We have no device that can measure presence or absence of consciousness. This is also referred to as the "hard problem" in consciousness studies. We can study brains and learn all kinds of interesting and practical things about them, their functions and dysfunctions, but this does not get us nearer to understanding what subjective conscious experience is or how the brain creates it. We know that a diseased or damaged brain may lose function or consciousness, ultimately resulting in death, but we do not know what consciousness per se is at the level of the "neural code."

Some are optimistic that we are closing this explanatory gap, that we will soon come to understand the "neural code" and be able to translate the "machine language" of the brain into the "software applications" of human consciousness. Indeed, a lot of progress has been made in understanding how the brain functions. Scientists have probed, prodded, tested, measured, dissected, and scanned lots and lots of brains, both human and animal. Scientists have also developed a remarkable pharmacology of new drugs to treat depression, schizophrenia, and other disorders.

Progress in the neurosciences raises other interesting philosophical questions, which necessarily overlap with religious and theological concerns. First, there is the question of reductionism and how far it can go. If we can reduce certain mental phenomena, say, mystical experiences of enlightenment, to neurological processes, does that mean that we have adequately explained the experience and can dismiss it? What happens if we invent ways to stimulate these peak experiences at will? If the brain is a deterministic system, then how can we talk about free will, moral responsibility, and creative choice? If personality is intrinsically linked to brain chemistry, should we reject the dualism between brain and mind, body and soul? In treating mental illness, should we "waste time" with talk therapy or simply treat these illnesses with medications? Do the cognitive neurosciences import assumed values and perspectives that are more ideological than empirical? And what of bioethical issues that arise in the context of neuromedicine? This is just a short list, and we are going to revisit some of these questions below and in the discussion to follow. The hard question remains: What is consciousness? Can we fill in the explanatory gap between the neurosciences and subjective experience? And what in particular is the nature of religious experience from the perspective of the neurosciences?

Science does not need to solve all these philosophical problems. That, I would argue, is not the job of science, but rather the task of scientifically informed philosophers and theologians. Science can and does continue to plod along in its methodical manner. The neurosciences move ahead by formulating small questions and then constructing experiments to try to answer them. The neurological basis of religious and spiritual experiences is certainly an interesting question, and it has recently been the subject of fascinating research in laboratories and debate in academe and in the media. There are a number of ways to tackle the question:

1. disease and injury-based studies
2. surgical studies
3. functional imaging studies
4. psychotropic drug studies
5. developmental studies

1. Disease and Injury-Based Studies

As already mentioned, many insights about the brain are derived from the study of brain disease and injury. There may be a link between mental illness and religiosity, for instance, in the case of schizophrenia, in which psychotic episodes often have religious content. Indeed, for many decades, the psychiatric community classified all religious content as delusional or neurotic in its earlier versions of the *Diagnostic and Statistical Manual of Mental Disorders (DSMMD)*.[4] That is happily no longer the case. The psychiatric community has slowly come around to recognizing that religious experiences among patients may be a sign of strength, a resource in healing, not necessarily pathological.[5]

There is a lot of interest in the role of the frontal lobes in religious experience. Traumatic injuries to the frontal lobes have a profound effect on a person's personality, impulse control, and complex-thought processes. The seat of cognition, however, does not work alone. It is part of a complex network, left, right, inside out, and all around. V. S. Ramachandran, a neuroscientist at UC San Diego, has focused on left temporal lobe epilepsy, which is frequently associated with religious visions during seizures and a preoccupation with religious issues between seizure episodes. Ramachandran speculates that Saint Paul, Mohammad, and other prophets and sages were afflicted with left temporal lobe epilepsy.[6] He notes that "God may be the ultimate confabulation of the Left Hemisphere of the brain."[7]

There are other mental defects that manifest themselves in otherwise mentally healthy individuals. For instance, with Charles Bonnet syndrome, people have complex visual hallucinations of people, animals, or objects not actually present. With Capgras syndrome, otherwise mentally healthy individuals have delusions that people around them have been replaced by imposters.

Another, much more common mental disorder is known as sleep paralysis. Probably many of you have had the experience of waking up at night unable to move and with the strong sense of someone else in the room. The presence-in-the-room is typically perceived to be a demon of some sort, and the experience is generally terrifying. This is such a common experience that it has many names, folk stories, and mythological explanations in diverse cultures around the world. Neuroscientists now have an etiology for sleep paralysis, but one could easily imagine how this experience or others would help give rise to religious beliefs in demons, ghosts, or the devil.[8]

There is one other neurological disorder that is worth mentioning. Synesthesia is a condition that might be thought of as metaphoric thought on steroids. It typically involves things like hearing sounds and seeing colors, reading numbers and seeing colors, seeing colors and hearing sounds. Perhaps one in a thousand humans has some form of synesthesia in varying degrees. It is not necessarily unpleasant. Indeed, far from being a disorder, it can be seen as a mental strength. As we would expect, many creative artists have synesthesia.

Synesthesia may be linked to a much more common mental functions that all of us employ every day, the ability to make and use metaphors, of which both religion and science are important subsets.[9] A metaphor is the combination of two unlike things to create a new meaning. Shakespeare writes that "time is a beggar," and now we have a new insight into time. You may have noticed that I have used several metaphors from the computer sciences to illuminate the neurosciences—neural "code," neural "machine language," mental "software," neural "networks," and so on. Science also uses metaphors. In some sense, all human language is derived from metaphors.[10] Religion can be thought of as something like the metaphoric confabulations of synesthesia, where people observe nature and hear the voice of God or see the Buddha-nature in all things.[11] These confabulations, however, are not necessarily devoid of insight and value, truth and profundity.

2. Surgical Studies

Surgical studies are much more limited because doctors cannot ethically open up someone's brain and start poking around, like, say, a mechanic fixing a car or a technician fixing a computer. The occasion to do surgery on live humans is typically to remove a brain tumor, a risky operation. Because the brain has no sensory nerves and cannot feel pain, brain surgery is typically done on conscious humans, which means you can ask them questions during the surgery. In the 1950s, Wilder Penfield, a Canadian neurosurgeon, electrically stimulated different regions of patients' brains during surgery and asked patients to describe any sensations. Stimulation of the right temporal lobe caused patients to hear voices and see apparitions. Around the same time, Robert Heath of Tulane University induced intense pleasure in psychiatric patients with electrodes implanted in the septum, a minute region just above the hypothalamus. He also induced multiple orgasms in a female patient by injecting the neurotransmitter acetylcholine directly into her septal region. These kinds of studies would not be allowed today by internal review boards at medical schools, and rightly so, but they were illuminating and suggestive. Certainly, every neuroscience course and textbook today still present the work of Penfield and Heath.

Based in part on these kinds of studies, Julian Jaynes proposed a unique theory of religion in his 1976 book *The Origin of Consciousness in the Breakdown of the Bicameral Mind.* Jaynes speculated that there were structural changes in the human brain some ten thousand years ago. He suggested that the bundle of nerves connecting the two hemispheres of the brain, the corpus callosum, may not have been as developed as it is today. In our ancestors' brains, the left hemisphere, acting as the primary seat of language and identity, would misattribute signals originating from the right hemisphere to an external source and thus imagined ghosts or gods.[12]

Brain-surgery research continues on nonhuman animals; but, alas, lab rats, dogs, and monkeys cannot verbally report to us on their subjective experience. Nevertheless, we learn a lot about how their brains function, information that is then correlated with human brain function. We are also embarking upon a new era of electrical-implant machines to help patients with Parkinson's or other brain disorders, as well as electrical implants to help quadriplegics to control computers with their thoughts alone. All this will have implications for our understanding of religious and spiritual phenomena, some of which may have been best prefigured in science fiction novels.

3. Functional Imaging Studies

New noninvasive technologies now allow us to look inside the brains of humans without adverse risks to the patient. Improvements in these technologies measure actual brain functions while the patient is performing limited tasks or having an experience and compare these states to some baseline image. These are referred to as functional brain-imaging studies. The earliest form of such techniques used electroencephalographs of brain waves, as well as measures of autonomic activities such as heart rate and blood-pressure changes, for instance, as used in early meditation studies. You are probably familiar with the term "biofeedback device," which was popular in the 1970s. This approach, however, has been compared to trying to understand human speech by listening to the sound of a sports stadium.[13] The new technology is much more powerful, but not without its limitations. There are three new techniques for functional brain imaging, and each has different strengths and weaknesses.

PET scans, or positron emission tomography, use a radioactive tracer injected into the bloodstream of the subject to measure oxygen flow, glucose consumption, blood utilization, or neurotransmitters in different regions of the brain. This indicates which areas of the brain are most active during any given experience or activity. The injection provides a freeze frame at a particular moment and is followed by the actual scan of the brain. The problem with the PET scan is that the tracers are present for only a few minutes, so the patient needs to be already in the scanning device before the injection occurs. Hospital scanning devices are not particularly conducive to having profound mystical experiences that can then be measured by the machinery.

Another category of imaging technology is fMRI, which stands for functional magnetic resonance imaging. The advantage of fMRI is that it does not involve injecting radioactive tracers into the bloodstream of the patient. The disadvantage is that it involves placing the patient inside a claustrophobia-inducing machine that makes loud banging noises, only slightly more tolerable than listening to a jackhammer. Again, this is not an atmosphere particularly conducive to contemplative practice or religious devotion.

The functional imaging technology most suited to research on religious and spiritual phenomena may be the SPECT scan, which stands for "single photon emission computed tomography." This uses a longer-lasting radioactive tracer. Typical research design has the patient outfitted with an IV and a button so he can self-inject the tracer at what he subjectively considers to be the peak experience in meditation or prayer. This can be done in a comfortable room in the hospital near the SPECT scan machine and can involve the use of ritual objects, incense, chanting, prayer, and so on. After the peak experience and the tracer's "snapshot" record of brain activity at the time of injection, the subject can then be put into the scanning machine to measure brain metabolism from the tracer "snapshot" some minutes earlier.

Andrew Newberg and Eugene D'Aquili pioneered this research with religious subjects. Their first study involved eight American Buddhists trained in Tibetan meditation and three Franciscan nuns. They observed increased neural activity in the prefrontal cortex and decreased activity in the posterior superior parietal lobe. The latter is connected with the ability to navigate the physical self in an external world. They hypothesized that the decreased activity in posterior superior parietal lobe was linked to the experience of nonduality described by the subjects. Newberg and D'Aquili call this experience "Absolute Unitary Being."[14] They maintain that "mystical experience is biologically, observably, and scientifically 'real' rather than 'wishful thinking' " and go on to speculate:

[We] saw evidence of a neurological process that has evolved to allow humans to transcend material existence and acknowledge and connect with a deeper, more spiritual part of ourselves perceived of as an absolute, universal reality that connects us to all others.[15]

4. Pharmaceutical Interventions

Psychotropic or psychedelic drugs have long been part of human religious practices in diverse parts of the world. The authors of the Hindu Vedas received inspiration from the drug soma, which is thought to be derived from psychedelic mushrooms, such as psilocybin-containing mushrooms or fly agaric, perhaps in combination with cannabis or other substances. The ancient Greek Eleusinian mysteries also involved the use of some kind of psychedelic drug. Tribal shamans from Africa, Asia, and the Americas used psychotropic drugs as part of their rituals. The Native American Church in the United States won a Supreme Court case to ensure its right to use peyote in its religious observances. The urge for intoxication is not limited to humans. Chimpanzees, elephants, parrots, and other species deliberately ingest fermented fruit and other intoxicants. The UCLA psychopharmacologist Ronald Siegel speculates that the desire for intoxication is "the fourth drive" after hunger, thirst, and sex.[16] The suggestion in this line of research is that perhaps religion is founded on this desire to "get high."

Ergot, a fungus that contaminates rye, wheat, and barley, also has psychotropic properties and was probably used intentionally as part of the Eleusinian mysteries. It has also caused many accidental poisonings in human history. Ergot epidemics were known as St. Anthony's Fire in the Middle Ages and may be linked to incidents of mass hysteria and hallucinations. The synthesis of LSD (lysergic acid diethylamide) in 1942 by the Swiss chemist Albert Hoffman was based on an ergot derivative.

In addition to LSD, modern science has synthesized a large number of new psychotropic and psychedelic compounds. Some prefer to use the term *entheogens*, meaning "God-inducing," to describe this class of chemicals, because of their ability to induce intense mystical experiences. The most common and quite potent drugs are

- mescaline—3,4,5-trimethoxyphenethylamine
- LSD—lysergic acid diethylamide
- DMT—5-methoxy-dimethyltryptamine
- MDMA—3,4-methylenedioxy-N-methylamphetamine, commonly known as Ecstasy

All these chemicals bear some resemblance to endogenous neurochemicals in the brain such as dopamine, norepinephrine, serotonin, and opiates. DMT, a powerful psychedelic drug, can also be produced naturally in the human brain. The ritual use of these drugs and others in religious ceremonies is quite extensive. In the 1950s and 1960s, mescaline and LSD were used to treat more than forty thousand patients for a variety of illnesses, and over one thousand papers describing these treatments were published in peer-review journals. But then came the excesses of Timothy Leary and the hippies, and the drugs became controlled substances, their use illegal in most countries.[17]

It is not clear what we learn about religion and spirituality by using and studying these drugs. Are they a shortcut to enlightenment or simply a drug-induced experience with no greater significance? Are other kinds of religious rituals and practice simply different methods for inducing these kinds of experiences that basically harness the brain's capacity to hallucinate? It is worth noting that we do discover some "form constants" in these drug-induced experiences, for instance, the recurrence of mandala-like geometric patterns in hallucinations.[18]

Psychopharmacology is powerful stuff, so we should not be too dismissive. A lot of drugs provide powerful relief for clinical depression, schizophrenia, and other ailments. Drug companies continue to research, discover, and invent new compounds. The prospects for new spiritual drugs are intriguing and disconcerting.

One thought experiment proposed by my colleague Jeremy Sherman involved an imagined compound that would disrupt the somatic nervous system, such that if you did not pay attention to and consciously will your breathing, you would soon die. This imagined drug would have no side effects and would last for only a few hours. No longer would a person need to spend years learning meditation techniques in a monastery. A few hours under the influence of this pill and you would achieve instant satori (or die).[19] Maybe mysticism, enlightenment, whatever you want to call it, is just a neurochemical state that can be induced by rigorous training in a meditative tradition or a simple pill taken on a Sunday afternoon.

5. Brain Development

Brains grow and evolve throughout life, but especially in childhood. In the second year of life, the brain of a human baby is only about 50 percent developed. The maximum size of a brain is reached in adolescence around the age of sixteen. Different parts of the brain mature at different stages. There are periods of high dendrite and synapse formation and other periods of pruning in which the number of neurons and synaptic connections is reduced. Some neuronal connections are enhanced through the formation of lipid sheaths around the axions that speed and strengthen neural transmissions. This process is known as myelination, the conversion of gray-matter neurons into white-matter neurons. Myelinated neural connections play a much more important role in mental processes than do unmyelinated neural connections.

Humans have universal dispositions to learn language, music, and religion; but the specific language, genre of music, and religious tradition are matters of the geography and culture of birth. All religions also use music and language, so these connections may be more than incidental to the development of brains and religions.

There appear to be developmental biases that predispose humans to believing in God or other supernatural personalities. Young children tend to assume that all objects in the world are manufactured for a purpose, and that these objects also have a creator.[20]

It may be that adolescence is a particularly important time for the transmission of religion, that there is a neurological disposition and evolved expectation that cultures utilize. This can be seen in the prevalence of rites of initiation. Seventy percent of the cultures studied by anthropologists have some formal adolescent–initiation practice. Some are for males only, some for females only, and some for both. These rites of passage generally involve separation from family and community, seclusion, physical hardship, psychological stress, deprivation of food or water or sleep, and sometimes also torture and body mutilation. These initiation rites precede marriage, reproduction, and adult responsibilities and rights within the social group.[21]

It may be that those cultures that do not have a formal adolescent-initiation ceremony do so at great risk to their well-being and survival. Adolescents have a way of initiating themselves in the manner of *Lord of the Flies* or the "ragging" rituals at universities in the absence of a formal adult initiation.

Problems and Issues

There are a number of problems inherent in these neuroscientific studies of religious and spiritual phenomena. First and foremost, religion is a complex neurocognitive experience that includes rituals, social groups, and a variety of other dimensions that are not easily replicated in a laboratory setting or isolated in individual human minds. Nor is it clear that all religious experiences are neurologically comparable. Talmudic studies, involving reading, analysis of text, and lively debate, may not be the least bit comparable to a Pentecostal experience of speaking in tongues. The contemplative practices of a Sri Lankan Buddhist may not be comparable to Hindu Bhakti devotions. Practicing Hatha yoga asanas in India may not be the same as Catholic self-flagellations at Good Friday observances in the Philippines. Listening to Bach cantatas at a Protestant church in Leipzig may not be the same as listening to Gamelan music played at a village temple in Bali. None of these phenomena is easily replicated in a laboratory. Science necessarily tries to simplify in order to pursue manageable research. Most of the neuroimaging studies focus on some kind of meditative or contemplative practice simply because it would be hard to study anything else in a hospital radiology department.

A fuller taxonomy of religious experience needs to be developed, detailed, and correlated with different brain states and cognitive theories of religion. Note that the list below does not necessarily indicate discrete experiences and can be combined in any number of ways in actual religious persons:

1. Interpretative experiences: understanding some event or circumstance to be religiously significant, as in serendipity, synchronicity, good or bad fortune;

2. Quasi-sensory experiences: auditory or visual experiences of the divine;
3. Revelatory experiences: receiving some insight about ultimate reality;
4. Regenerative experiences: a healing or catharsis in which problems or anxiety dissipate;
5. Ethical-moral experiences: grasped by moral obligation to act in the face of suffering or injustice;
6. Aesthetic experiences: an intense spiritual experience of beauty in nature or art, music, or ritual;
7. Intellectual experiences: an intense engagement in learning and problem-solving that takes on a spiritual dimension, for instance, in the moment of discovery or comprehension;
8. Ecstatic experiences: as in energetic devotional prayer, particularly in group context, perhaps not unlike a rock concert;
9. Numinous experiences: an encounter with Spirit that is Wholly-Other, being in the presence of God;
10. Oneness experiences: loss of distinction between self and world, nondual sense of unity with God and the universe.[22]

Another problem in the neuroscientific study of religious and spiritual phenomena is the tendency to draw ontological conclusions from these studies, typically either to validate or disprove some religious doctrine. This is philosophically bogus; one cannot prove or disprove the existence of God by studying someone's brain. A neurological correlation does not equal causation or ultimate explanation. So what if Mohammad or Saint Paul had temporal lobe epilepsy? If God wants to use that mechanism to transmit His revelation, then so be it. Every thought we have, including scientific thoughts, also has measurable brain states. We can use a SPECT scan to study the brain of a physicist while he works on equations. We would learn lots of interesting things about the brain of a physicist, maybe generalizable to all physicists, perhaps also to all equations, but we would learn nothing about whether the physics is true.

Let us use a playful analogy and imagine what the neurosciences of sports might look like. There are a lot of different sports and we cannot study them all, so we are going to simplify by looking only at cricket. Still, cricket turns out to be really complicated, so we are going to need to simplify some more. We are not going to pay attention to the business of cricket, to the rules of the game, to the social practices and enculturation of cricket as a sport among the youth, to the fanatical fans in former British colonies, or to the complicated numerology of the sport. It is just too much; so we are going to focus on the neurological correlates of cricket. But whose cricket brain are we going to study, that of one of the boys from the Sunday pickup game in the village where I taught in Sri Lanka or, perhaps better, that of a professional player of cricket on the national team? We assume that a neuroscientific study of a cricket exemplar will be more revealing, so we select Sanath Jayasuriya of the Sri Lankan National Team to be our subject for a neuroimaging study of cricket, assuming that this is generalizable in some way to all cricket players, indeed to all sports. Before the big match, we outfit Jayasuriya with a remote-control IV, so that we can inject him with radioactive tracers in the midst of batting one of his cut-short shots during a big game. He swings the bat and hits a big one; unfortunately, now we have to stop the game, in order to whisk Jayasuriya away to the laboratory and put him into the SPECT scan. Don't worry: the game can resume in half an hour because we will have finished the scan and can begin our analysis comparing his base-state brain with his cricket-state brain. No doubt we would learn something interesting about Jayasuriya's brain, but we would be nowhere near understanding the phenomenon of cricket. We would not know whether his brain is the same as other cricket players' brains or, for that matter, the brains of other athletes playing other sports—say, tennis, golf, or baseball. It might be that brain scans of the fans watching the match would reveal the same neurological correlates, given the phenomenon of mirror neurons, but we would need to test this.

From a strictly neuroreductionist point of view, we would not really know whether cricket was "real" or merely a "subjective" experience. It seems that the object of cricket is more concrete and objective than the objects of religion, but is that really so? You can take the neuroscientist to a cricket stadium and tell her, "Behold, here is cricket." As an outsider, she probably has not acquired an appreciation of the game and will not understand the complicated rules. The object of cricket is to have fun, you might explain. Our neuroscientist would then have to ask, "What is fun?" Similarly, I could also take the neuroscientist to the monastery, the temple, the church, the synagogue, or the mosque, and say, "Behold, here is religion." But she would still ask, "What is the object of all this activity? God, enlightenment, what's that?" There is no "objective" reason, in either case, to divert so much time and energy, passion and skill, into either activity, whether cricket or religion. So, the neuroscientist postulates that maybe it has something to do with the brain states of cricket players and fans or the brain states of the religious believers, as the case may be.

Let's push this reductio ad absurdum one step farther. What is the objective reality of the brains of a neuroscientist while they do neuroscience? The British geneticist J. B. S. Haldane (1892–1964) came to the same conclusion in thinking about the brains of scientists in general:

> It seems to me immensely unlikely that mind is a mere by-product of matter. For if my mental processes are determined wholly by the motions of atoms in my brain, I have no reason to suppose that my beliefs are true. They may be sound chemically, but that does not make them sound logically. And hence I have no reason for supposing my brain to be composed of atoms. In order to escape from this necessity of sawing away the branch on which I am sitting, so to

speak, I am compelled to believe that mind is not wholly conditioned by matter.[23]

As the Buddhist philosopher Alan Wallace points out in his book *The Taboo of Subjectivity* (2000), we still do not understand the mind:

> Despite centuries of modern philosophical and scientific research into the nature of the mind, at present there is no technology that can detect the presence or absence of any kind of consciousness, for scientists do not even know what exactly is to be measured. Strictly speaking, *at present there is no scientific evidence even for the existence of consciousness!* All the direct evidence we have consists of nonscientific, first-person accounts of being conscious.[24]

Uncorroborated first-person accounts of anything do not count as adequate evidence in a court of law or in the sciences. These need to be correlated and corroborated by other evidence. The "I" cannot be trusted. Science leaves us with something like the Buddhist doctrine of *anatman* or no-self, a subtle and paradoxical doctrine in Buddhism. We have sawn off the branch on which we sit. Perhaps we need to rethink science and, with it, the neurosciences from the bottom up.

The Emergence of Mind

The problem is that science lacks an adequate metaphysics for incorporating both mind and matter. While this is an issue I will explore in more detail in chapter eight, it is useful to discuss some of these metaphysical and philosophical issues in our present context. Today, an informed metaphysics and philosophy of science needs to go beyond reductionism and materialism. We cannot really talk about science anymore without discussing emergent properties of phenomena and different levels of organization. The human brain is only one example of emergence in nature, but an extraordinary one to be sure. A single neuron may be beautiful to the discerning eye of a neuroscientist, but it is pretty stupid all by itself.

The concept of emergence says simply that *the whole is more than the sum of its parts.* We can learn a lot of interesting things about a brain cell by studying its parts and its chemistry. A quick perusal of the typically heavy undergraduate textbook on neurosciences should be adequate to demonstrate just how much we have learned in the last century through this kind of reductionist approach. That being said, the neuron itself could not be predicted or adequately described solely on basis of its constituent components. Nor can a brain be adequately understood by listing its parts. The human brain is an emergent phenomenon, both in its ontogeny—developmental biology—and its phylogeny—evolutionary biology.

Mind is also an emergent phenomenon. Mind cannot exist without a functional brain, but you could never predict consciousness on the basis of an exhaustive reductionistic description of the brain. Nor does mind-brain really do anything by itself. An isolated mind-brain would be a terrible waste. To reach its potential, a mind-brain requires an entire body, vocal chords, oppositional thumbs, tools, languages, families, societies, cultures, and nature.

It is not just "soft" concepts like mind-from-brain that burst the reductionist dream of a mechanistic account of complex phenomena. There are ample examples of emergent properties throughout the sciences. From the surface tension of water in a glass to superfluidity and superconductivity in a physicist's lab, the behavior of huge numbers of particles cannot be deduced from the properties of a single atom or molecule.

A Musical Interlude

Let us imagine a scientific study of music, in this case, classical choral music. Our case study will be Johann Sebastian Bach. We will examine in scientific detail one of Bach's Cantatas, BMV 99—"Was Gott tut, das ist wohlgetan."

Our first approach will be to examine carefully the paper on which this cantata was written. We will study the chemical composition of the paper and the ink in which the score was written. We can also study the semiotic development of the notation system used and the music theory behind it. This is all relevant to the subject matter, but it is not likely we will discover much of interest about Bach, his cantata, or our experience of listening to it.

Another approach will be to study the physics of acoustics and the instrumentation. This cantata calls for string and wind instruments and, of course, a choir. This is going to lead us into some interesting directions, including questions about how the human ear and vocal chords function, but we are still not going to learn much about Bach or this cantata.

Another approach will be neurological. We will place you under an fMRI or PET scan to try to ascertain through neuroimaging analyses the effect on your brain of listening to this cantata. Technically, we are also going to have to do a lot of comparative work here with other sound-perception and music-perception studies to isolate what is unique, if anything at all, to listening to this particular work, as opposed to other sounds, musical pieces, and genres of music. No doubt we might learn lots of interesting things, at least about your brain, because it is not clear yet that another subject, say, a Chinese or Indonesian person unfamiliar with the genre or even the tonal structure, would have the same neurological experience when listening to this Bach piece.[25]

Another approach would be to employ a mathematical analysis of the music itself. With Bach, in particular, there is clearly not only a musical genius composing, but also a mathematical genius. So this might lead to some interesting insights, including computer programs that can generate "original" scores in Bach's style.

We could also take a historical approach, considering Bach's life and time, his musical influences, his biography, and his musical and perhaps mathematical genius. This may be more instructive than studying the chemical properties of the paper on which the cantata was written or the physics and physiology of acoustics. Here, the level of analysis better fits the topic, not that the physics and physiology are wrong or uninteresting in themselves.

A truly "scientific" study of the cantata would surely also reflect on the philosophical, religious, and theological significance of this work, compare it to the other two hundred cantatas that Bach wrote for the liturgical calendar, and wonder about Bach's own religious beliefs. What does it mean to assert "Was Gott tut, das ist wohlgetan" ("What God does is done well")? How does the music reinforce the message? What influence does Bach's music and theology have on us today? How do we feel when we listen to this song or perform it?

Our scientific analysis of a single composition by Bach can be posed on many different levels and can lead us in many different directions, including into interpretative humanistic disciplines not normally thought of as scientific. Furthermore, none of these directions and levels of analysis necessarily conflicts with each other. The only problems arise when we insist on a single, valid level of analysis to the exclusion of others. For instance, a neuroscientist might insist that brain science is the only valid level of understanding the phenomenon of Bach's music.

In this discussion of a new science of music, we see many intriguing parallels and problems common to the proposed new sciences of religion. This is why I keep coming back to the necessity and wisdom of a non-reductive functionalist study of religion.

Dangers and Opportunities

There is a lot of exciting research still to be done and some brilliant people devoting themselves to this research. There are enormous benefits to be realized on the road ahead. For instance, all traditions recognize that there is religious deviance, but they do not agree on how to classify it. Neuroscientific research may give us better tools for distinguishing between pathological religious persons and normal, healthy religious persons.

There are also some dangers that we should recognize. The neurosciences can be used ideologically to denigrate religion, as was the case in the psychiatric community in the early years of the profession. More worrisome is that the neurosciences may provide insights that might make religious euphoria easily obtained or religious brain-washing easily manipulated. This danger applies not just to drugs but any foolproof technique that can guarantee religious ecstasy or obedience. The notion that someone might take a pill and achieve eternal bliss without any side effects might well spell the end of our species's evolution and quite possibly inaugurate the beginning of our extinction. It is not clear what we would do if everyone were happy and euphoric all the time, one with the universe, what Newberg and D'Aquili called Absolute Unitary Being. What would motivate us to struggle and be creative?[26]

Sometimes getting what we want is really bad. I take comfort, and, of course, some pain, in a faith that we will never really understand the human mind-brain, certainly not in a way that we can mechanistically control or easily transform it to some desired end. The mind-brain is just too complicated with too many feedback loops to expect certain results.[27] The mind-brain is an example of a complex distributed system, extremely powerful and creative, but because of its complexity, not something that can be understood and controlled. In the end, we will be saved from ourselves by this very complexity, which does not mean that people will not try to discover or invent the fountain of youth and the key to eternal happiness.[28] Buddhism, for instance, claims to be such a foolproof technique, but after over 2,500 years, *samsara* (loosely translated as "the wheel of endless birth, death, and rebirth") continues. We have not all achieved nirvana and are unlikely to do so. It is perhaps the questing after enlightenment or God, rather than the actual achievement of enlightenment or finding God, that is the most wholesome and transformative aspect of religion. In that quest, there is no reason not to invite science, including the neurosciences, along for the ride. We have a lot to learn from each other.

In closing, it is worth recalling the words of William James:

> Let empiricism once become associated with religion, as hitherto, through some strange misunderstanding, it has been associated with irreligion, and I believe that a new era of religion as well as philosophy will be ready to begin. . . . I fully believe that such an empiricism is a more natural ally than dialectics ever were, or can be, of the religious life.[29]

Empirical research on religious and spiritual phenomena is not only healthy for each of our traditions separately, but it will also help us better understand each other in an increasingly globalized religious world. James writes that a science of religion "can offer mediation between different believers, and help to bring about consensus of opinion."[30] Instead of religion's being something that divides us, more and better religion can be something that unites us, here in our increasingly diverse communities and throughout our increasingly globalized world. The neurosciences of religion can certainly help us along that road.

It may also be that religions can teach science a few interesting tricks. Buddhism, for instance, has been studying the mind for a long time and has its own taxonomy of mental states. What are the neurological cor-relates to these states? Might this be a useful taxonomy in other religious traditions? Would this Buddhist taxonomy be useful in the cognitive neu-rosciences? Not coincidentally, many Western neuroscientists turn out to be practicing Buddhists.

Given the profound connection between embodied self and personal-ity, is it appropriate to use metaphysical dualisms such as body and soul or atman and anatman? What happens to our theologies and philosophies if we reject these dualisms, as science seems to suggest we must? We will return to these questions in later chapters.

CHAPTER SIX

The Medicine of Religion

The study of the relationship between religion, spirituality, and health is now an important field of medical research and a growing area of public interest. The challenges of conducting rigorous scientific investigation in this area provide an interesting case study in the complexity of the phenomena and the problems inherent in the sciences thereof. Here again, we will see the utility of taking a nonreductive functionalist approach to the new sciences of religion.

Health can be defined as "the state of being free from illness or injury." The verb "heal" means "to cause a person to recover from an illness or injury." Both terms derive from the German word *heilen*, which has the original meaning "to be whole." Certainly, most religions would define "wholeness" of body, mind, and spirit as the *sine qua non* of their spiritual teachings. Similarly, the Latin word for health, *salus*, from which we derive the words *salubrious* and *salutation*, also has spiritual connotations, as it serves also as the root of the English word *salvation*. The point is that health and healing have always been major concerns of all religious traditions. A quick Google search of the word *healing* resulted in 94,000,000 links mostly to spiritual and alternative medicine sites.

In this chapter, we will take a careful journey, summarizing an enormous field of literature. I begin by talking about (1) the problem of definitions and how difficult it is to operationalize "religiosity" or "spirituality" in medical research, (2) the problem of measurement, and (3) the challenges in good research design. We will explore (4) some of the salient research results, including (5) random, double-blind studies of distant intercessory prayer. We will touch briefly on (6) secular versions of spiritual therapies, before moving on to discuss (7) complementary and alternative medicine (CAM) and why it is often excluded from the research on spirituality and health. We will consider (8) the growing field of psychoneuroimmunology, which moves us beyond epidemiological statistical correlations to thinking about causal pathways in the mind-brain-body that might provide a naturalistic account of the efficacy of spirituality and religiosity in promoting health. I will discuss (9) the role of placebos in medicine and argue that these are significant in all medical therapies, whether they are scientific, spiritual, or alternative therapies. All this raises issues about (10) medical ethics, which we will touch on briefly, before considering (11) some of the scientific and theological controversies around this field. Finally, I will propose (12) the concept of a deep "semiotics of health" and why the psychosocial-somatic dimensions of health and healing should receive much more attention in research and clinical practice in the future.

1. The Problem of Definitions

One of the first problems we encounter in trying scientifically to study the medical efficacy of religion in health and healing is the problem of definitions. In the context of the United States, with its great diversity of religious beliefs and practices, this is no simple matter. If there were religious uniformity, then we would simply define religion as the dominant orthodox beliefs and practices. In the United States, we also encounter a large percentage of the population who professes to being "spiritual, not religious." We assume this means people affirm certain unspecified religious attitudes but choose to distance themselves from the institutional and historical manifestations of organized religious groups. Hospitals and clinics in the United States must attend to the medical needs of a great variety of patients with diverse religious backgrounds, so the research community has tended to distinguish between religion and spirituality. In a more homogeneous religious culture, this distinction would not have the same importance.

In 2001, Harold Koenig, David Larson, and Michael McCullough published the *Handbook on Religion and Health*, which served as a review of the research literature in the field. The authors defined religion as

> an organized system of beliefs, practices, rituals, and symbols designed (a) to facilitate closeness to the sacred or transcendent (God, higher power, or *ultimate* truth/reality) and (b) to foster an understanding of one's relationship and responsibility to others living together in a community.

They went on to define spirituality as

> the personal quest for understanding answers to ultimate questions about life, about meaning and about relationship to the sacred or transcendent, which may (or may not) lead to or arise from the development of religious rituals and the formation of community.[1]

In both these definitions, we see many problems in the use of multiple abstract and metaphysical terms that would be difficult to operationalize in scientific research. Whatever religion and spirituality may be, they are heterogeneous and multidimensional. In everyday language, these words may be employed without much rigorous reflection, but scientific research demands much greater precision. The spirituality of an Iranian Sufi mystic may have no relevance to the spirituality of a Nigerian Christian Pentecostal or that of an American Tibetan Buddhist. The organization of the respective communities, including their beliefs, practices, rituals, and symbols, may bear little resemblance. Furthermore, these beliefs and practices are always in transition, not fixed, and are subject to many variations and mutations in our increasingly global civilization and in specific local contexts. The problem of developing a precise definition is particularly troublesome for scientific researchers but need not trouble lay people as much. There are other common words and profound concepts that do not lend themselves to rigorous definition: for instance, try defining the words *love* or *justice*, *zero* or *infinity*.

2. The Problem of Measurement

If we cannot even define the terms, how then are we to measure them? Science can proceed with research despite ambiguity about the terms. Such is the case with much of economics, in which many of the yardsticks used in econometrics also import questionable assumptions. For instance, if I total my car in an accident and have a hundred thousand dollar medical bill, this is "good" for the GNP, even though it represents an avoidable and terrible loss of capital and labor. In economics, however, even a faulty yardstick can yield interesting results if it is used consistently over long periods of time to generate large data sets, as long as those results are not overinterpreted. Or at least, so the economists tell us.

The challenge in studying the medicine of religion is in correlating the subjective experiences of patients with the objective measures of body states offered by scientific medicine. There are now several decades of research efforts by psychologists and sociologists in developing research instruments to measure spirituality and religiosity. In 1999, Ralph Hood and Peter Hill published *Measures of Religiosity*, which reviewed and critiqued numerous validated research instruments. There are many different surveys and questionnaires used to measure spirituality and religiosity. All of them involve self-reporting, which often results in overreporting and other distortions.[2]

One example of a questionnaire used to measure the subjective experience of religiosity and spirituality was developed by the Fetzer Institute, from whose website you can download the questionnaire and documentation. Fetzer's *The Multidimensional Measurement of Religiousness/Spirituality for Use in Health Research* (1999) identifies twelve dimensions of religiosity and spirituality: daily spiritual experiences, meaning, values, beliefs, forgiveness, private religious practice, religious/spiritual coping, religious support, religious/spiritual history, commitment, organizational religiousness, and religious preference. The documentation is some eighty pages. The brief version of the survey consists of thirty-eight items, most of which are multiple choice. The Fetzer questions were included in the 1997 and 1998 General Social Survey, which provided "validation" and correlation to other socioeconomic and demographic data.[3] A quick read of the questionnaire shows how out of place this instrument would be in the context of many Asian countries and other contexts, where "belief in God" or "participation in a congregation" may have nothing to do with religiosity and spirituality as practiced and understood by the majority of religious people.

3. Research Design

Social-scientific research is difficult, much more difficult than physics I would argue, because humans are so complicated. Take, for instance, the study of the connection between smoking, cancer, heart disease, and mortality. Why did it take so may years to establish this connection? The consequences, higher mortality rates, do not inevitably occur as the result of an action. The consequences do not appear immediately. The consequences can occur in the absence of any action whatsoever, that is, non-smokers also die of lung cancer and heart attacks. And the consequence is measured as a probability. In these circumstances, it is difficult to make scientific causal inferences.[4]

To these uncertainties, we must now add deep commitments to worldviews and ideologies that people are generally not open to questioning. The operative psychological term here is "cognitive dissonance avoidance," which includes commitments that researchers and patients alike have to particular metaphysical assumptions. We will explicitly address this challenge in the next chapter on "The Narratives of Religion." Studies are further complicated by other factors such as optimism or pessimism, skepticism or trust, respect for authorities, and the selection of which authorities to trust.

Indeed, merely by studying a person, we change the person and the results. This is referred to as subject-expectancy effects. Studies invariably have sample biases in the self-selection of people willing to participate in the studies. Researchers also introduce their own biases into studies. Experimenter-expectancy effects also include self-interest, as researchers necessarily invest enormous amounts of time and money conducting their studies, and their future funding and careers depend in part on the success of these studies. Positive results are more likely to be published. Negative and null results tend not to enhance one's scientific career. Finally, there are societal and institutional biases on the part not only of the journals and professional societies but even on the part of whole cultures. One is not likely to encounter a null or negative study of ayurvedic medicine conducted by Indian researchers or a null or negative study of acupuncture conducted by Chinese researchers.[5]

The outcome—better health—is often poorly defined and might have nothing to do with religion and spirituality as the independent variables. Perhaps better health habits of religious people might account for their greater health and longevity, for instance, in reduced use of tobacco and alcohol. Perhaps nonreligious people who do not use tobacco or alcohol have as good or better health than a comparable religious group.

There are also numerous confounding socioeconomic biases. Comparing the health of Episcopalians, who tend to be higher in socioeconomic status, to the health of Southern Baptists, who tend to be lower in socioeconomic status, would dramatically skew the research results because socioeconomic status is causally linked to health. A well-crafted research project must account for and minimize the impact of these confounders, and this is not easy.

Another research-design problem is in defining and establishing a control group. Given the broad understanding of religiosity that I introduced in earlier chapters, it is not clear that there is such a thing as a "nonreligious" control. The only question is what kind of religious identity a person might have. Nor is it easy to specify religiosity or spirituality as a medical intervention resulting in specific outcome variables. Below we will discuss the challenges of using double-blind, randomized control trials (RCT) in the study of religious and spiritual interventions in health care.

I have already mentioned some of the definitional biases, but the research is also full of theological biases. Most of the research conducted in the United States assumes Protestant Christianity as normative and, in so doing, emphasizes amorphous "belief" as the significant variable to be studied, whereas the outward expressions of piety, that is, behavior, may be more important than the actual beliefs.

In an attempt to minimize trying to measure subjective and variable belief, spirituality-health researchers have tried to substitute an "objective" measure of religiosity. They define frequency of church attendance as the measure, rather than more subjective self-assessments such as those found in the Fetzer questionnaire. Regular church attendance is hypothetically objective, but people tend to overreport this, if they attend church at all. Regular church attendance does seem to be correlated with better physical and mental health. Indeed, some studies suggest that it may add seven years to one's life expectancy.[6] Of course, here too the measurement may not be generalizable. If a pious Muslim prays five times per day every day, does this mean that he has exponentially better health than a Christian who only prays once a week? Perhaps the health efficacy of "church attendance" has nothing to do with spirituality or religiosity per se and is really correlated to greater social support. Perhaps we would get similar or better results for groups that belonged to weekly bridge clubs or bowling teams, as compared to the general population. Certainly, a lot of research correlates social support with better physical and mental health. In general, people who are socially isolated have a much more difficult time of it in life. Robert Putnam takes on this dynamic in his book *Bowling Alone*:

> As a rough rule of thumb, if you belong to no groups but decide to join one, you cut your risk of dying over the next year in half. If you smoke and belong to no groups, it's a toss-up statistically whether you should stop smoking or start joining. These findings are in some ways heartening. It's easier to join a group than to lose weight, exercise regularly, or quit smoking.[7]

Remember, so far we have only discussed epidemiological studies that are observational in nature and seek statistically significant correlations. Religiosity and spirituality are not guaranteed to work for any particular individual. In that respect, we cannot make any meaningful predictions for any individual about the impact of religion and spirituality on her health.

In this type of epidemiological research, several statistical fallacies must be avoided. The so-called Texas sharpshooter fallacy is a clustering illusion. The metaphor is of a near-sighted marksman aiming at the side of a barn (somewhere in Texas). He squeezes out ten shots and then goes to the barn after the fact and conveniently draws the bulls-eye target, locating it where the bullets have already hit. With poorly specified outcome variables in the research design, it is always possible to interpret the significance of the results after the fact, bending the interpretation of the results to fit post hoc hypotheses.

A similar statistical fallacy is known as the shotgun fallacy. Here, again shooting at a barn, because it is hard to miss, our marksman shoots shotgun pellets at the wall. This results in scattered bullet holes on the barn side. After the fact, the shooter draws his XY coordinates on the barn side and discovers patterns in the many bullet holes. If you have enough data points, you are bound to get some kind of pattern.

Most of these studies assume some stable expression of religiosity on a daily or weekly basis; but sometimes, people have extraordinary religious experiences that happen once in a lifetime. Perhaps these dramatic spiritual transformations also have significant health benefits, though little research has been conducted on this.[8] One example of a dramatic spiritual transformation is the near-death experience, about which it would be interesting to collect cross-cultural data and build naturalistic hypotheses.[9] Unfortunately, here too we are confronted with the problems of self-reporting and the anecdotal nature of the data.

4. Research Results

The upshot of all this research is the establishment of a mostly positive correlation between religiosity and health. These studies are primarily observational in nature and, thus, cannot control for the exposure to religious activities and beliefs. They are plagued with problems of self-reporting, but this is true of most social-scientific studies, and these distortions can be critically examined, minimized, and improved.

It appears that religiosity and spirituality benefit blood pressure and the immune system, decrease depression, and lower mortality rates. Religion offers better physical health, better mental health, and longer survival.[10] These correlations are difficult to attribute causally to one specific aspect of religion and spirituality. They may be the result of better health habits, increased social-support structures, or improved psychosocial strengths such as self-esteem; or perhaps the belief structures themselves provide some health advantage. Note that all these possible explanations are naturalistic and do not invoke any concept of supernatural intervention, which is not the domain of legitimate scientific research and, I venture, never will be.

As already noted, the research conducted in the United States so far is mostly biased toward mainline Protestant Christianity. Many modalities of religion and spirituality are ignored or excluded, including Roman Catholic healing traditions and many folk practices. The exceptions to this bias are meditation studies. Meditative practices, generally derived from Eastern religious traditions, lend themselves to controlled laboratory interventions. Meditation has numerous measurable health benefits, and these studies are more reliable.

One study, which seemed to minimize confounders and examined the health impact of religiosity in a non-Christian and non-American context compared religious and secular kibbutzim in Israel. The kibbutz, as you know, is a socialist agricultural community, in which property is held in common, meals and childrearing are generally conducted in common, and the land is cultivated in common. It is a unique lifestyle, to be sure. Most kibbutzim are secular socialists and do not observe Jewish religious practices and beliefs. Some kibbutzim, however, are intentionally religious and make religious observation a central part of their cooperative lifestyle. The comparison of religious to secular kibbutzim allows us to ignore many socioeconomic confounders that would complicate other kinds of studies. The sixteen-year prospective study of 3,900 persons living in eleven religious and eleven secular kibbutzim was also matched for geographic location, quality and types of regional hospitals, number of members over forty years of age, and the dates of establishment. The results were striking. Over sixteen years, the religious kibbutzim had a 50 percent lower mortality rate (69 to 199 between 1970 and 1985).[11] We must still ask whether this might be the result of lower consumption of tobacco and alcohol at the religious kibbutzim. Might this result be because of increased social support at the religious kibbutzim? Our study must probe deeper to isolate religiosity per se as the independent variable in these impressive health outcomes. Of course, if we expand our time frame sufficiently, the mortality rate in either kind of kibbutz, as in life, will be 100 percent.

Several intriguing studies have been conducted by Gail Ironson, M.D., Ph.D., and her team at the University of Miami. They had been working with a group of long-term HIV/AIDs patients, managing their disease with an antiviral "cocktail." Ironson divided the patients into two groups—those who believed in a punitive, judging God and those who believed in a loving, forgiving God. There were not enough patients to do a similar group for nonbelievers. A blood test allowed her to measure T-cells, indicating the strength of the immune system, and to measure the viral load, indicating the strength of the disease. Those who believed in a punitive and judging God had lower T-cell counts and higher viral loads, indicating poorer health. Those who believed in a loving and forgiving God had higher T-cell counts and lower viral loads, indicating better health. Here we have strong evidence at least in one small study that religiosity is not only important but can have positive or negative health impact depending on what type of God one believes in.[12]

5. Distant Intercessory Prayer Studies

Christians regularly pray to God on behalf of other people. In many Christian traditions, this is a regular part of the service, praying for political and church leaders, praying for peace in the world, praying for those in prison or impoverished, and praying for those who are sick. This is called intercessory prayer. One does so for oneself also in times of need. Many Christians believe that intercessory prayer works, that God answers prayers for health and healing. Many Christians also engage in faith-healing rituals, most famously in charismatic Christian groups, where the minister lays hands on an individual and effects spontaneous cures. While some of these faith healings have been unmasked as the work of charlatans staged with accomplices in the audiences, this is not necessarily always the case. There is lot of anecdotal evidence that some of these spontaneous healings do occur, for instance, in some cancer remissions, with or without the help of a charismatic healer.

Accordingly, there has been a lot of interest in intercessory prayer studies in the United States. In contrast to the epidemiological and observational studies we considered above, it is possible to set up scientifically rigorous, randomly assigned, and double-blind studies of distant intercessory prayer. This is to be distinguished from other forms of intercessory prayer, where the patients know that others are praying for them on Sunday mornings, as well as perhaps visiting their homes and hospital rooms to pray in person. The efficacy of this kind of intercessory prayer can be accounted for as a form of social support, which has long been correlated with better physical and mental health. Distant intercessory prayer studies can be constructed with the highest standards of clinical research, whereby the effect of the prayer, if any, is isolated as an independent variable.[13]

In the largest and most rigorous of such studies, Herbert Benson and a team at the Mind/Body Medical Institute studied 1,802 patients who had received coronary artery bypass grafts (CABG). The researchers proposed to measure the rates of complicated recoveries from the bypass surgery. The patients were assigned to three groups: those receiving no intercessory prayer, those told that they may or may not receive intercessory prayer, and those who knew they were receiving intercessory prayer. The conclusion was that "[i]ntercessory prayer itself had no effect on complication-free recovery from CABG, but certainty of receiving intercessory prayer was associated with a higher incidence of complications." The higher incidence of complication with those who knew they were receiving the intercessory prayer was attributed to possible higher anxiety about being prayed for.[14]

There is no indication that distant intercessory prayer works, except in the cases of research fraud and fabrication.[15] Note also that the outcome variables in many of these studies are not well defined; nor are there any naturalistic mechanisms that would explain a positive correlation should it ever be discovered. Richard Sloan, PhD, an important skeptic of the connection between religion and health, writes:

> Significant problems characterize all aspects of these studies. At the level of the treatment variable, the inability to understand the characteristics of prayer make it impossible to determine with certainty the degree of exposure to the putative therapeutic agent, a problem which does not exist in randomized controlled trials. At the level of the outcome variables, there is a different kind of uncertainty: the inability of the IP (Intercessory Prayer) researchers to specify the outcomes likely to be influenced by IP leads to a shotgun approach that violates standards of statistical analysis. Finally, the absence of a persuasive mechanism linking IP to outcomes has led to assertions about the revolutionary nature of IP "findings" that are greatly overstated and fail to appreciate the nature of true scientific revolutions.[16]

These studies do not consider the health benefits for the people who engage in the intercessory prayer on behalf of the sick patients. Here, I suspect we will find significant data that correlate with better physical and mental health for the prayer providers, if not the prayer recipients. There is a whole line of research suggesting that altruism, that is, other-regarding thoughts and behavior, is indeed good for one's health.[17] In that sense, engaging in intercessory prayer may be good for the person doing the praying on behalf of others.

6. Secular Versions of Spiritual Therapies

Many health-care researchers have tried to separate the spiritual-healing technique from the spiritual beliefs. We now have a variety of secular therapies that are devoid of religious or spiritual content. Herbert Benson, M.D., was one of the first to adapt meditation techniques to clinical practice. Meditation can be shown to produce all kinds of healthy outcomes—reduced stress, lower blood pressure, better pain management, and recovery from addiction and compulsive behaviors. Benson founded the Institute for Mind-Body Medicine and regularly hosts continuing-education conferences for health-care professionals at which they explore these and other links between spirituality and health.[18] Similarly, Jonathan Kabat-Zinn, M.D., has adopted Buddhist practices to promote a technique he calls Mindfulness Meditation, which is devoid of specific Buddhist content like the Four Noble Truths, the Eight-Fold Path, and the notions of *samsara* and nirvana. Again, many mental and physical health benefits have been realized in this secularized meditation.[19]

Different schools of hatha yoga have proliferated in the United States. It is safe to say that more people practice hatha yoga in the United States today than in India, though it is approached more as a form of exercise and meditation than as a spiritual practice. Hatha yoga has been used, for instance, to treat posttraumatic stress disorder (PTSD) among war veterans, as well as numerous orthopedic problems.[20]

Therapeutic Touch was developed by Dolores Krieger in the 1970s, a professor of nursing at NYU. She was interested in faith healers and came to believe that the technique of laying-on-of-hands could be used in non-religious healing practices as well. Krieger writes, "I became convinced that healing by the laying-on of hands is a natural potential in man, given at least...the intent to help heal another, and a fairly healthy body (which would indicate an overflow of prana)."[21] It would not be unusual today for students at a nursing school in the United States to be exposed in formal course work to the theory and practice of Therapeutic Touch.

An interesting area for further research would be studying the differential impact of secular meditation versus spiritually focused meditation on health and healing, for instance, with people dealing with cancer. Below I will argue that every psychosocial, spiritual intervention should be individualized based on the patient's beliefs and preferences.

7. Complementary and Alternative Medicine

There is a major split in the United States between those who study the health effects of religion and spirituality and those who are interested in CAM, but the latter is also strongly correlated with spiritual beliefs and practices. This can be seen as both Protestant Christian and Western medical biases on the part of the spirituality and health researchers. For instance, David Hufford points out that the *Handbook on Religion and Health* contains only one entry in the index for "alternative medicine" and refers to it in the text as "unconventional."[22] Koenig et. al. write that public demand for "psychosocial-spiritual care...is not being met by traditional sources... [and that] has opened the door to a whole host of charlatans and alternative medicine practitioners."[23] Obviously, the use of the term *charlatans* is extremely prejudicial, perhaps appropriately so in many cases, though in most case I doubt the CAM practitioners are so motivated.

CAM encompasses many different traditional healing therapies from around the world, so it would be difficult to classify it as one thing. It includes ayurveda, acupuncture, reiki, homeopathy, diverse herbal medicines, chiropractics, diverse forms of massage therapy, and other traditional medical therapies. These may or may not involve highly standardized practices. Acupuncture is now a very formalized therapy requiring training and certification. This recent standardization allows it to be studied scientifically. It is not clear, however, that the same applies to Chinese herbal medicines. In the case of standardized CAM, it is possible to do rigorous scientific investigation, for instance, isolating active ingredients in herbal therapies and accounting for them through naturalistic mechanism.

Acupuncture is an interesting case in point. It was originally received in the West with a great deal of skepticism. Chinese acupuncture was standardized in China during the Cultural Revolution in the 1960s. The traditional Chinese physiology of meridian points and channels, however, bears no resemblance to anything in modern scientific physiology or histology. The concept of Qi-energy is metaphysical and cannot be measured scientifically. Yet acupuncture works in many instances, including on animals in veterinary labs, who are presumably not exhibiting a psychosomatic effect. Acupuncture has been shown to have modest beneficial effects for many patients in many thousands of scientific studies. Nor does one need to believe in Chinese metaphysical and spiritual concepts for acupuncture to work. As the National Institutes of Health (NIH) consensus statement noted,

> There is sufficient evidence of acupuncture's value to expand its use into conventional medicine and to encourage further studies of its physiology and clinical value... [T]he data in support of acupuncture are as strong as those for many accepted Western medical therapies.[24]

Here, we have a case of a CAM therapy that has been disconnected from its spiritual belief structure and used in a different cultural context as a medical technique. Think for a moment how difficult it would be to conduct a placebo–controlled trial for acupuncture. It is easy to construct such a study on pharmaceutical products that are ingested or injected, but much more complicated when the therapy involves needles being inserted in one's body. R. Barker Bausell has helped design and conduct sham-acupuncture procedures used in placebo-controlled studies and is much more jaundiced about the efficacy of acupuncture.[25]

Many CAM therapies represent themselves as medical technologies. For instance, herbal therapists frequently advocate their therapies as biochemical. Drink two of these special teas and call me in the morning! But this biochemical understanding is rarely the view of the practitioners, who generally have some spiritual understanding of vital energy trans-ferred from the plant to the patient, as is the case in traditional Chinese herbal medicine.

CAM therapies have been collected over thousands of years of human experimentation in diverse cultures. There may be some great ancient dis-coveries and intuitions to be sifted out of the enormous diversity of drugs and procedures. The history of medicine up until the last century, how-ever, is essentially the history of the placebo effect.[26] The impact of CAM is surely partially/probably/predominantly psychosomatic, but then I will argue that all medical therapies are such. We should be open to the idea that there may be effective naturalistic reasons that some of these thera-pies work, remembering humbly that much of what is practiced under the rubric of scientific, physicalist medicine is not evidence based but an ongoing experiment with probabilistic results and unknown long-term consequences. Remember also that in those cases where physicalist medi-cine offers no cure of chronic illness, CAM therapies and their spiritually related cousins do provide at least a kind of relief for suffering patients.

8. Neurological Pathways

One of the most exciting areas of research with enormous implications for the field of religion, spirituality, and health is the study of causal path-ways within the mind-brain-body that are implicated in all aspects of our health. Here we begin to understand the complex naturalistic mechanisms that explain how our thoughts and beliefs actually affect bodily func-tions. We can now move from "weak" epidemiological and observational studies of spirituality and health to "strong" understandings of the actual chemical and physiological pathways in the mind-brain-body that trans-late these beliefs and practices into improved bodily functions.

The mind-brain communicates with the body through the nervous system, as well as through chemicals released into the bloodstream. Somatic nerves regulate volitional movement. Autonomic nerves regulate the organs and functions of the body, maintaining homeostasis through largely involuntary and unconscious processes. The mental act of decid-ing to wiggle my big toe, even as I type this sentence, utilizes executive functions in the brain. This is an example of what might be called "top-down" causation, in which a "higher order" complex system, my voli-tional mind-brain, regulates a "lower order" system, the muscles in my big toe, as well as the typing of this sentence. The impact of religiosity on the physiology and health of the body is a much more complex example of this top-down causation, even though the beliefs and practices are not simply volitional and will also harness many autonomic and unconscious functions of the mind-brain-body.

It is well established that volitional activities and psychological states of people alter their brain chemistry, for instance, by fostering the release of endorphins, oxytocin, dopamine, opioids, serotonin, and adrenaline. These and other powerful hormones are involved in all aspects of brain and body function, controlling all aspects of reproduction, including sexual behavior, spermatogenesis, ovarian cycle, fetal development, giving birth, lactation, maternal behavior, and fight and flight reactions to danger. Neuroendocrines are involved in our responses to external stresses and internal infections. They are involved in our metabolism— eating, drinking, and digesting—and regulate how this intake is used. Neuroendocrines are implicated in the normal, healthy functioning of the body, as well as in many diseases. Psychoneuroendrocrinology is the study of how human behavior and thought are involved in these hormone fluctuations. Increasingly, we understand the complex chemical cascades that link human psychology and behavior to brain and body function. Moreover, these causal pathways are multidirectional systems. It is not simply that endogenous chemicals change our moods and behaviors; our moods and behaviors can also change our endogenous chemicals. We now know that placebos release endogenous opioids in the brain and that sham drugs can have real biochemical effects.[27]

A closely related field is psychoneuroimmunology, which tracks how psychological states impact the immune system. Here, too, scientists are tracing the causal pathways within the mind-brain-body. They now have a detailed understanding of how external stress in your life is converted through a chemical cascade in your brain into glucocorticoids and how this hormone then affects antibodies in your bloodstream, thereby impairing the full functioning of your immune system. We now have a causal model for how stress can make you sick.[28] Clearly, our mental state can impact our health and healing in negative ways and, therefore, also in positive ways. Religiosity and spirituality certainly impact our mental states. It will be interesting to see whether we can design spirituality-and-health research to track how religiosity impacts these psychoneuroimmunological systems.

9. Placebo Studies

Within the field of religion, spirituality, and health, as well as CAM, researchers do not like to talk about placebos. For instance, there is no mention of placebos in the index of the monumental *Handbook of Religion and Health*, which reviews some 1,200 studies. Calling something a placebo is widely perceived to be a criticism, indeed an insult, in the contemporary research climate. Prayer may have a placebo effect for the patient, but it is not "real" medicine. Ayurvedic herbal medicine may have a placebo benefit for the patient, but it is not evidence-based medicine, tested with the rigors of random-controlled studies. Given that rigorous, evidence-based, scientific medicine is itself quite a new phenomenon in the history of medicine, it seems rather regressive to celebrate the placebo, but I think this disparagement of placebos is a terrible mistake. Placebo studies offer us a naturalistic understanding of the link between spirituality and health. Indeed, placebo effects are involved in all medical therapies, orthodox scientific or alternative. Placebos may be the most effective and important tool in any healer's toolbox, though, as we will see, they raise many complex medical and ethical problems.

Placebos are referred to as subject-expectancy effect, but they are more complicated than just substituting a sugar pill for an active drug therapy. Randomized controlled trials are regularly conducted by the pharmaceutical industry to test the efficacy of a new drug treatment. A group of patients is typically divided into three groups: those who receive the active drug, those who receive the placebo drug, and those who receive no intervention and for whom the natural progression of the disease is allowed to take its course. The studies are "blind" because the subjects do not know whether they are receiving the active drug or the inactive drug, the latter typically being a sugar pill. "Double-blind" means that the clinicians interacting with the patients also do not know who is receiving the active therapy. A National Institute of Health study concluded that the placebo effect yields beneficial results in 60 to 90 percent of diseases, including angina pectoris, bronchial asthma, herpes simplex, and duodenal ulcers. Placebos have been used successfully in sham knee surgery. Placebos have been linked directly to the spontaneous release of opiates in the brain. Placebo response rates vary from 0 to 100 percent in virtually every clinical condition studied. The placebo response is both universal and unpredictable.[29]

How placebos work turns out to be a very complicated question. Who does what to whom, how, where, and when are all parts of this complexity. Are the patient's responses to the sham treatment or inactive drug specific effects for which the treatment was administered, nonspecific side effects unrelated to the treatment, or unintended and serendipitous effects. Remember that the therapeutic context is always already a highly ritualized situation for patients and physicians, full of differential meanings, power dynamics, vulnerabilities, expectations, and symbols. Placebo effects may be in part conditioning effects. Like Pavlov's dogs, we have been conditioned through a lifetime of television shows, advertising, and visits to doctors' offices, hospitals, and pharmacies to have certain unconditional metabolic responses to conditioned behavioral stimuli, for instance, the taking of a pill. Placebos may reflect a patient's desire to cooperate and please the physician. Nor are placebos necessarily always positive. Sometimes referred to as "nocebos," negative expectations can also play havoc in health and healing, as in the anecdotal cases of people walking into a hospital to visit a patient and having heart attacks on the way in.

RCTs assume that the placebo effect in the intervention and control groups will be nearly identical and, therefore, cancel each other out, leaving the independent therapeutic effect. This claim cannot be proven; indeed, it can be refuted. And yet, RCTs are the methodological gold standard for drug trials. An NIH study concluded that a "placebo response" can amplify, diminish, nullify, reverse, or even divert the action of an active drug. This is important because it shows that the placebo response is just as significant in the case of "real" medical therapies as it is in cases of "inert" dummy drugs and sham treatments.[30] Antibiotics and apparently acupuncture work whether you believe in them or not, but they work better if you believe in them. Double-blind experiments have blinded researches to the profoundly psychosocial somatic dimensions of humans.[31]

10. Medical Ethics

The use of placebos in medical research and therapy is controversial on ethical grounds; and these ethical problems apply also to medical research and therapy using spiritual interventions or complementary and alternative medicine.[32] Medical ethics has established standards for informed consent and disclosure, which have legal import in court cases involving malpractice. Such standards do not apply to CAM practices, but it is only a matter of time in the United States before malpractice lawsuits will be brought against CAM providers. One sees the effects of this new legal and ethical environment in the ads for pharmaceutical products that now include disclosure of side effects and risks in taking a drug. In modern clinical trials, participants must know in advance that they are part of a drug trial or research protocol and that they may receive an active drug/treatment being tested or a placebo drug/treatment. The clinician and the patient must balance the treatment and research objectives. If a standard treatment exists for the disease being studied, then it would be unethical to substitute a placebo for that standard treatment as this would deny the patient known cures for her medical dysfunction or disease. Nor is it a simple matter to define a control group in such studies, who are presumably excluded from any treatment. Clearly, if a standard treatment exists for the disease being studied, and especially if it is a serious disease, then withholding that treatment would not be in the patient's interest, however much the researcher would like to collect the comparative data.

In addition to informed consent and full disclosure, medical ethics seeks to advance the patient's interests and views of health and healing. Of course, the patient's views and interests are also shaped by his spiritual and psychological concerns and perspectives. The physicalist medical paradigm does not address the patient's subjective meaning paradigm. How the physician relates to patients is now a topic of medical education and professional ethics. Many have advocated that physicians take a spiritual assessment of their patients as part of their treatment, and protocols have been developed for doing so. If the patient is a Jehovah's Witness or a Christian Scientist, that knowledge is directly relevant to the clinical context and therapeutic options. Many worry, however, that the taking of spiritual assessments is a slippery slope toward physicians and nurses encouraging those religious beliefs. Spiritual care in medicine is more appropriately the role of hospital chaplains and religious communities, not doctors and nurses who are not trained to provide spiritual counseling and support.[33] Furthermore, modern clinical practice operates in the context of religious pluralism. Many religious persons have exclusivist understandings of their beliefs. If hospitals and private practices were segregated by religious affiliation, this would not be such a problem, but imagine the danger of manipulation and coercion if an Evangelical Christian physician were doing a spiritual intervention on a Hindu patient and trying to convert him to Christianity in the process. Nevertheless, survey studies seem to suggest that patients prefer to be treated holistically, in a manner that recognizes that health and healing are more complicated physically, emotionally, psychologically, and spiritually than getting a car repaired by a mechanic.. These studies suggest that simply taking a spiritual history is often intervention enough.[34]

Religions may promote virtues that are relevant to the practice of medicine and the healing of patients. These might include honesty, self-control, love, joy, peace, hope, patience, generosity, and diligence. And yet, writes critic Richard Sloan, it is not the business of physicians to promote these values:

> These values are virtues to be sure but we have no evidence that they are associated with better health. And questions should arise about whether it is the business of physicians to promote them, regardless of their merits as a whole. Suggesting that it is the business of physicians to make recommendations about the values that their patients hold represents an arrogant and unwarranted extension of the role of a doctor.[35]

This seems to me to be an extreme position. Physicians need to be cognizant of healthful behaviors—exercise, social support, attitudes, compliance, and so on—and self-destructive behaviors of their patients—smoking, drinking, social isolation, and so on. This is more acutely so in the mental-health professions. Indeed, a whole new field of positive psychology is now developing around promoting character strengths and virtues, rather than simply treating mental illness.[36] Still, we should be mindful of arrogant physicians treading in areas where they are not necessarily trained and where they may lack the very virtues and values that should be promoted.

11. Controversy

The research on the medicine of religion is full of problems, as is medical research in general. I have presented a cursory overview of many of these problems—self-selection biases, residual confounding factors, measurement error in the self-report of attendance, and data dredging of large data sets. These studies often have vague definitions of dependent and independent variables and what the predicted outcome variables are. For instance, outcome variables might deal with diseases such as hypertension, cardiovascular disease, cerebrovascular disease, cancer, depression, suicide, marital instability, delinquency, substance abuse, or schizophrenia; but within each of these disorders, we could specify numerous subvariables. Within cardiovascular disease, for instance, there are multiple variants like improved functioning, adherence to treatment, diminished health concerns a year after cardiac transplantation, length of stay in ICUs, length of stay in the hospital, pain medication required, arrhythmic events, blood pressure, functional status, disability, and blood lipids.[37] It will be extremely difficult to correlate, let alone establish, a causal relationship between a spiritual intervention and any of these specific outcome variables.

The controversies extend into the domains of epistemology and theology. Even when meaningful correlations are established between religion, spirituality, health, and healing, we must decide whether these are the results of local, naturalistic efficacy yet to be discovered or the results of supernatural efficacy, which is presumably outside the domain of scientific investigation. In the case of the latter, we must also then question the goodness and justice of a God who intervenes to heal some sicknesses, while letting others suffer and die. This is known as the theodicy question. Many theologians reject the idea that God intervenes in curing some and damming others, which is not to say that prayer does not change the person doing the praying.

12. The Semiotics of Health

The correlations between religion, spirituality, health, and healing are ancient and modern concerns. Recent observational studies indicate a significant, mostly positive connection between religiosity and better health, though it would be difficult to isolate what aspect of religion and spirituality plays the significant role. Is it a matter of improved lifestyle, more social support, better psychological coping, positive attitudes, or perhaps something in the beliefs and rituals themselves? We now have plausible biochemical models for how nonphysical, psychosocial effects can influence the brain chemistry and the immune system. Experimental studies are much more difficult in the case of religiosity and health but, in certain limited cases, can be constructed.

I have emphasized a pervasive psychosocial somatic dimension of all healing practices, whether they be modern scientific therapies, prayer interventions, or alternative therapies. In closing, I want to argue that these psychosocial somatic dimensions are not isolated in the mind-brain-bodies of the patients but distributed through the cultural context of

a society. Recent research on the social contagion of health habits and
behavioral diseases strongly supports this conclusion, though without
clarity about the mechanism by which psychosocial-behavioral-somatic
contagion occurs.[38]

Placebos are encoded by cultures; otherwise. they would not exist
in patients' mind-brain-bodies. There is a culture of modern scientific
medicine that encodes the popping of pills as effective placebos, along
with white coats, stethoscopes, and the examination room as symbols
and liturgy in the culture of sickness and healing. This is reinforced from
childhood on in the rituals of visits to doctors and pharmacists, the act of
taking pills at home, ubiquitous advertisements in the media, and television medical dramas from *Doctor Kildare* to *Gray's Anatomy*. In Chinese
culture, acupuncture is similarly reinforced and encoded as effective therapy. Placebos are always culturally specific, albeit in an increasingly globalized market. We can refer to cultural encoding of placebos as the deep
semiotics of health.[39]

The question, then, is how to improve and enhance the semiotics of
health in a clinical context and in a broader cultural context. How do we
better utilize the placebo effect to create better health outcomes, noting
that we must do so without also selling snake-oil therapies? I imagine
that one of the most interesting areas of research and clinical practice will
focus on harnessing the patient's own mental powers to create powerful
endogenous transformations in her endocrine and immune systems. The
wisdom of CAM and spiritual interventions is that the more elaborate the
healing ritual, the more effective the placebo effect.[40]

CAM debunker Bausell ends his book *Snake Oil Science* with a curious
section titled "How to Select a Placebo Therapy That Works." Bausell
writes, "If you suffer from an unrelieved chronic condition, I sincerely
hope that you (or medical science, conventional or alternative) will someday discover something that will help you." But in the mean time, try a
placebo! Bausell recommends shopping around for the "best" spiritual
or CAM therapies and therapists: "Once you've started the therapy," he
continues, "embrace it... with all your heart and soul."[41] Here, Bausell
is affirming the ancient wisdom of the second-century physician Galen,
whose strange theories dominated medical practice for over a millen-
nium. Galen noted, "He cures most successfully in whom the people have
the most confidence." Indeed, even today after all the critical analyses
and best scientific practices, it helps to have blind faith and your fingers
crossed. In the next chapter, we will introduce this concept as "the second
naiveté." Hope heals; ritualized hope in groups heals more effectively.

Is there a way systematically to study, ritualize, and individualize these
psychosocial-somatic interventions as a supplement to the standard scientific treatments, when such treatments exist? This would require clinicians to customize the context of health care to the culture of each
particular patient. An intake questionnaire might be used to provide each
patient with symbols, rituals, objects, music, and care, alongside of the

best medical practices, to enhance the patient's ability to harness the placebo effect to promote healthier outcomes. For one patient, it might be a cross by his bed and Gospel music on his iPod; for another, it might be recitations from the Qur'an and a comfortable place to perform *salat*; for yet another patient, it might be photographs from her pilgrimage in the Himalayas and the sound of running water, while another might want a small shrine for Lord Buddha on her nightstand and a soundtrack of chanting monks. To this we can add photographs of family and friends. New technologies make it possible to customize the spiritual-clinical environment with an infinite variety of scriptures, poems, music, images, and videos, even in a crowded hospital context. If the placebo effect is so powerful, then we should be trying to harness it to realize better health outcomes.

The Magic of Medicine

The late psychiatrist Thomas Szasz was a fierce critic of what he saw as the new religion of modern science, especially in the field of medicine, particularly in psychiatry. Szasz understood the men in white coats to be a new secular priesthood, writing, "[F]ormerly, when religion was strong and science weak, men mistook magic for medicine; now, when science is strong and religion weak, men mistake medicine for magic."[42] The most important take-away from this discussion of the medicine of religion is that there has always been, and I venture always will be, a bit of magic in the practice of medicine. All health and healing are partially psychosocial-somatic in universal and unpredictable ways. Psychosocial-somatic effects are in part instances of top-down causation in which "spirit" acts on mind, mind acts on brain, brain acts on body, and body acts on disease through the endocrine and immune systems. Religion, in this view, is an attempt to take conscious control over this dynamic. Psychosocial-somatic healing and the semiotics of health are examples of a nonreductive and functional dimension of religion and spirituality. All people and philosophies are implicated in this dynamic, which we increasingly understand in scientific causal pathways.

Practitioners of modern scientific medicine need to become self-critical in recognizing this deep semiotics of health, including in their own culturally encoded context, and become proactive in ethically harnessing these psychosocial-somatic therapies in promoting the well-being of their patients, themselves, and their societies. The medicine of religion is minimally this deep semiotics of health, from which we cannot extract ourselves, even in the practice of modern scientific medicine. This material semiosis of health—spirit-mind-brain-body-society—is traditionally the domains of religion, where significant expertise has been accumulated over the millennia. Through the medicine of religion and the tools of modern science, we might learn how better to harness this "magic" in creating better health outcomes for our patients and ourselves.

Religion from the Bottom Up

C H A P T E R   S E V E N

The Narratives of Religion

Even as the natural sciences challenge the literal plausibility of ancient religious cosmologies and the accounts of miracles in these narratives, so too the historical sciences challenge the literal plausibility of sacred scriptures as actual historical record. We need to begin by reexamining and rethinking the interpretation of these sacred stories from the bottom up. Believers believe that their stories are true, for instance, that Moses was a real person who led the Hebrews out of slavery and received the Torah directly from God on Mount Sinai or that there really was a Prince Siddhartha Gautama who searched for and found enlightenment in the sixth century B.C.E. Moreover, they believe that contained in these ancient stories is information vital to contemporary humans. In fact, the historical evidence for either of these stories from the ancient past is quite sparse and filtered largely through centuries of oral history, mythological elaborations, and sectarian biases before they were even recorded in written form by religious partisans.

Antireligious skeptics might argue that these ancient books might best be assigned to some dusty shelf in the library for historians doing archival research. They imagine that these religious texts will be as unimportant in future generations as Aztec and Greek mythologies are in our time. The vast majority of humans, however, hold on to these scriptures as sacred, as profound revelations, as precious guides to the mysteries of life and death. How should we read these ancient narratives—the Torah, the New Testament, the Qur'an, the Vedas and the Upanishads, the Buddhist Pali Canon and the Mahayana Sutras, the Tao Te Ching and the Confucian Analects? How do we understand the stories of religion, be it as outsiders looking in at foreign religions or as thoughtful believers reconsidering our own tradition?

In this chapter, we will travel into a border realm between the human sciences and the humanities, employing historical and textual studies, as well as psychological and philosophical analyses.

Historical Source Criticism

Historical critical studies of sacred texts began in eighteenth- and nineteenth-century Europe and should be understood as an extension of the scientific method to the study of scripture. The primary focus of these studies was the Bible, though attempts had been made to apply these methods to other sacred texts as well.[1] In this approach, the Bible is treated as a text created by humans in particular historical and cultural contexts to advance different human purposes. Careful philological analysis of ancient languages is combined with archeological and historical research to decode the probable authorship and purposes of different material in the biblical anthology. This is in sharp contrast to treating the Bible or some other scripture as the inerrant word of God, as promoted by religious fundamentalists. Historical criticism understands the Bible, and by implication all other sacred scriptures, to be a compilation of texts constructed intentionally from previous layers of Judaism, borrowed from sources in other cultures in the region, and containing portions intentionally inserted by unknown priests and scribes for political and theological purposes over many generations. The redaction of the Bible is, thus, a kind of whisper down the lane in which real persons and events are mixed with fantastic elaborations and imaginations. What begins mostly in oral transmission is eventually written down in bits and pieces, though further transformations occur in the hands of generations of scribes who recopy and edit the text. These fragments are then selectively remembered and preserved based on the interests of those who follow. Eventually it is redacted into a single authoritative sacred text. Politics, personalities, and power play a role at each stage of this evolution. The authors and editors may be inspired by God, directly or indirectly, but in no sense should the Bible be taken as an accurate historical chronology or an actual account of ancient Judaism, first-century Palestine, and the history of the early church. The Bible is as much a political and ideological document as it is a spiritual and philosophical document. It is of enormous historical import but is itself not an actual history. This scientific approach to reading the Bible, and by implication all other sacred texts, is referred to as higher criticism, source criticism, or simply historical criticism.

For many believers, historical criticism of scripture is simply heretical. Today, however, even pious and conservative Christians and Jews have adopted and adapted the insights of historical criticism, albeit within a confessional framework (there is essentially no comparable historical criticism of the Qur'an by pious Muslims today). Historical criticism does not necessarily lead to atheism, but it does make the hermeneutics of the sacred more complicated than the supposed transparency presumed by some fundamentalist readers. For instance, the modern Catholic catechism states:

> In order to discover the sacred authors' intention, the reader must take into account the conditions of their time and culture, the literary genres in use at that time, and the modes of feeling, speaking and narrating then current. For the fact is that truth is differently presented and expressed in the various types of historical writing,

in prophetical and poetical texts, and in other forms of literary expression.[2]

By way of example, let us take a closer look at what historical criticism says about the redaction of the New Testament. First, the authors of the four Gospels are not actually known, though tradition attributes these to Mark, Matthew, Luke, and John. The Gospel of Mark is thought to be the oldest, probably written mid- to late first century C.E., long after the death of Jesus and the ministry of Paul. Note that the language of the Gospels is Greek, while Jesus and the disciples spoke Aramaic and presumably read and prayed using biblical Hebrew within the larger context of a Greco-Roman-dominated Mediterranean civilization. The Gospel of Matthew was written by an unknown author who apparently borrowed and elaborated from both the Gospel of Mark and an unknown source called Q by the scholars. Matthew's Gospel was written in the late first century, perhaps a generation after Jesus's death. The Gospel of Luke has a similar ambiguous genealogy. The Gospel of John is thought to have been written by someone who had no direct connection to the historical Jesus. Paul, who should be credited as the real founder of Christianity, had no direct knowledge of the historical Jesus. His letters, and the letters attributed to Peter, James, John, and Jude, were written before the Gospels and make almost no reference to the Gospel accounts and sayings of Jesus. Many of the letters are thought to be pseudepigraphal, meaning that they were written by others and falsely attributed to Paul.

Many ancient manuscripts were discovered in the late twentieth century in Egyptian Coptic churches. These ancient manuscripts, sometimes just fragments thereof, are known as the Gnostic Gospels and include the gospel of Thomas, the gospel of Mary, and the gospel of Judas. These were presumably excluded from the redaction of what we now call the New Testament for political and theological reasons, the details of which do not matter for this discussion. And while history has passed on Paul's letter to Priscilla of Ephesus, we do not have Priscilla's letters to Paul. What is preserved, included, and excluded and why are profoundly important questions.

The redaction of the New Testament was a politically and theologically charged affair that only began in the fourth century in a series of synods, most notably the Synod of Hippo in 393 C.E. The churchmen—at this point, they were all men—met to choose the canon some 350 years after the death of Jesus in what had by then become the imperial church of the Roman Empire. They selected the texts to be included in the anthology that we now call the New Testament. They resolved discrepancies between different copies of the same text, remembering that these manuscripts were all hand-copied over many generations. The result thereof is now immortalized, widely translated, and mass-produced as the New Testament, an anthology touched and transformed at many stages by the hands of partisans and politics. The New Testament is not a history textbook. Indeed, by contemporary historical standards, there is precious little

independent corroboration to establish even the existence of the historical Jesus. It seems more likely that Jesus is a composite personality, even
as Christianity is a mixed movement, drawing from multiple cultural
sources including Jewish mythological and Greek philosophical overlays
in the context of first- and second-century Roman civilization.

These insights from historical criticism are not necessarily a showstopper
for thoughtful and committed Christians. In terms of traditional trinitar-
ian theology, the historical Jesus is not all that essential and in any case can
only be known through the Holy Spirit. The Father is too transcendent
to be known directly. Jesus, the incarnation of God, came to bridge that
gap and effect a cosmic reconciliation between the transcendent Father
and humanity. After Jesus's death and Resurrection, the Holy Spirit steps
in as the primary relationship that Christians have with God. It is only
by the inspiration of the Holy Spirit that one can understand the Bible or
come to know Jesus and the Father. Remember also that the church, the
collective of Christians, is now also understood to be the Body of Christ.
It was not until the Protestant Reformation, the translation of the Bible
into vernacular languages, and the mass reproduction of the Bible with
the new printing press that reading and interpreting the Bible became a
central dimension of Christian piety; so, for most of Christian history, the
Bible actually plays a minor role in Christian faith and practice. All this is
to repeat that many thoughtful Christians embrace historical criticism and
continue to be pious believers.

Still, other problems remain in interpreting the doctrine of Creation,
the stories of miracles, and the promise of resurrection. It is not the purpose of this book to delve deeply into a single tradition and engage in
reconstructive theology or modern apologetics. Others do so today to
varying degrees of satisfaction. At this stage, we need only point out that
every sacred text from antiquity, at least as we work from the bottom up
and the outside in, is the product of human minds, human hands, and
human societies. In many cases, these texts have been passed on in oral
tradition before they were committed to writing. In the case of the Pali
Canon, the earliest Buddhist manuscripts, these were passed on orally for
some 300 years before they were committed to writing. The Qur'an and
the Hadith were passed on orally in a single generation before they were
committed to writing. The Book of Mormon was apparently invented
whole cloth out of the imagination of Joseph Smith Jr. in 1830. Any or all
these sacred scriptures may be inspired by God, but they are selectively
remembered, transcribed, interpreted, and passed on by humans.

The Storied Nature of Humans

What are we to make of all these sacred texts with their complex origins?
How should we read them today? Is there some truth to be found therein,
as their followers so fervently proclaim?

One option for scriptural interpretation is to read the Bible and other sacred texts as rich sources for archetypal stories. Here, we draw on some of the insights of Sigmund Freud, C. G. Jung, Claude Levi-Strauss, and their many followers. In this approach, the conflicts and dynamics between the characters in the Bible, the Jataka Tales, the Bhagavad Gita, and other scriptures are psychologically profound but not literally true. Of course, such an approach finds large portions of these scriptures irrelevant in the contemporary context and also accords them the same status as other myths, fairy tales, and great literature from around the world. This approach seeks contemporary, true-to-life profundities in sacred stories but does so with an eye to ambivalence and uncertainty, conflict and cathar-sis, and the construction of powerful symbols and shared meanings.

We also find in scriptures codes of moral conduct. These can be analyzed independently of the mythological context for their wisdom and practi-cality. Of course, there is often a large gap between the ideals preached by religions and the real behavior of religious persons. Nevertheless, the moral teachings of religion may be a source of ethical intuition worthy of serious philosophical and empirical reflection.

Finally, we find in scriptures metaphysical points of view, which may be philosophically important, independent of the larger mythological frame-work in which they are originally presented. For instance, on each day of creation in Genesis 1, God repeats the word *tov,* meaning "good." On the last day of creation, when "God saw everything that he had made," including the humans, God pronounces the universe *tov me'od,* or "very good" (Gen. 1:31). In its parts, the universe is "good," and on the whole, the universe is "very good." This is a normative orientation to the uni-verse; independent of whether there is a creator God and independent of the new scientific cosmology, this is a really interesting philosophical question. What does it mean to say that life is good or not? How might one live differently based on how one answers that question?

It is interesting to observe that the way humans tend to answer these big questions is through stories. If we zoom out again and think about the whole phenomenon in the broadest categories, we observe that humans are profoundly storied creatures. For generations, humans gathered around hearth and fire to tell and retell stories. Much of cultural trans-mission was in the form of storytelling. Today, people are more likely to gather around the cool glow of the television, but we are no less storied. Some imaginary calculations of the amount of time and money spent today on the entertainment, news, and publishing industries should give us pause to think about how central storytelling is to our humanity. To this we can add everyday interactions with friends and families, in which we recount events and share gossip. By my rough estimation, we spend perhaps 50 percent or more of our waking hours in storytelling. Humans make stories but, in some sense, are also made by our stories.

Many contemporary thinkers have argued that there is a deep nar-rative structure of human thought.[3] The psychologist Jerome Bruner argues that "it is through narrative that we create and recreate self-hood, that self is a product of our telling and not some essence to be delved for in the recesses of subjectivity."[4] Narratives are not just a matter of individuals creating their inner and social self; narratives are also what bind societies and cultures together. They are how we integrate events and actions through time into meaningful patterns. They specify cause-and-effect relationships and organize these into coherent wholes. Narratives tell us which events and actions are significant and which can be ignored. The interrelationship of events in our lives is explained by these narratives.

Stories always have normative content, describing what is important, what is unimportant, what is better, what is worse, what is good, and what is bad. Our sense of meaning and purpose and our values and motivations are based on these narratives. Charles Taylor argues that stories about self and society are how humans construct the "horizons of meaning" that form the critical background for social relations and life choices. Narratives always represent a kind of movement in moral space. They are our way of constructing coherence and continuity in our lives.[5]

Moral reasoning is not as much a matter of propositional logic and rational choice as some modern philosophers have argued;[6] rather, we make moral judgments based on the analogical applications of powerful stories.[7] Whether it is the story of the Ring of Gyges, the Good Samaritan, the Jataka Tales, or the story of our revered grandparent, we apply these mini-narratives to new situations in the course of our life. If we do the right thing, it is generally not because of a lot of philosophical reflection and rational cost-benefit analyses, but rather because of a moral teaching we learned from a story. Mini-narratives are nested together into larger stories, stories within stories. It is stories, all the way down.

The most important stories that humans tell, retell, and reframe are the ones people do not generally recognize as stories at all. These are referred to as "metanarratives."[8] These master stories are the stuff of ideologies, religions, nationalisms, and cultures. People do not even recognize them as stories but rather tend to take them as an unarticulated background, the taken-for-granted truth, the way things really are.

In discussing religion and politics with someone with very different assumptions and beliefs, the debates can quickly become heated. There is a profound gap between the parties in such debates, so much so that they often do not agree about the relevant facts, let alone interpretations of these facts. For instance, a fundamentalist Muslim will refer only to the Qu'ran, the Hadith, and his particular reading of world history as relevant background for the debate. A fundamentalist Christian will refer only to her particular understanding of the Bible. A Communist approaches economics and world history with a very different set of assumptions from that of a free-market capitalist. Palestinians and Israelis have very different understandings of the relevant histories and facts regarding the history of their conflict. In Sri Lanka, there are the tragic competing narratives

of the Sinhalese Buddhist nationalists and the Tamil separatist nationalists, each with its own reading of history and a long list of grievances.
In these moments of profound disagreement, both sides are confronted
with incomprehensibility of the other's worldview and assumptions. In
such arguments, one has the distinct feeling of beating one's head against
a wall. "How could someone else be so stupid and stubborn," one tells
oneself. They, the Other, do not even recognize what is obvious to you.
They must be irrational, evil, inhuman—so begins the escalating spiral of
ideological violence.

Entangled Narratives

Modern humans, perhaps more than at any other time in history, are
caught up in a web of entangled narratives. Globalization and communication technologies have brought the world of differences into our
living rooms, classrooms, and communities. People wage culture wars
within and between civilizations based on these narratives, religious and
otherwise, which, for the most part, they do not even recognize as stories. What intellectual tools can help to mediate between these competing stories? People disagree about the good life and, in so doing, tend to
demonize those with different visions of that life here at home and around
the world.

Christian Smith explores these conflicts in *Moral, Believing Animals*.
In a chapter titled "Living Narratives," he offers a dozen examples of
contemporary metanarratives, each presented in about 200 words—
the Christian narrative, the Militant Islamic Resurgence narrative, the
American Experiment narrative, the Capitalist Prosperity narrative, the
Progressive Socialism narrative, the Scientific Enlightenment narrative,
the Expressive Romantic narrative, the Unity with Brahman narrative,
the Liberal Progress narrative, the Ubiquitous Egoism narrative, and the
Chance and Purposelessness narrative. Not only do explicitly political and
religious movements have metanarratives, but even competing schools
of thought in sociology, economics, and psychology assume the form of
metanarratives. These short statements of competing worldviews make
for an excellent seminar discussion or role-play for students. I imagine it
would also be a useful exercise for world religious and political leaders.

What one discovers very quickly is also disturbing on a deeper level.
There is no simple way to adjudicate between these competing worldviews and world doings. Given a certain set of assumptions, any particular
metanarrative becomes difficult, if not impossible, to refute. Indeed, once
captured by a particular worldview, it is possible to rationalize just about
anything and everything within that worldview. Soon, all facts seem to
bolster one's assumptions because the facts that matter are dictated by the
narrative. This is what I mean when I use the term "solipsistic rationality."
People tend to select facts and the interpretation of those facts carefully

based on their metanarratives. Smith writes:

> The problem with a narratological understanding of human persons—
> and probably an important reason modern people resist thinking of
> themselves as ultimately storytelling and believing and incarnat-
> ing animals—is that it is difficult rationally to adjudicate between
> divergent stories. How do you tell which one is more deserving of
> assent and commitment than others? The American Experiment nar-
> rative will probably appeal to more readers of this book than the
> Militant Islamic Resurgence narrative. Why? Because objective,
> empirical evidence proves that it is a truer story? Not really. For what
> *is* evidence is *itself* largely made significant, if not constituted for us,
> by our narratives.[9]

Let us examine one of the metanarratives from Smith's book in detail.
This is the narrative of the Community Lost, and it appears in different
religious and cultural idioms:

> Once upon a time, folk lived together in local, face-to-face commu-
> nities where we knew and took care of each other. Life was simple
> and sometimes hard. But we lived in harmony with nature, laboring
> honestly at the plough and in handicraft. Life was securely woven in
> homespun fabrics of organic, integrated culture, faith, and tradition.
> We truly knew who we were and felt deeply for our land, our kin,
> our customs. But then a dreadful thing happened. Folk community
> was overrun by the barbarisms of modern industry, urbanization,
> rationality, science, fragmentation, anonymity, transience, and mass
> production. Faith began to erode, social trust dissipated, folk customs
> vanish. Work became alienating, authentic feeling repressed, neigh-
> bors strangers, and life standardized and rationalized. Those who
> knew the worth of simplicity, authentic feeling, nature, and custom
> resisted the vulgarities and uniformities of modernity. But all that
> remains today are tattered vestiges of a world we have lost. The task of
> those who see clearly now is to memorialize and celebrate folk com-
> munity, mourn its ruin, and resist and denounce the depravities of
> modern, scientific rationalism that would kill the Human Spirit.[10]

This is a nostalgic narrative of the tragedy of modernity, industrialization,
and globalization. It offers a backward-looking romantic view of history. In
the old days, people were better, life was better, local communities mattered. The basic structure of this narrative is repeated by many Christians,
Muslims, Hindus, and other cultural idioms. In Sri Lanka, we see this narrative functioning in romantic readings of the *Mahavamsa* and the idealiza-
tion of "tank, temple, and paddy." There is also a potent contemporary
ecological version of this narrative articulated by some in the environmental
movement, who might have us all return to Neolithic village life.[11]

It is important to emphasize that humans can hold multiple narratives, sometimes mutually exclusive. We mix and match. The conservative Roman Catholic narrative is incompatible with the narrative of liberal democracy, but that does not prevent most conservative Roman Catholics from being enthusiastic supporters of liberal democracies. The Christian narrative appears incompatible with capitalist virtues, but that does not prevent Christians from living the bourgeois life. The ecoromantic narrative appears incompatible with much of modern technology, but that does not prevent environmentalists from using soon-to-be-obsolete laptops and flying around the world to enjoy ecotourism. The Theravada Buddhist narrative is incompatible with Sinhalese nationalism and militarism, but, of course, that is just like *samsara*. Each generation reinterprets these narratives in different situations, even as each generation is also constituted by these received stories. People are not passive recipients of these narratives but active reinterpreters. Embodied in these narratives are symbols and meanings that acquire motivational power—the religious icon, a flag, a book, or a people.

The idealized past of the Community Lost narrative above contrasts sharply with progressive, future-oriented narratives, for instance, the Scientific Enlightenment narrative or the Capitalist Prosperity narrative. This nostalgia narrative is woven into many of the fundamentalist religious movements today, whether in the East or West, the North or South. One can argue with this nostalgia, but evidence alone cannot compel someone to believe otherwise. Like all the narratives Smith describes, it involves a certain reading of history and a certain set of assumptions about what really matters in life.

As the historian Eric Hobsbawn reminds us, "History is the raw material for nationalist or ethnic or fundamentalist ideologies. . . . If there is no suitable past, it can always be invented. . . . The past legitimizes. The past gives a more glorious background to a present that doesn't have much to celebrate."[12] Of course, history is another form of storytelling, narrative in structure, always ideologically oriented toward some present reality and context in which the author lives, thinks, reads, and write. That is why the rewriting of history will never end. In a hundred years, people will still be writing new books about the American Civil War, the French Revolution, and the Anuradhapura kingdoms of ancient Sri Lanka, offering new insights and interpretations for new times.

Even science is a bundle of stories. There are short stories about particular research projects and the history of entire disciplines. There is the new cosmological narrative of a dynamic universe and an evolving planet. And then there are interpretations of these scientific stories, a distinction we will return to in the next chapter. Smith presents the Scientific Enlightenment narrative in this abridged form:

For most of human history, people have lived in the darkness of ignorance and tradition, driven by fears, believing in superstitions.

Priests and lords preyed on such ignorance, and life was wearisome and short. Even so, gradually, however, and often at great cost, inventive men have endeavored better to understand the natural world around them. Centuries of such inquiry eventually led to a marvelous Scientific Revolution that radically transformed our methods of understanding nature. What we know now as a result is based on objective observation, empirical fact, and rational analysis. With each passing decade, science reveals increasingly more about the earth, our bodies, our minds. We have come to possess the power to transform nature and ourselves. We can fortify health, relieve suffering, and probe life. Science is close to understanding the secret of life and maybe eternal life itself. Of course, forces of ignorance, fear, irrationality, and blind faith still threaten the progress of science. But they must be resisted at all costs. For unfettered science is our only hope for true enlightenment and happiness.[13]

This Scientific Enlightenment narrative must be distinguished from the content of science. The facts of science do not necessarily result in this interpretation, as we will see below. This metanarrative of scientism becomes one of many possible metanarratives competing for our allegiance. We can chose the Christian narrative, the Islamic Resurgence narrative, the American Experiment narrative, the Capitalist Prosperity narrative, the Progressive Socialism narrative, the Community Lost narrative, the Expressive Romantic narrative, the Unity with Brahman narrative, the Liberal Progress narrative, the Ubiquitous Egoism narrative, the Chance and Purposelessness narrative, or many other foundational stories all tinged with a religious-like faith that structures what we see as true and good. We find ourselves at a relativistic impasse. There appears to be no way to adjudicate between the narratives of Palestinians and Israelis, of Sinhalese Buddhist nationalists and Tamil separatists, of Islamic militants and the West, science and religion, the future utopic enthusiasts of progress and the nostalgic utopic conservationists of nature and tradition. If there is no possibility of mediating between these metanarratives, then we are left with the prospects of brute force being the last judge between ideologies, political parties, nations, and religions. If might makes right, we will all be losers in the twenty-first century.

How, then, do we understand passionately held commitments to different religious and ideological worldviews? I would call the discussion above observational. With the exception of certain scientific knowledge, and even then only provisionally and quite narrowly, there is no immediate way to adjudicate intellectually between competing metanaratives. These stories structure our thought and behavior in many profound ways, both political and personal. We have reached the so-called postmodern moment in scholarship. This relativistic impasse is actually philosophically mandated by rational analysis and reflection in the context of our contemporary world.

Which of these stories is worthy of our affirmation and support? Which narrative has the power to convince, convert, and transform? Which religion does one choose? Whose politics should one support? Which stories of self, society, and cosmos are we willing to risk all for when push comes to shove? I turn to the field of philosophical hermeneutics to try to find a way out of the relativistic impasse. I believe the philosophy of interpretation offers us a way out and a path forward. In the end, I will advocate what I call "intellectual nonviolence" or, more simply, humility. This path is not without risk, but it offers the greatest promise for discovering truths that transcend our many varied stories. In the next chapter, I will argue for the possibility of a more all-encompassing metanarrative, in part by embracing the evolving scientific cosmology, which affirms but also transcends the many competing narratives mentioned above.

The Antics of Hermes

Hermeneutics is the philosophy of interpretation. Problems of interpretation are endemic in scriptural studies, translation, law, history, literature, and the social sciences. The word *hermeneutics* derives from the Greek god Hermes, who was the messenger god, mediating between the gods of Mount Olympus, the mortals, and the gods of the underworld. Hermes is something of a trickster god, using his role as messenger to confound and confuse. So the "-neutics" of Hermes is not a simple matter. How one interprets sacred scripture, translates from a foreign language, applies case law, constructs history, and reads a work of literature can lead one in very different directions with sometimes contradictory results.

Interpretation is also central to political theory and social action. Interpretation is central to the narrative creation and recreation of self and society.[14] In this section, I will use the work of Paul Ricoeur on hermeneutics to develop these ideas, with a view to developing a hermeneutic of our competing visions of ultimate reality.

Paul Ricouer takes the philosophical debate between Hans-Georg Gadamer[15] and Jürgen Habermas[16] as a point of departure. Gadamer rejects classical German hermeneutics by arguing that every reading of a text begins with a prejudgment. There is no possibility of objective interpretation because all readers begin with a set of assumptions and prejudices.

The author's original intention is no longer accessible and not necessarily all that important, in part because like the reader, the author is not transparent to himself. There are hidden meanings in a text about which the author himself may be unaware. Humans are not objective to themselves, neither as writers nor as readers. Self-knowledge requires effort and is never absolute. Creative works of authors and artists have a life of their own separate from the intentions of the creator. Gadamer looks toward a "fusion of horizons" between the world of the author, the text itself as something now disconnected from the author and his world and the life of the reader in a different time and place.

Habermas was critical of Gadamer's subjectivization of hermeneutics and its relativistic implications and held out for a critical and objective reading of the text. Remember that the text stands in for much more than simply any old book; it also refers to society, history, and culture, as well as to religion. Habermas comes out of the German socialist tradition so is committed to the possibility of social-scientific theories of society that allow critical and objective judgments to be made. To give so much weight to the reader's prejudice does not allow for the possibility of scientific objectivity in hermeneutics.

Always the creative synthesizer, Paul Ricoeur explores and expands the dialectic between Gadamer and Habermas. The hermeneutical circle, as expounded by Gadamer, moves in three stages. It begins with the *understanding* that we already bring to the text, the prejudices of the reader in her particular historical and social context. Just to pick up a book already means that the reader has a background in reading, but whether that book is Plato's *Republic*, the Gospel of John, Bhagavad Gita, Shakespeare's *Richard III*, Dante's *Inferno*, or the *Communist Manifesto* is already determined by a cultural and historical situation that valorizes the text and orients the reader to its significance or the lack thereof. Ricouer agrees with Gadamer that we cannot escape these prejudices and that they need not be seen as simply negative.

The second stage of the hermeneutical circle involves *explanation*, the work of reading, comprehending, analyzing, and interrogating the text. Here, critical theory can help, though which critical theory we use is also partially determined by our prejudgments. For instance, if we take a psychological approach to the text, we might choose from any number of competing theories—employing Freudian object-relation theory, Jungian archetypal theory, Frankel's logo theory, or others. In part 1 of this book, for instance, we used multiple analytic theories to try to explain what religion might be and how it works. Which analytic theory we adopted—economic, evolutionary, neuroscientific, or medical—acted as a kind of prejudgment, structuring what we understood to be significant about religious and spiritual phenomena.

This analytical stage then gives way to the third stage, our *appropriation* of the reading, a new interpretation based on the new data acquired and new relationships observed in a close, critical reading of the text. Through this increased familiarity with the text, we now end up with a deeper understanding. We have achieved what Gadamer refers to as "a fusion of horizons." Should we read the text again, our understanding will be enriched by previous readings. This, then, is the hermeneutical circle—understanding, explanation, and appropriation leading to deeper understandings as the world of the text and the world of the reader interrelate and inform each other.

Ricouer recognizes along with Habermas that the hermeneutical process so described can become a vicious circle, in which the prejudices of the reader dictate certain dogmatic readings over and over again. The *explanation* employed is preselected to predetermine the *appropriation*. Such is the case for many in the reading of sacred scripture or ideologically informed readings of history. Ricouer's solution is to interject the possibility of a willful *distanciation* from one's prejudices, a kind of temporary suspension of judgment. This is what we did in part 1 in our phenomenology of religion, when we imagined the possibility of standing outside a tradition as an objective observer of the phenomenon. Ricouer renames the three stages as *prejudgment, configuration,* and *refiguration.*

Ricouer seeks in part to reverse the relationship between text and reader. Instead of reading a "passive" text, we should allow an "active" text to read us, informing and transforming our world with new insights and understandings. To do so, we must become expectant readers of powerful texts. Critical theory is very much part of this active process, but it will not give us simple objectivity. By all means, use French-Russian structuralist theories, Marxist critical theories, psychoanalytic theories, feminist theories and gender analyses, postcolonial theories, Foucauldian power-knowledge analyses, postmodernism, and so forth—just do not cling to these theories dogmatically. When our critical theories begin to predetermine our interpretations, we must try something completely different with different ideological baggage and analytic possibilities. This suspension of judgment and shifting of standpoint are the keys to opening up the hermeneutical process into a hermeneutical spiral. Figure 7.1 below is a schematic presentation of this dynamic.

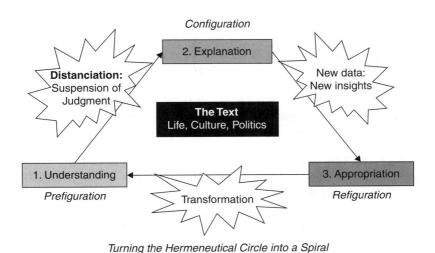

Turning the Hermeneutical Circle into a Spiral

Figure 7.1   The Hermeneutical Circle.

Returning to the many narratives of religion in our global civilization, we can see that the hermeneutical process is involved here too. The
Christian metanarrative, for instance, can be a closed, fundamentalist
circle, in which each reading of the Bible and the tradition simply rein-
forces the prejudgments and prejudices with which we began. This kind
of hermeneutics can be thought of as solipsistic rationalism because it does
not allow extraneous data into the interpretation. On the other hand,
Ricoeur holds out the possibility that the Bible can also "read" us and
offer new critical and transformative insights into the text and the world.
Any sacred scripture or great work of literature offers up both possibilities,
making them enduring texts. Ricoeur writes:

> [I]t is not true that all interpretations are equal. The text presents a
> limited field of possible constructions. The logic of validation allows
> us to move between the two limits of dogmatism and skepticism. It is
> always possible to argue for or against an interpretation, to confront
> interpretations, to arbitrate between them and to seek agreement,
> even if this agreement remains beyond our immediate reach.[17]

Even within a closed culture or dogmatic ideology, the sacred stories
and guiding metanarratives are open to competing interpretations, some
better, some worse, some more probable, and some highly improbable.
The hermeneutical circle need not be a vicious circle. The text can "read"
us and transform our lives with new insights. Religious fundamentalism,
it has been argued, is never really closed. Religious fundamentalism insists
on *intratextuality*, to be sure. This focus on a single text, however, does not
mean that all fundamentalists agree with one another. Among Christian
fundamentalists, for instance, there are disagreements about the correct
reading of the Bible. Nor do all Muslim fundamentalists agree with each
other. While the Bible or the Qur'an can be read as the infallible word
of God, the reader does not have an infallible mind.[18] Nor is the meaning of the sacred scripture necessarily to be found in its plain meaning.
Orthodox rabbis, for instance, affirm that there are at least seventy correct
readings of every verse of the Torah. What characterizes fundamentalists
is their insistence that "their disagreements would be bounded by the final
arbiter, the text, as interpreted by the principles of intratextuality."[19]

In a sense, we are all fundamentalists, though we may not be as clear
about what specific text is relevant to solving our disagreements. We hold
certain metanarratives to be true and rarely do we question these fundamental assumptions. They structure how we think, our motivations,
meanings, values, and symbols. We feel strongly about these metanarratives and derive our sense of purpose and self-worth inside these entangled
stories. If we operate within the framework of a single story, whether it
be religious or ideological, then we are as intratextual as the fundamentalist Christian or Muslim. But even here, we should not expect uniformity. Think for a moment about all the sects that have been spawned by

Communism over the years, even though they share most basic assumptions about dialectical materialism, class struggle, and world history.

Our challenge today, however, is so much more complicated than the intratexual hermeneutics of a single sacred tradition. We live in this global civilization and are confronted with many different entangled narratives. These entangled narratives are not just global; they are local, as I observe everyday on the streets of New York and the campuses of universities. Often we inhabit multiple and conflicting narratives of self, society, and cosmos. Where should our allegiances be? How do we mediate between conflicting narratives? The exploration of narrative social psychology and philosophical hermeneutics may give us more insights into how these processes work, but are we any closer to adjudicating between these different worldviews?

Ideology and Utopia

Here, I return to the work of Paul Ricoeur and his seminal book *Lectures on Ideology and Utopia* in order to find a partial solution and way forward.[20] As Ricoeur emphasizes, the words *ideology* and *utopia* in common usage have negative connotations. Ideologies are always false ideologies. The use of the term is normally pejorative. Utopias are unattainable fantasies. Indeed, it can be argued that some of the worst tragedies in human history have been committed promoting ideologies and pursuing utopias. Religions fall into these categories.

The negative connotations of these terms were first popularized by orthodox Marxists. Ideologies were contrasted with the "science" of Marxism. Utopias, like religion, were denounced as "the opium of the masses." False ideologies and false consciousness were contrasted with the true "science" of dialectical materialism.

As typologies, ideology and utopia would appear to be distinctly unrelated. Ideologies tend to be authorless; their content is extracted from many sources. They present a picture of reality, trying to mirror and reproduce a social order as "natural." Ideologies function to legitimate "what is" in a particular social group. They are the mechanism by which societies integrate their members around a certain set of values, beliefs, symbols, and traditions. Ideologies are societies' way of controlling and programming social harmony and change. The term itself is always polemical. It is always someone else's ideology that is denounced. The "good guys" are not ideological.

Utopias, however, are different. They seek to redescribe "what is" in a way that disrupts the existing order. Utopias seek to transfigure society in a way that highlights the gap between ideals and the existing reality from the perspective of "nowhere" and, thus, produce a vision and motivation to change society or abandon it. Utopias are presented as fictions by acknowledged authors. The term was coined by Sir Thomas More to title his book *Utopia* (1516) about a fictional island with the perfect society. We can list a number of works and authors in this genre: Francis Bacon's *New Atlantis* (1627), James Hilton's *Lost Horizon* (1933), B. F. Skinner's *Walden Two* (1948), Aldous Huxley's *Island* (1962), and Robert Heinlein's *The Moon is a Harsh Mistress* (1966). While the word *utopia* also has a sometimes pejorative association, the inclusion of modern science-fiction books in this list should alert us that the genre also has some popular appeal. From a broader perspective, all religions promote some kind of utopic possibility—eternal life in heaven, a blissful end to suffering, or complete wisdom and knowledge. The hope and promise of religions are always utopic in some fundamental sense.

Ricoeur is only too aware of these distinctions—ideology as a dysfunctional distortion of reality and utopia as an escapist fantasy to an alternate reality. He argues, however, that both terms also have a positive, integrative function in the realm of social transformations and cultural imagination. Ricoeur writes that "[t]he organizing hypothesis is that the very conjunction of these two opposite sides or complementary functions typifies what could be called social and cultural imagination."[21] He builds this argument by exploring the work of Karl Marx, Louis Althusser, Karl Mannheim, and Clifford Geertz. Ricoeur constructs a three-stage correlation of ideology and utopia, moving from negative to positive understandings.

In the first stage, both appear in their negative form—ideology as a distortion of reality and utopia as a fantasy incapable of dealing with reality. In the second stage, ideology serves to legitimate the status quo precisely because the political system falls short of its claims of legitimacy due to internal contradictions. For instance, the president of the United States, or of Sri Lanka for that matter, used the "war on terrorism" as a justification to consolidate political power and enrich his political allies. We will come back to this example later. In this second stage, utopia can be seen as an attempt to expose this contradiction, to show that "what is" could be otherwise, indeed much, much better. Drawing on the work of Geertz, Ricoeur argues that in the third stage, ideology is always necessary and serves the positive role of integrating humans within social groups. There is no ideologically free way to look at the world. By virtue of being social and symbolic creatures, we need powerful meaning systems to bind us together in functional groups. In this third stage, utopia functions as a form of social imagination that allows societies to imagine alternate futures, to critique the present, and, thus, to open up the hermeneutical circle into a progressive spiral. Ricoeur's correlation of ideology and utopia is presented in Table 7.1.

It is helpful to consider an example of this process, so we can see the role of ideology as *distortion*, *legitimation*, and *integration*, along with the reciprocal role of utopic thought as *escapist*, *oppositional*, and *imaginative*. This interplay between ideology and utopia is directly linked to vision of the good life and the good society, whether it be in preserving or

Table 7.1   The Correlation of Ideology and Utopia

Ideology	Utopia
1. Ideology as distortion of real social life	1. Utopia as escapist, pathological inability to deal with real social life
2. Ideology as legitimation of status quo to fill the gap between the *claims for* and *belief in* the legitimacy of a system of power	2. Utopia as a challenge to authority and power in an attempt to unmask the gap in the *surplus-value of meaning* claimed by ideology
3. Ideology as positive and necessary *integration* of individuals within cultural groupings	3. Utopia as *social imagination* that opens up the possibility of a critique of status quo from "nowhere," which turns the hermeneutical circle into a dynamic spiral

transforming some status quo. In varying degrees, we should expect all ideologies and all utopias to manifest all these aspects, both positive and negative.

In the United States, the "war on terror" was the ideological justification for an imperial presidency; the abrogation of many constitutional principles; and the use of torture, militarism, and an ill-considered invasion of Iraq on what turned out to be specious grounds. Note that the "war on terror" was also used at home to reward political allies, demonize and silence critics, and consolidate political power. The rationale for invading Iraq changed over time during the Bush administration. Originally a plan to deny Saddam Hussein weapons of mass destruction, it turned into a movement to liberate the people of Iraq from a dictatorship and bring democracy to the region. These noble principles might just as well been invoked for invading Tibet or Zimbabwe, but there are no particular U.S. national interests in Tibet or Zimbabwe, unlike the huge oil reserves in Iraq. So there is a gap between the claims of the government to the people when asking for their support. Here, we see the use of ideology as both distortion of reality and gap in legitimation.

The positive function of ideology as integration is perhaps most easily seen in the days and weeks following the September 11, 2001, attacks. The country was united in common cause, indeed united with the sympathies of the entire world, in ways we have rarely experienced. Unfortunately, there is nothing like a threat from outside to unite a people with a common purpose. The symbols and ideals of the United States, our flag, and our "way of life" were and continue to be evoked to serve the function of integration, binding a people together in common purpose, indeed asking soldiers to make the ultimate sacrifice for the group. No society will long persist without some ideology of identity that integrates individuals within a common culture and shared motivations.

Utopic processes were running parallel to these ideological processes. We were asked not just to fight a war against terrorism in self-defense, but also to fight a war of liberation that would bring democracy to Iraq and its neighbors. The idea of implanting Jeffersonian democracy in Iraq can be seen in retrospect as a fantasy disconnected from history and context, a pathological dream in its inability to deal with the profoundly different social realities and history of that country and region. The vision of democratic reforms of governments in the Middle East was certainly in contrast to many decades of U.S. foreign policy in the region, which had supported these very dictatorships, including the dictatorship of Saddam Hussein. The vision from "no-where" of Iraq and the Middle East transformed into liberal democracies is certainly inspiring social imagination. Why should the peoples of the region not enjoy better government, the same kind of government that we enjoy, based on fundamental human rights, the balance of power, impartial rule of law, and the concept of social contracts? It was and remains a noble vision, however unrealistic in the short-term.

We could spell out in similar detail how ideology and utopia correlate and function in contemporary Israel, Iran, India, Indonesia, or elsewhere, but I will leave that to others. The point is that all religious and political movements exhibit both ideological and utopic dimensions. Nobody escapes ideology, and ideology implies some utopic vision of the good life. The same could be said about our personal lives. I have a set of stories about my life journey, some of which may be distortions and legitimations of flaws and failures; but without these stories, there would be no integration of self. These stories are also part of my own utopic vision of my good life, a life that I strive to realize, involving hoped-for career successes and fulfilling personal relationships.

It is important to note that dystopia, a negative story, has the same function as utopia in this correlation with ideology. George Orwell's *1984* is a powerful critique of totalitarian governments rendered through a work of fiction. We might think also of the *Left Behind* series, written by the Evangelical Christian authors Tim LaHaye and Jerry Jenkins, as dystopian. *Left Behind* is a series of sixteen books offering a fictional account of the Second Coming of Christ and the biblical Armageddon set in the contemporary world. The series is perhaps the most popular book by sales in the United States over the last decade, albeit within a conservative Christian subculture.[22] The point is that dystopias, religious or secular, can also function as critiques of business-as-usual and a form social imagination for an alternative future, recalling Ricoeur's three-stage analysis. Dystopic novels play a prophetic role in the critique of ideology and the status quo.

As an exercise, try writing two different stories about the future, one as a utopic vision and the other dystopic. Both would serve as critiques of the status quo and forms of social imagination. Both would be correlated to different ideological projects in society today. Making these visions explicit would actually help clarify what is at stake in the contemporary debates about good governance, the hoped-for end of wars, the issues of cultural identity, economic development, environmental protection, and the motivation and pursuit of the good life. Indeed, what I fear most for people in the world today is growing learned helplessness. In the end, whatever ideological program that can present a positive and yet realistic scenario for the future is most likely to succeed in winning public support. Our visions of the future, both personal and political, are partially self-fulfilling prophecies, because without the vision, it is difficult to create the motivations and sacrifices necessary for transformation.

A Privileged Hermeneutics?

So far, we have postulated the centrality of narratives to human self-understanding on both individual and societal levels. We have explored a hermeneutical framework for thinking about these stories involving pre-figuration, configuration, and refiguration, along with the possibility of open-ended and evolving readings of these foundational stories. We have considered the correlation between ideology and utopia, looking at both positive and negative dimensions of each, and their roles as distortion/escapism, legitimation/critique, and integration/imagination. The guiding question is how this analysis might help us in our central task in the twenty-first century, the task of judging among the many conflicting, entangled narratives—religious, ideological, and social-scientific—that compete for our loyalty and commitment.

There will be no simple resolution of this conflict. One possibility is to renarrate someone else's metanarrative within a broader framework, showing how it fits within a larger context and thereby redefining its significance within a different political and moral paradigm. This is what Alasdair MacIntyre attempts in *Three Rival Versions of Moral Enquiry*. He begins by giving a fair and thorough presentation of the three competing schools of thought about moral nature—scientific, postmodern, and traditional. He ends by advocating his own Catholic Thomist tradition, drawing on both Platonic notions of transcendence and Aristotelian notions of natural dispositions. He asks:

> Is there any way in which one of these rivals might prevail over the other? One possible answer was...that narrative prevails over its rivals which is able to include its rivals within it, not only to retell their stories as episodes within its story, but to tell the story of the telling of their stories as such episodes.[23]

This is a standard movement in apologetics, in which one projects commonality with an opponent, shows what is wrong with the Other's position, and then projects a solution within one's own ideology by showing how one's religion, politics, or psychology can explain the failings of the Other. In its crass form, this mode of argument involves psychologizing the Other. Because of their false consciousness or their ignorance of the real story, they do not understand the truth that you are privileged to have and patient enough to share with them. Too often, apologetics is more about convincing oneself of one's own righteousness than about honestly seeking to understand and convert another, let alone risk the chance that you yourself might be converted in turn. The dialogue of apologetics gives rise to an arms race of each side's trying to relativize the other through ever-expanding analyses.

Still, a dialogue of apologetics is better than using brute force to compel submission, if not ascension. In the process of apologetic dialogue, there is always the possibility that new insights will emerge, that the Other may be recognized as partially right, that relationships will evolve, and that the hermeneutics will spiral out to something new and unexpected for both parties. After all, sometimes the missionary goes native, without ever setting out to do so.

Speaking of brute force, it is important that we realize that our entangled narratives are not all competing on an equal footing. There are real power disparities in the world that empower certain stories and marginalize others. One hermeneutical option advocated by some is the notion of a "preferential option for the poor."[24] Originally formulated as part of Liberation Theology in South America, it has become an important part of Catholic social teaching, but need not be seen only within a Christian framework. Because the poor are downtrodden and oppressed, lacking dignity, the basics of subsistence, and a voice in political and economic decision making, our religious and political hermeneutics should always begin with their well-being and betterment as our point of departure.

There are other versions of this interpretative approach in which other oppressed groups are hermeneutically privileged, even as they are socio-economically disadvantaged. Women, postcolonial societies, and ethnic-minority groups can all claim special insights into the interpretation of social, political, economic, and cultural issues, precisely because of their location on the margins of power. In the "master-slave" relationship, notes G. F. W. Hegel, the slave has a better understanding of the social reality than the master.[25] This "standpoint epistemology" argues that the marginalized and oppressed have a better understanding of the true nature of social relationships than do the privileged and the powerful. The feminist philosopher Sandra Harding equates standpoint epistemology with "strong objectivity."[26]

While this might be a useful heuristic for considering our entangled narratives, it turns out to be a bit more complicated. Is an African American woman from the ghetto more oppressed by being a woman, by being black, or by being poor? A poor white man in West Virginia laid off from his job is also oppressed, but what if he beats his kids and was himself abused as a child? The white woman of privilege and education in New York City who experiences sexual violence or workplace discrimination is also oppressed. And none of these oppressed Americans has it quite as tough as a family living off the garbage dumps in Sao Paulo, Brazil. Pretty soon, our standpoint epistemology degenerates into a calculus of comparative oppressions and runaway identity politics. Nor is it the least bit clear who is authorized to speak on behalf of these multiple oppressed identities and what privileges thereby ensue in the name of fighting for the oppressed. In practice, we are soon back to ideology as a mask used to claim and justify political power and privilege. Nor are the oppressed simply innocent or the powerful hegemonic. Finally, we cannot say for certain which metanarrative will actually best relieve the lives of the oppressed. Global capitalism, for instance, can be seen either as a means by which "the rich get richer, while the poor get poorer" or as an engine for economic growth and new technologies that have dramatically increased life expectancy and standards of living throughout the world. Good things happen for bad reasons; bad things happen for good reasons; and often our reasonable thinking and good intentions are not up to the task at hand. Standpoint epistemologies get us closer to adjudicating between different metanarratives, but not far enough.

In addition to the dialectics of ideology and utopia and the necessity of critical explorations from the periphery of social power, we can also observe the centrality of emplotment in all metanarratives. Following the work of the historian Hayden White, we note that all historiographies, indeed all metanarratives, employ modes of emplotment. These insights apply to different interpretations of religious narratives as well. White lists romance, comedy, tragedy, and satire as the four basic tropes employed by historians, indeed by all storytellers.[27] Our utopic stories about the future tend to be romantic, painting a picture of something with which we should fall in love. Nostalgic stories that idealize the past are also romantic stories. Perhaps not enough has been done with comic renderings of history and the future, but comedies and tragedies are really two sides of the same coin. Both comedies and tragedies involve some irreducible conflict. Comedies end with the synthesis of opposites, typically a marriage, while tragedies lead to the elimination of an opposite, typically a death. In academe, we have grown more cynical and are more likely to use satire and irony as the plot structure of our metanarratives. Certainly, existentialist and Stoic readings of history and life tend toward the ironic and the tragic. Postmodernism despairs of telling grand narratives, so its deconstructions become endlessly ironic readings of history.[28] Part of what makes adjudicating between our entangled and conflicting metanarratives difficult today is that we do not know how it all turns out in the future. We cannot prove historical predestination, even though metanarratives assume some inevitable future outcomes, good or bad, based on current choices and beliefs. The choice of emplotment, White argues, is an arbitrary, free choice of the historian, though the basic facts remain the same. How convincingly historians weave their story plots depends on the use of evidence and their rhetorical skill.

A Humble Hermeneutics

Presumably, the adjudication of competing, entangled religious and ideological narratives is a matter of knowing truth as well as something about goodness and beauty. We want to know which story or set of stories is most worthy of our support. If our goal is to know truth, at least as much truth as any one human might acquire in a lifetime, then we need to adopt a hermeneutics of humility. I call this hermeneutics of humility "intellectual nonviolence," and it should not be equated with political nonviolence or pacifism, as we will see below.

Intellectual nonviolence can be defined as *noncoercive habits of thought*. It recognizes that the most reliable truths are more likely to be found outside oneself, in interpersonal, cultural, biophysical, and historical networks. Truth is more often found *outside*, in the complex distributed systems of culture and nature, much more than is found *inside* the 1.3 kilograms of any single human mind. To arrive at truth, we need a new kind of intra- and intertextuality that embrace multiple metanarratives, that explore many situated knowledges of culture, class, gender, history, and ethnicity. We need to try on multiple ideologies and utopias. This hermeneutic is less about converting others and more about becoming converted over and over by an appreciation and appropriation of the metanarratives of others. In a sense, this entire book aspires to instantiate this hermeneutic by bracketing sectarian truth claims, adopting an intentional distanciation, and exploring multiple explanatory strategies, all in the expectation of some new synthesis in a more complete and more wholesome fusion of horizons.

The greatest untruths will always be the unconscious lies that we tell ourselves, the mistaking of our own limited perspectives for the Absolute. Reinhold Niebuhr summed it up best when he quipped that the doctrine of original sin is the only empirically verifiable doctrine of Christianity.[29] To avoid sin, we should be humble, rigorous, courageous, and creative in pursuing truth (and beauty and goodness), wherever it leads. And the goal of intellectual nonviolence is to set out in as many different directions as possible and to be converted multiple times to diverse metanarratives, inhabiting their truths, forgiving their failures, taking the best, and leaving the rest.

Whatever God (or the God's eye view of truth) might be, we humans are neither omnipotent nor omniscient, neither reliably compassionate nor unfailingly merciful. Human identities, norms, and actions are forged through the confluence of different stories, powerful symbols, causal patterns, divergent reasons, universal passions, existential terror, and transcendent hopes. New insights are often gained from unexpected sources. Even in the pathos and tragic maladaptations of inhumane extremes, there are important truths to be learned: there but for the grace of God (or circumstance) go I. Thus, the central tenet of intellectual nonviolence is that it is never permissible to demonize the Other, especially those we find the most repugnant and threatening. In the words of Jeffrey Stout, professor of religion at Princeton University, we must resist our tendencies "to block the path of moral inquiry and social criticism...by narrowing one's focus too quickly, reducing one's ability to recognize complexity and ambiguity or to experience moral ambivalence."[30]

For these reasons, this hermeneutics of humility sits uneasily with different forms of political correctness and religious fundamentalism. Too often, people become captive to taken-for-granted metanarratives. Ideology and power politics are substituted for authentic spirituality, penetrating philosophy, and compassionate curiosity. We all tend to fall back on our own patterns of dogmatic thought, manifested in political correctness, insularity, and lack of rigor. The real adventure in the hermeneutics of truth is to inhabit as many different metanarratives as possible, while recognizing one's own inevitable partiality.

"Civilization," wrote Reinhold Niebuhr, "depends upon vigorous pursuit of the highest values by people who are intelligent enough to know that their values are qualified by their interests and corrupted by their prejudices."[31] Civilization, then, depends on pursuing the highest values by temporarily bypassing one's prejudices and ignoring one's self-interest to see the world from another's perspective. Indeed, ascertaining what these "highest values" are also requires a hermeneutics of humility.

Intellectual nonviolence is not the same as political nonviolence. Pacifists can be as captivated by their own insular, self-righteous metanarrative as the next person. Their utopia can be an escapist fantasy. Intellectual nonviolence does not rule out the use of violence, though it would do so with a very different attitude. When other options are exhausted, there will always be situations necessitating the use of force, including physical and lethal violence. The trouble is that state-organized violence tends to presuppose, indeed is always preceded by, ideological violence and epistemic distortions. In war, as the saying goes, truth is the first casualty. By the humble hermeneutics proposed here, one must resist the tendency to demonize and dehumanize. One must always seek the humanity in one's foe and in oneself to embrace both the tragic and ambiguous in all conflicts. This is perhaps the practical implication of the understanding of universal sin and postmodern finitude. None of our metanarratives alone is adequate; all our entangled narratives woven together provide the most complete picture. This weaving of different perspectives into a richer, more encompassing life narrative is analogous to the distributed wisdom of economic markets. Indeed, it is analogous to the distributed creativity of life itself.

Nations and individuals will continue to be faced with the need to kill in self-defense, overthrow tyranny, prevent tragedies, and promote greater goods; but in the process, we need not also commit intellectual violence. Prolonging individual lives and postponing death are always relational values presupposing some greater purposes in human life that transcend mere longevity. What might those greater purposes be? How much risk are we willing to take? How much risk can we avoid? How can we most effectively promote noble purposes? What are these noble purposes? How can we pursue these together to our mutual benefit? For this vision of story weaving and truth seeking to be realized, it is necessary to suspend disagreements temporarily and inhabit someone else's metanarrative, entering into the intratextuality of their "one true story," to see what might be gleaned in the hope of building more vectors toward transcendent truth.

Intellectual nonviolence is about epistemology, not sentimentality. It is about maximizing our potential for knowing truth in our short lifetimes, perhaps even transcendent truths. It is a hermeneutics for reading, debating, and learning that requires rigor and reciprocity. It is not passive. Paradoxically, it also requires intolerance and arguments, but also honesty, principles, pragmatics, and always the real risk of conversions. These are virtues and values that I believe central to the mission of higher education, excellent philosophy, authentic religion, and the very soul of science.

In all probability, power will continue to be the mediator and adjudicator between our entangled narratives in the twenty-first century. In that respect, it is better to get clear about what you believe and be pugnacious in arguing its validity. Single-minded advocacy gets the job done, although there is no guarantee that one is actually right or that one will actually achieve one's aims. It does seem as if the self-certain narratives have the upper hand in the world today, while the less self-certain of us are more paralyzed with too many options and complex analyses. "Things fall apart; the centre cannot hold," wrote William Butler Yeats in 1919. "The best lack all conviction, while the worst / Are full of passionate intensity."

Ricoeur notes the same dilemma in prose form. The hermeneutic of suspicion in modern academe has rendered us paralyzed, unable to take effective action. He advocates a "second naiveté" after all the critical analyses are done, when we refigure and reappropriate our understanding of the text:

> This process of suspicion which started several centuries ago has already changed us. We are more cautious about our beliefs, sometimes even to the point of lacking courage; we profess to be only critical and not committed. I would say that people are now more paralyzed than blind.[32]

Is it better to commit blindly to a single, "true" story and therein find both conviction and courage? Not if we also want to commit to a true story, for the truth is found in a transcendent fusion of horizons that we can approach but never reach. We are left, then, with multiple and evolving convictions, but with no less need for courage, because the ongoing adjudication of our competing, entangled narratives is not without risk. The practice of intellectual nonviolence can be ineffective. It can be easily shouted out and down, drowned in the din of media-amplified ideological extremes. True, understanding from whence this "passionate intensity" arises, as well as this "lack of conviction," may make us more effective agents of truth and transformation, but we cannot escape the dangers. These are not just any risks; these are existential risks. Ricoeur warns us:

> It is too simple a response, though, to say that we must keep the dialectic running. My more ultimate answer is that we must let ourselves be drawn into the circle and then must try to make the circle a spiral. We cannot eliminate from a social ethics the element of risk. We wager on a certain set of values and then try to be consistent with them; verification is therefore a question of our whole life. No one can escape this. Anyone who claims to proceed in a value-free way will find nothing.[33]

Intellectual nonviolence is also how science works, when it is at its best. Science should not impose its preconceptions on the phenomena; rather, it should let the experiments and observations tell their own story and which hypotheses are right or wrong, better or worse. Scientists need to get out of the way of the phenomena, as they enter their own humble hermeneutical circle, such that new and often unexpected readings of the "book of nature" can emerge. Good science is altruistic fidelity to the phenomena. It does not impose itself on reality but makes a space for many different realities of nature to tell their own authentic stories. Scientists carefully translate the languages of particles, proteins, and people in the manner most authentic to the phenomena.

All stories of history and self involve facts. All texts are limited fields of interpretation, a specified construct of sentences, characters, and plot. Texts, histories, and self are open to multiple interpretations constrained by the specificity of facticity. Science has discovered a new set of facts that encompass all our different stories and, thus, provide a new context for interpreting our entangled narratives. This shall be the topic of our next chapter as we work from the bottom up.

CHAPTER EIGHT

The New Religion of Science

In our bottom-up approach to exploring religious intuitions and truth claims, we will now consider contemporary science to see how far we can climb from science to the sacred without invoking special revelation. I call this "the new religion of science," but not in the sense of scientism, the faith of philosophical naturalism. I am not the reincarnation of Auguste Comte; this is not a resurrection of the Enlightenment project of replacing the old religions with science. Our ambitions are more modest, more interesting, and more compelling. Instead of replacing or displacing the "old" religions, we look to reinterpret and reinvent them through a constructive dialogue with contemporary science, supposing that the received traditions have intuited, experienced, discovered, and transmitted important insights into ultimate reality. This is a theology of nature from the bottom up, initially without reference to revealed scriptures and received traditions. We shall take nature as understood by contemporary science as the primary revelation to be read and interpreted in religious categories. Contrary to popular belief, contemporary science is actually conducive to certain religion-friendly interpretations. Approaching religion through science will help us get closer to some of the truth claims intuited by religions over millennia that inform religious belief and behavior.

This approach provides an important service to contemporary religions as they seek to adapt to new realities in our global civilization. The distinction between science and the interpretation of science needs to be more sharply drawn on both sides of the religion-science divide. Good science is the precondition to the responsible interpretation of science by philosophers and theologians, clergy and laity, believers and practitioners of all kinds. The world desperately needs the constructive integration of scientific realities and religious systems of meaning, if we are to meet the challenges of the twenty-first century.

The actual history of all religions involved similar periods of reinterpretation and reinvention, so there is historical precedence for this enterprise in intellectual and religious history. For instance, Islam, Judaism, and Christianity were all dramatically transformed in the medieval period through the rediscovery of and encounter with the "lost" writings of Aristotle, Plato, and others. Aristotelianism was the best science at the time. The adoption of this science required some interesting theological adaptations on the part of the three Abrahamic faiths.[1] Similarly, the rise of neo-orthodoxy and fideism in the modern period can be seen as a reinterpretation in reaction to the remarkable success of mechanistic and materialist science in the nineteenth and early twentieth centuries.[2] Today, the sciences are very different, so the plausible religious interpretations of science will also be quite different.

Is Science Simply Another Story?

First, we must ask why we should privilege science in this inquiry. Is not science just another story, like all the other stories that we considered in the last chapter? Why should we let science make claims on the interpretation of sacred scriptures and received traditions? Religious fundamentalist, postmodernist, feminist, and postcolonialist hermeneutics are all inclined to argue that science is simply another story, indeed one infected with many modes of domination and oppression.[3] To answer these objections means that we must consider the philosophy of science.

The philosophy of science has long been preoccupied with distinguishing science from nonscience based on some notion of a unique epistemology. The idea of science as a privileged way of knowing, however, is widely rejected today in philosophy. This does not mean that anything goes in the domains of science. Far from it!

Remember, though, that the philosophy of science is to the practice of science what linguistics is to speaking a human language. Just as one can be competent in speaking a human language and know nothing of linguistics, one can be competent in science and know nothing of the philosophy of science.[4] Both linguistics and philosophy, however, turn out to be extremely useful when we get into the realm of translations between languages and domains. Metalevel understandings and explanations of the phenomenon, be it science or language, require that we enter into these rarified disciplines.

Let us begin a brief tutorial in the philosophy of science with Aristotle, who laid out four types of causative relationships exhibited in the universe: *formal, material, efficient,* and *final*. The *formal* refers to the plan or structure of a thing; the *material* refers to the matter of a thing; the *efficient* refers to the dynamic or initiating power of a thing; and the *final* refers to the goal or end. The universe as a whole, or any of its component parts, can be framed within these four causative relations; in so doing, we see how modern science broke with earlier traditions.[5]

The medieval worldview emphasized the formal and final causative features of things, from whence the universe arose, its formative structure or idea, and to what end it was going, its goal and purpose. The modern scientific worldview emphasized the material and efficient causative features and gradually came to reject consideration of formal and final causations as nonverifiable speculation that supported socially and scientifically regressive superstitions and social structures.[6] This corresponds with Comte's "positive" understanding of science and reality. At first glance, it appears that this formulation provides a simple and clear demarcation between science and nonscience.

Fast forward now to your science classes in high school, where you were probably introduced to something called the "scientific method" or, more philosophically, the hypothetical-deductive method. The claim is that modern science is based on a method—in other words, an epistemology or way of knowing. We begin with a hypothetical inference, conduct empirical observation, and then employ deductive reasoning to verify our initial inference. The hypothetical-deductive method begins by posing a problem or inferring a theory about reality and then formulating this as a question for verification. This hypothesis is tested through empirical observations. The results of these structured observations lead to the acceptance or rejection of the theory based on deductive or logical reasoning about the sequence of events and their apparent causal relationships.[7]

This formulation of the scientific method is naively accepted by most scientists and science educators, but few philosophers of science today consider this adequate. On closer examination, this description of science as an epistemology fails to distinguish science from nonscience. As so described, my dog is a scientist when trying to solve dog problems like how to provoke me to share some of my food with her from the dinner table. As so described, a religious person is also a scientist, where creeds and beliefs serve the same function as theories that are tested through lived experiences from which rational deductions lead to verification or falsification. The so-called hypothetical-deductive process turns out to be a tautology and represents very muddy water in the philosophy of science. The problem lies in the tricky "logic" of induction. "The theory of Induction," wrote Alfred North Whitehead, "is the despair of philosophy—and yet all our activities are based upon it."[8]

In this abbreviated tutorial in the philosophy of science, we need to fast forward through the logical positivism of Moritz Schlick (1882–1936), to the falsification theory of science advocated by Karl Popper (1902–1994), and to the theory dependency of observations of Willard Quine (1908–2000) and Hilary Putnam (b. 1926), among others.[9] The end result of this rational and empirical reflection on the nature of science was the collapse of positivism and formalism in the philosophy of science. There is no way to define science abstractly as a particular and uniquely privileged epistemology. Fortunately, none of these philosophical debates has in any way hampered science from making tremendous discoveries over this same time period, an important point to which we will return.

Enter now Thomas Kuhn (1922–1996) and his 1962 book *The Structure of Scientific Revolutions*. Kuhn applies historical, causal analysis to the developments of modern science and, in so doing, unleashes a revolution of his own. Kuhn turns the analytic tools of science on itself in search of causative formative factors within the development of science. He uses "science" to study science, not as some idealized epistemology but as an actual, historically dependent process. To say that the developments and results of modern scientific inquiry are socially and historically contingent, and not simply the product of a universally verifiable method of inquiry, was a radical move at the time. It contributed mightily to the intellectual dethronement of science in the humanities. Fortunately, none of this intellectual tempest in a teapot really hindered the exponential advance of the scientific enterprise in the ensuing decades, because, as previously stated, you do not need the philosophy of science to do good science. Philosophy of science, however, is essential when it comes to interpreting science, which is the purpose of this chapter.

Not only is the practice of science theory-dependent, Kuhn argues, but the observations are also theory-dependent. In those moments in history when two theories collide, the data cannot always be appealed to as a final arbitrator between conflicting theories. Kuhn does a historical analysis of what he calls "scientific revolutions" or "paradigm changes," in which there is no rational basis to choose the new paradigm over the old because there was an underdetermination in the observational data. He defines scientific revolutions to be "those non-cumulative developmental episodes in which an older paradigm is replaced in whole or in part by an incompatible new one." In these instances in the history of science, the choice between the old and the new paradigms "cannot be determined merely by the evaluative procedures characteristic of normal science, for these depend in part upon a particular paradigm, and that paradigm is at issue."[10]

Kuhn's work is filled with historical examples of how these paradigm changes have actually functioned in the real practice of science. In subsequent decades, his approach unleashed a vast quantity of new scholarly research on the history, anthropology, sociology, and psychology of science. Feminists, postmodern, and postcolonial studies of science all draw on Kuhn's basic insight, as they seek to deconstruct the underlying "irrational" and "oppressive" forces operating within the actual practice of science.[11]

What "the theory dependency of observation" means in the common parlance is "I wouldn't have seen it, if I hadn't believed it." And therein lies its problem. However compelling Kuhn's arguments may be, his social-constructionist approach to science, and those who have followed in his footsteps, has been criticized as subjectivist, relativistic, and irrational.[12] Kuhn responds that he is not subjectivist in an individualistic sense but in an intersubjective-group context and that, within a given group, the discourse is highly structured, rule-governed, and rational. This is something more akin to the way language communities function, though Kuhn leaves us uncertain about the possibility of translation between incommensurate scientific paradigms.[13]

Within a given scientific paradigm, what Kuhn calls "normal science" or "puzzle solving," there is a deductive-thought process with rules for "rational" discourse. Between scientific paradigms, however, the rationality of one group makes no sense to a group that follows an incommensurate paradigm. In this formulation, science can be seen as just another story, which we are free to believe or not. Thoughtful religious doubters of evolution, for instance, draw heavily on Thomas Kuhn (as well as Karl Popper) to justify their rejection of evolution. So too do those who seek to rationalize some complementary and alternative medicine practice as a "paradigm shift." Unrealistic epistemological abstractions, social constructionism, and postmodernism have gotten us in a real philosophical pickle and led to some unfortunate confusion and heated debates.

A purely social-constructionist model for the history and philosophy of science tends to render the predictive, practical, and explanatory results of scientific inquiry as miraculous and unintelligible coincidences. The physical reality of the "external" world has a kind of "facticity" that the "internal" realm of "mere" human sensation-perception-preference-ideology does not have. When physicists design nuclear power plants or physicians administer antibiotics, there is more going on than simply "incommensurate theory-dependent observations" with some other worldview. When we log on to the Internet or use fossil fuels that are 200 million years old, we affirm the reality of science, although we may not understand this reality. There is a dangerous schizophrenia in contemporary technoscientific civilization. In his last book, *The Demon-Haunted World*, the late astronomer Carl Sagan wrote:

> We've arranged a global civilization in which most crucial elements profoundly depend on science and technology. We have also arranged things so that almost no one understands science and technology. This is a prescription for disaster. We might get away with it for a while, but sooner or later this combustible mixture of ignorance and power is going to blow up in our faces.[14]

The miracle of science is that, in spite of our all-too-human imperfections, which scientists possess in equal distribution as the rest of humanity, science continues to progress and evolve evermore factual insights into the workings of the universe and ourselves. Science is a self-transcending learning process, but how does it work? One implication from our discussion so far is that we might better teach the actual history of discovery, the methods and madness of real scientists, rather than teach the abstract formulation of some imagined hypothetical deductive method.

All that being said, we still need to account for why the actual content of science is reliable knowledge. And with that, why and how should it be thought of as privileged knowledge? While there is no unified scientific epistemology, it turns out that science is a unified body of knowledge, knowledge that also turns out to be an interesting new metanarrative of the universe and ourselves. Yet the interpretation of that metanarrative, we will learn, is open to many possibilities. How and where do we draw the line between the content of science and the interpretation of science, given that we propose to reinterpret science in religious categories and need some rules for doing so?

Critical Realism

The consensus in the philosophy of science today might be called pragmatic operationalism or instrumentalism. In this view, there are many different scientific specializations, each one having its own methods and history of discovery. Different sciences have different rules of evidence and verification, different peer-review processes and standards, different professional associations and journals. Depending on what one wants to study, one pragmatically poses questions as appropriate to the phenomenon. The established science then makes its way down into disciplinary textbooks, which are regularly expanded and updated. There is no grand unified epistemology of science, but within the many domains of science, there are exponentially more reliable facts.

Most philosophers of science also now recognize that the traditional fact-value distinction is bogus. This distinction has been prominently mapped onto the science-and-religion divide. Science is supposed to be about facts; religion is supposed to be about values. Science answers "what"; religion answers "why." Science, however, is not a value-free enterprise (and religion, for that matter, also makes truth claims).

Science is best when it comes with a passion for rigor and debate. Scientists exhibit an intrinsic fascination with how things work. Most scientists presuppose a profound commitment to studying natural entities from the microcosmic to the macrocosmic that they perceive to being endlessly fascinating. They share amazement at the intricate, beautiful, and elegant structures of stuff, life, and consciousness. In other words, the universe that science studies is filled with intrinsic values, though scientists are at a loss for words to say why this is so. Scientists preach a passion for truth wherever it leads. Thou shalt not cook the data. Science thrives in a spirit of competition but also in highly evolved cooperation. Scientists preach humanistic purposes informed by the best knowledge obtainable and promote codes of ethics, such that the powers unleashed through science benefit and not harm humanity or the unique and precious planet that we inhabit. When scientists are at their best, they practice what I call "altruistic fidelity to the phenomena," a phrase we will need to unpack later. These values often put science at odds with authorities, be they religious, corporate, or governmental.

Of course, this is an idealized account of science and scientists. Science is also a very messy business. There are egos and interests involved. Personalities, power, and politics are also part of the often-chaotic process. There are Promethean tragedies enacted and feared, terrible possibilities unleashed, powers and principalities supported by the applications of science. Scientists can be corrupt. They can also blindly follow money or ideologies. Scientists may also possess increased powers of selfish rationalization. They tend to be overly compartmentalized in their lives. Their myopic visions can become dogmatic propositions. They are humans, after all, and exhibit all the flaws and failings that we encounter in other domains of human life. Science is always social, political, personal, economic, cultural, and historical. In spite of this, the miracle of science is that there is a progressive unfolding of reality, a process that allows for self-transcending knowledge, if not always appropriate wisdom and noble purpose.

I want to propose that the problem with the social-constructionist account of science, and its postmodern and postcolonial offshoots, is that it draws the circle of intersubjectivity too narrowly. A purely social-constructionist account of science, for instance, fails to explain why physicists came to accept quantum mechanics in the 1930s, when none of them wanted to believe it was true. The phenomena can trump the community's dogmatic preferences, indeed often do. If we include all nature as part of the intersubjective community, the phenomena playing an active role in the conversations of scientists, then the problem of philosophical relativism disappears. Philosophical anthropocentrism is the downfall of social constructionism. Nature-centrism rescues social constructionism and gives us a more robust, realist, and critical philosophy of science.

Critical realism then leads to the concept of symbolic realism. To grant the nonhuman an active "voice" in our scientific conversations requires a more expanded understanding of "language" and ultimately also a new metaphysics.[15] I call this *symbolic realism*.[16] In this view, nature is already "linguistic" through and through. If nature were not already symbolic and filled with semantic meanings, we could not be a linguistic species. Nature teaches us how to speak our own human languages in the coevolution of our nature-body-brain-minds-languages-cultures over millions of years.[17] The innate intelligibility-intelligence of nature is itself the precondition of any science of nature. Science, then, is a particular genre of translation projects in which scientists listen carefully to natural phenomena and try to translate their languages into symbolic systems that we can understand and use. The dominant metaphor for seeking scientific truth shifts from "seeing" to "listening."

I define science as altruistic fidelity to phenomena; in other words, selfless listening to the "voices" of natural phenomena. We can say, for instance, that rocks participate in the science of geology by way of presenting themselves as a limited field of plausible interpretation at different levels of analysis. Leave the rocks out of geology and we cannot understand the geologists. And, yes, of course, the geologists are profoundly influenced by social, economic, political, cultural, and historical factors; but without the rocks, mountains, volcanoes, plate tectonics, earthquakes, erosion, fossils, chemistry, radioactive dating, and the rest, there would be no geologists. Science is about trying to put the phenomena first—hence the fidelity and the altruism. In the next chapter, we will explore a new metaphysics based in part on these insights, as we work toward a new concept of transcendence.

By including natural phenomena as active participants in the explorations of science, an obvious though neglected perspective in scientific philosophy, we strengthen pragmatic instrumentalism, social constructionism, and critical realism in our philosophy of science. Note that this new philosophy of science is not unlike our proposed nonreductive functionalist approach to religions. Science cannot be reduced to a single epistemology; instead, it is a diversity of methods that function and sometimes dysfunction in specific contexts.

The upshot of this truncated discussion of the philosophy of science is perhaps a new definition. Science is (1) different methods for detecting patterned phenomena and explaining causal relationships, (2) applied by communities of specialists (3) in rigorous "dialogue" with phenomena, (4) always implicated in lived historical contexts and limitations, (5) resulting in a self-correcting, self-transcending, and progressive learning process that (6) makes strongly objective truth claims, (7) which facts are pragmatically verified in practical applications. We will further expand this definition of science below.

Reductionism and Holism

Typically, science tries to understand a phenomenon by taking it apart, by trying to see how the constituent components work to create the whole. This is reflected in the etymology of the word *science*, which derives from the Latin *scire*, to know, probably akin to the Latin *scindere* "to split" and the Sanskrit *chyati*, "to cut off." Recall that the etymology of the word *religion* is the Latin verb *religare,* "to bind together." So, in the etymology of these two words, *religion* and *science*, we have some indication of conflict but also a necessary relationship. Science is to split apart; religion is to bind the parts together. The concepts of reductionism and holism are embedded in the very etymology of the two words.

For instance, in the science of botany, we might see what plants are made of with our microscopes and other tools, noting the existence of differentiated cells, the chemical composition of these cells, the molecular processes inside the cells, the genetic structure of different plant species, the taxonomy of different plants, the interactions of plants with their environment, and the evolution of a plant over eons. The working assumption is that a plant, or any phenomenon, is best understood by a reductionist approach, one that takes phenomena apart, seeing how all the pieces fit together. The science of botany would further assume that the causal influences that give rise to the particular plant in question are all material; there are no mystical vitalist forces behind living things, just a lot of complicated chemistry underneath the biology and physics underneath the chemistry. Science works by pursuing causation from the bottom up, even if the scientist herself is an example of causation from the top down.

Let us look at an example from simple-cell biology, the inner life of a bacteria as described by Bill Bryson in his remarkable book *A Short History of Nearly Everything*:

> Blown up to a scale at which atoms were about the size of peas, a cell would be a sphere roughly half a mile across, and supported by a complex framework of girders called the cytoskelton. Within it, millions upon millions of objects—some the size of basketballs, others the size of cars—would whiz about like bullets. There wouldn't be a place you could stand without being pummelled and ripped thousands of times every second from every direction. Even for its full-time occupants the inside of a cell is a hazardous place. Each strand of DNA is on average attacked or damaged once every 8.4 seconds—ten thousand times in a day—by chemicals and other agents that whack into or carelessly slice through it, and each of these wounds must be swiftly stitched up if the cell is not to perish. The proteins are especially lively, spinning, pulsating and flying into each other up to a billion times a second. Enzymes, themselves a type of protein, dash everywhere, performing up to a thousand tasks a second. Like greatly speeded-up worker ants, they busily build and rebuild molecules, hauling a piece off this one, adding a piece to that one. Some monitor passing proteins and mark with a chemical those that are irreparably damaged or flawed. Once so selected, the doomed proteins proceed to a structure called a proteasome, where they are stripped down and their components used to build new proteins. Some types of protein exist for less than half an hour; others survive for weeks. But all lead existences that are inconceivably frenzied.[18]

A typical cell contains twenty thousand different types of proteins. A small cell contains perhaps 100 million protein molecules. The adult human body, for instance, contains some 10 trillion (10^{13}) cells in 210 tissue types. Remember that these all began as a single fertilized cell in your mother's womb, a cell that replicated and differentiated into these 210 tissue types in their proper organs, performing their proper function. In addition to these eukaryotic "human" cells that compose our bodies, there are perhaps 100 trillion prokaryotic cells living in our intestinal track (as well as on our skin.) This rich ecology of bacteria in our gut is symbiotic. They do not "belong" to us but are freeloaders who happen to add a lot of value, as we do to them.[19] This is pretty amazing stuff, and most of what is described above is new to science. Fifty years ago, not much of this was known in any detail.

We can learn a lot of interesting things about a cell by studying its parts and its chemistry. A quick perusal of the typically heavy undergraduate textbook on cell biology should be adequate to demonstrate just how much we have learned in the last century through this kind of reductionist approach. That being said, the cell itself could not be adequately described solely on the basis of its constituent components, even less so the phenomenon of the particular plant. The plant is an emergent phenomenon, both in its ontogeny—developmental biology—and its phylogeny—evolutionary biology. To this we must add ecological systems in which the plant both contributes to creating the selective environment and is also acted on by the selective environment in a fine piece of circular logic. Ecology, we are told, is a "subversive science" precisely because it is about emergent phenomena and does not fit the dominant reductionist paradigm in science.[20] The concept of emergence says simply that *the whole is more than the sum of its parts*—in this case, an ecology is more than the sum of all the species within a bioregional system, just as a cell is more than the sum of its proteins and other chemical processes.

While we have learned a lot about how a cell works, the unified phenomenon of a cell could hardly be predicted by studying its 100 million parts, and much less so could the phenomenon of your personhood be described by separately examining the 10 trillion cells in your body. As science has acquired exponentially more knowledge through reductionism, it has also increasingly embraced robust concepts of emergence as essential to scientific explanation.

Emergence is not just "soft" concepts from cell biology and ecology that burst the reductionist dream of a completely mechanistic account of complex phenomena. From the surface tension of water in a glass to superfluidity and superconductivity in a physicist's lab, the behavior of huge numbers of particles cannot be deduced from the properties of a single atom or molecule. In accepting the Nobel Prize for Physics in 1998, Robert Laughlin noted:

> The world is full of things for which one's understanding, i.e. one's ability to predict what will happen in an experiment, is degraded by taking the system apart, including most delightfully the standard model of elementary particles itself. I myself have come to suspect most of the important outstanding problems in physics are emergent in nature, including particularly quantum gravity.[21]

Materialism and Information

To say that one is a materialist today requires some explication, because matter turns out to be rather bizarre stuff. Atoms are not fundamental; they are divisible, on the first order, into protons, neutrons, and electrons. Far from being "matter," the atom turns out to be mostly empty space on a scale difficult to conceptualize. The single proton at the center of a simple hydrogen atom is something like a baseball sitting on the pitcher's mound at Yankee stadium, and the single electron is not even the size of a flea buzzing around in a "probability space" at the farthest edge of the stadium. If we break these atomic components down further, we end up with other subatomic particles whose "materiality" is rather strange indeed. Materialism reduced to this level of "matter" disintegrates into forces and fields, entangled relationships, and ephemeral existence—quarks, leptons, electrons, neutrinos, photons, gluons, W & Z, and gravitons.

Reductionism and materialism, however useful as methodological approaches in science, self-destruct as philosophical propositions when we push them to the limits of the very small, the very fast, the very cold, the very hot, the very dense, the very large, and the very complex. Frankly, it is embarrassing that otherwise brilliant people think nothing of invoking "materialism" today as one of the hallmarks of science. The concept of materialism deconstructed itself with the advent of quantum mechanics and particle physics. None of this means that we are compelled to adopt some form of supernaturalism, but the fundamental nature of nature turns out to be fantastically super.[22] The physicist-philosopher Varadaraja V. Raman describes the current state of affairs:

> Thus, instead of supernature, science unveils *subnature*: a world in the core of palpable matter. Physics has penetrated into the substratum of perceived reality and discovered a whole new realm of entities there, beyond the imagination of the most creative minds of the past. Through sophisticated labyrinths of theory and mathematics, aided by an array of experimental ingenuities, science has uncovered a microcosm that is abundant in minute bits which are not like sand grains, but are smeared out mini-clouds of electric charge and other properties.[23]

Today, an informed philosophy of science would also need to talk about information as a metaphysical concept. The previous metaphysics of science took space-time and matter-energy to be fundamental. To this we add the four nuclear forces, the laws of thermodynamics, some algorithmic processes, an element of randomness, and presto! We have the universe built from the bottom up that science has been so successful at explaining and describing from the microcosmic to the macrocosmic in all its stunning complexity. The oddity in all this new talk of information from scientists is that information does not fit into that mid-twentieth-century paradigm. For instance, information is "immaterial." It is not a thing you can point to but a no-thing that must be metaphorically "read" by some-things, which some-things are apparently constituted by the no-thing in another fine piece of circular logic. An ontology and epistemology that looks to materialism and reductionism for its explanations of phenomena will have a hard time explaining information itself. Ironically, the very pursuit of this materialist and reductionist paradigm has led to its super-venience, but the character and nuances of this new metaphysical vision have barely been explored.

In physics, we now talk about the information states of quantum phe-nomena. In cosmology, we speculate about a preexistent mathemati-cal order, through which the cosmos unfolds. Challenge a hard-nosed, reductionistic physicist about his mathematics, and you are likely to find a soft-hearted Neoplatonist.

With the genomic revolution, biologists now also talk about informa-tion residing at the center of life processes. In cellular-signal transduction, the genomic "Word" becomes living flesh. Though species come and go in the evolutionary epic, much of the genomic memory of the past is retained in contemporary genomes. As new evolutionary niches are explored, the "figurative" becomes "literal," as new species are reconfig-ured by selection into new emergent possibilities, adding new chapters to the book of life.

The neurosciences today see the brain as an information-processing system. While no doubt beautiful to the discerning eye of a scientist, a single neuron is rather dumb. A hundred billion neurons in the human brain, however, wired in a massively parallel system, become potentially the most complex entity in the universe. The neurons fire in on and off states through the synaptic media to mediate every human experience and memory, including the self-transcending neuronal activities of sci-entists doing science. Laying down neural networks is another way of talking about encoding information, as the inside informational world of the brain maps with the outside informational world of nature, culture, and cosmos.

This new metaphysical movement in the sciences has largely been mediated by the computer as both tool and metaphor. Among diverse scientific disciplines, the real scientific revolution in the last decades of the twentieth century has been the ability to collect and analyze large data sets and to manipulate these data sets further through powerful com-puter simulations. Computers provide not just the tools for new scientific discoveries but also the new metaphors that now also dominate scientific discourse. Algorithms, binary code, hardware, software, and networks are terms that have traveled widely outside the domain of the computer sciences. Computational finitude, however, also points toward a com-plexity horizon that may thwart our unbridled desires for controlling and predictive knowledge.[24] The universe may be a single database, but it is so profoundly relational that the easy hackings of the codes by earlier science may soon be exhausted.[25]

This new relational, information-centered ontology arising in the sciences today provides a wonderful moment for the recovery and reinterpretation of traditional religious worldviews. Many religions have understood language to be in some way primordial to the material constitution of the universe. In Hinduism, the Upanishads talk of a primal word, *Om*, that functions as the creative source of all nature. In Jewish Midrash, the grammatical ambiguity of the first line of Genesis and the extravagant linguistic creativity of Elohim lead to philosophical speculation about a preexistent Torah, which God uses to speak reality into being. In medieval Judaism, this rabbinic tradition gave rise to the wild speculations and philosophical subtleties of the Kabbalah. The Greeks, including Plato, drew upon Heraclitus's notion of *logos*, viewing the embodied word as the fire that animated and ruled the world, to explain their understanding of primeval, material language. In the Gospel of John, Christians celebrate this Word or *Logos* in a radical incarnationalist vision of a cosmic Christ in whom and through whom all things come into being. Today, the universe is far grander than our ancestors could have possibly imagined, but somehow they seem to have already intuited the deep informational structure of the universe through which all things come into being.

Hierarchies of Explanation

At this point, we have a number of interesting categories in our new metaphysics of science. We have space-time, matter-energy, and information. We also have a powerful dialectic between reductionism and emergence. We have diverse methodologies for studying different types of phenomena. All these are in some sense both symbolic and real in that they can be intelligibly represented in the semiotics of human language. We can now introduce hierarchies of scale, time, and complexity into our reading of contemporary science.

The sciences are organized hierarchically from the microcosmic to the mesocosmic to the macrocosmic. You will recall from chapter two that August Comte already proposed such a hierarchy of the sciences, but we know so much more than he or his contemporaries could have imagined. At the bottom of the reductionist hierarchy is particle physics, which is required for atomic physics. The properties of atoms are necessary for simple and complex chemistry to arise. Chemistry is necessary for there to be biology, geology, and other mesocosmic sciences. Biology is necessary for there to be human consciousness and culture. Our sciences of religion enter into this hierarchy at this stage, but our new religion of science must deal with the synthetic interpretation of the entire cosmological hierarchy.[26]

Of course, a universe is required to contain the atomic particles and give rise to the properties of physics in the first place, a time and a place for all the complex, evolving stuff we see around us. So, we need a universe of space-time and matter-energy. In ways not fully understood, it also appears that the science of the very small, particle physics may tell us something important about the science of the origins of the universe as a whole, so the microcosmic and macrocosmic scales may loop back together. Particle physics turns out to be helpful in thinking about cosmological questions about the early universe.[27] This is the hierarchy of scale. Everything discovered by science is related in size.

There is also a hierarchy of time in the chronological unfolding of the 13.7-billion-year evolving universe. Stellar fusion creates the heavy elements, which then give rise to complex chemistry in second- and third-generation solar systems, which—at least on one planet—gave rise to life and consciousness. Thus, there is both a hierarchical scale and chronological unfolding of increased, emergent complexity in the sciences.

What emerged over time were layers of increasing complexity. In outline form, we can talk about seven stages, each of which has a new level of complexity and intensity. The earliest universe can be called the epoch of particles, which then leads to the epoch of galaxy formation. The epoch of stellar fusion leads to the epoch of planetary formation, and the chemical epoch leads to the epoch of biology. Most recently, we find ourselves in the epoch of culture, with the rapid evolution of intelligence and technology through collective learning. The previous epochs do not disappear. Subatomic particles, for instance, are present throughout, but new complexities are added onto the underlying structures.[28]

Eric Chaisson, who proposes this seven-staged schema, also calculates the energy-density flows at different levels of complexity. Energy-density flow is the amount of free energy flowing through a system in respect to its mass over time, in this case measured as erg per seconds per grams (erg s^{-1} g^{-1}). The earth's climasphere, which consists of the atmosphere and oceans, has roughly a hundred times the energy-density flow of a typical star or galaxy. Through photosynthesis, plants achieve an energy-density flow roughly a thousand times more than that of a star. The human body is sustained by a daily food intake resulting in an energy-density flow about twenty thousand times more than that of a typical star. Remember that we are comparing the ratio of energy consumed to mass of the objects. Here is another way to think of this. If a human body could be scaled up to the mass of our sun, it would be twenty thousand times more luminous (assuming it could obtain enough food energy!). The human brain, which consumes about 20 percent of our energy intake while constituting about 2 percent of our body weight, has an energy-density flow 150,000 times that of a typical star. And, finally, modern human civilization has an energy-density ratio some five hundred thousand times that of a typical star.[29] Energy-density flow turns out to be a useful way to think about emergent complexity.

In the background of this discussion of increasing complexity is the second law of thermodynamics, which states simply that entropy increases in any closed system. Without new sources of energy flowing into a system, the system will deteriorate into less complex, more diffuse states. In lay terminology, the second law of thermodynamics is the certainty of death and taxes. Everything tends toward equilibrious disordered states (e.g., death), while disequilibrious ordered states (e.g., life) can only be maintained by paying energy-intake taxes. In other words, there are no free lunches, and you work until you die.

The complexity of life on earth is ultimately sustained by the flow of energy from the sun to the planet, which energy is then captured by photosynthesis. The food we eat, and with which we think and act, is ultimately solar energy passed along through the food chain. Fossil fuels can be thought of as part of this photosynthetic energy flow. Contemporary ecoromantics get it partly wrong and partly right. There is always a cost to life, which we can refer to as the Great Eucharistic law: eat and be eaten. Without killing and harvesting energy from other sources, which means ultimately the sun, we would cease to exist. The slogan "reduce, reuse, recycle" is only partly right because what drives the evolution of increasing complexity on our planet and in the universe is actually "consume more energy in order to be more complex." The real evolutionary morality tale can be better summed up in the new aphorism "minimize entropy, maximize creativity." What environmentalists get right is the centrality of solar energy to our lives and the possibility that we can do complexity better, more elegantly, and less destructively. Note that sun-worshipping religions of the past intuited something profound about contemporary science and thermodynamics.

While nothing violates the letter of the law—the second law of thermodynamics—the actual evolutionary history of the universe violates the spirit of the law.[30] Science offers no adequate explanation for why the particular complexity we observe today should have evolved. Many other universes and many other types of complexity can be imagined. The observed complexification of the universe allows us to postulate a purposeful directionality in the universe. This purpose we shall tentatively characterize as increasing complexification. This inference can be made based on the observed history of the universe; the evolution of life on the planet; and the development of human culture, economics, science, and technology.

At this point, it is useful to distinguish between teleonomy and teleology. The latter refers to a goal to which something aspires, as in Aristotle's notion of final cause. Teleonomy, on the other hand, can be thought of as an implied trajectory based on past history and need not make reference to future purposes. The observed history of the universe—its teleonomy—is indicative of increasing complexification as the "purpose" of the universe—a possible teleology.

Skeptics will immediately retort that the trajectory of the universe is death, in either an entropic dispersal of matter-energy or a cosmic collapse in a so-called "Big Crunch." When the sun exhausts its nuclear fuel in another 4 billion years, we can well predict the end of the earth, if not sooner. Earth's complexity will eventually cease. The increased complex-ification that earth has experienced over the preceding 4 billion years is because of the energy flow from the sun. For the time being, the earth is not a closed system, so increasing complexity overrules the intractable necessity of entropy.

We do not really know, however, whether the universe as a whole is actually a closed system, though this is the default assumption in cosmol-ogy. The theistic hypothesis, of course, is that the universe is not a closed system, that there is some kind of force—mind or being—that transcends the universe. In this formulation, information may be the key to under-standing what it means to talk of God-by-whatever-name and the nature of divine intervention.[31] This divine intervention, however, would be something more like Adam Smith's image of an "Invisible Hand" at work within economic markets. We shall come back to this interpretation in the next chapter, when we further explore the implied purposes of the uni-verse, as we work from the bottom up toward God-by-whatever-name.

Emergence and Transcendence

The concept of emergence gets us closer to the possibility of certain reli-gious truth claims being plausible An emergent and layered understand-ing of science leads to different levels of explanation. Particle physics, for instance, is not the least bit helpful in doing botany. Indeed, particle physics has limited utility in even normal chemistry. Nor does knowing chemistry help an economist. The pursuit of a reductionist account of phe-nomena has *not* led to a grand unified theory of science but to now thou-sands of disciplines and specializations within science. As already detailed, there is no such thing as a "scientific method" true for all these different disciplines and specializations. Scientists try to solve particular problems within the parameters set by the phenomenon in question, pragmatically adopting the tools and methods most appropriate to that problem. There are levels of analyses; and biologists, or even economists, can safely know nothing about particle physics and still do excellent science.

There are different meanings of emergence in our bottom-up approach to transcendence. First, there is ontological emergence in evolution. New enti-ties come into being that previously did not exist. For a long time, there were no carbon atoms in the universe, but then stellar fusion created carbon. For a long time, there was no life in the universe, but, on at least one planet, com-plex chemistry catalyzed into a self-replicating, adaptive, and thermodynamic process. For a long time, there was no eyesight in the universe, but finally eyes evolved, and the capacity of sight emerged as a novel event in evolution. Ontological emergence entails epistemological emergence, different ways of knowing appropriate to different levels of reality and complexity.

The concept of emergence, as we have already examined, also means that different levels of reality require different scientific practices appropriate at each level. Emergence puts some limitations on reductionist explanations. For instance, emergence places philosophical limits on the claims of some social scientists to explain away religion reductionistically or, for that matter, any other complex human or natural phenomenon. Emergence is central to nonreductive functionalism because religion is an emergent phenomena both in its ontogeny and its phylogeny.

A robust understanding of emergence, and with it different levels of analysis and interpretation, opens up a possibility space within the soul of the scientific enterprise for religious notions of transcendence, the God-by-whatever-name mystery. We will tentatively define God-by-whatever-name as the set of all phenomena—past, present, future—as well as that which may also in some sense precede and transcend this universe. Contemporary science is actually more suggestive of some notion of transcendence than it is of atheistic materialism. There is a cultural lag in absorbing these insights on both sides of the religion-science divide.

While it is possible to think from the bottom up toward the possibility of God-by-whatever-name, it is not possible to think from the bottom up to establish God-by-any-particular-name of any specific revealed tradition. Science will not give us the God of Abraham, Isaac, and Jacob, or Jesus Christ, my Lord and Savior, or Allah and Mohammad as His Prophet (PBUH), the avatars of Brahma, or the Buddha Nature in All Things. Once we grant the possibility of a God-by-whatever-name, however, we should also grant the possibility, that this may also be a God-by-a-particular-name. Who are we to tell God what God can and cannot be in the realm of ultimate reality. Any such "god" that we could contain within our intellectual constructs would simply not be God. Top-down revelation is a real possibility. God may well "speak" to us in human languages and in very personal ways. Of course, the interpretations and faith commitments of particular religious communities are certainly self-serving on this point, but God may well enough choose one particular historical moment and one particular revelation to be the definitive text.

For instance, maybe the revelation received by Mohammad, PBUH, is indeed God's final revelation, given to an illiterate merchant in the language of Arabic some 1,400 years ago in the deserts of Arabia. Science cannot rule out that the God might choose to reveal herself to humans through certain privileged revelations, but science can put some parameters on the plausibility of different readings of those traditions. In other words, certain readings of the first chapters of Genesis or the Qur'an are just wrong, not that the Bible or the Qur'an are stupid—far from it. God, as often understood by traditional religions, seems rather small and parochial in view of what we now understand to be a fantastically large universe, but the concept of God is no less robust in light of contemporary science. There is a secular logic to religious exclusivism, as there is to human languages, which has to do with the dynamics of being human, even if it makes no sense for our bottom-up theology of nature. The logic of group selection in evolutionary psychology, the economics of irreversible choices, and the perennial psychological need for certainty in the face of cognitive dissonance mitigate against a truly universalist reinterpretation and reinvention of our received religious traditions. We will come back to this exclusivist-universalist challenge in the next chapter.

Just because nature turns out to be super, fantastically super, does not mean that it is "supernatural." And while much of science is also fantastically strange, this does not mean that every strange belief and practice humans have or have had is therefore true. Just because quantum mechanics is weird does not mean that every weird idea that people come up with is true, even if it is dressed up with the patina of quantum mechanics. Just because there is ontological emergence of novelty in the evolution of the universe does not mean every novel notion that people invent is true.

The concept of emergence creates a possibility space for a lot of strange beliefs and practices—the i-Ching, the Bible-code, Reiki, the Book of Revelations, astrology, parapsychology—but it does not mean that any of this stuff is, in fact, true. Should these paranormal processes actually exist, science will not be of much use in verifying "unnatural" emergent phenomena. Strictly speaking, miracles are possible within the metaphysical system that we are exploring here, but why postulate "miracles" unless they are based on one's own lived experiences? If one has a profound personal experience of a miraculous or mystical nature, one should not necessarily discredit these. And while emergent "unnatural" or "paranormal" phenomena may be possible in this framework, it is also important to recognize that certain interpretations of religion can also be falsified, as in the example of Young Earth Creationists promoting an alternative natural history of the planet based on uninformed biblical literalism and no serious understanding of science. Remember the scriptures are not true; they are profound.

In the same vein, we should not read popular-science writers as offering the necessary and correct interpretation of science. There is a difference between the content and interpretation of science, just as there is a difference between a sacred text and the interpretation of the sacred text. The dominant culture of science today reads the content of science with Stoic and Existentialist biases, what is called *scientism*. This is not a necessary interpretation, though like all fundamentalisms, scientism seeks to present its interpretation as the "one-true-story."

Let me give two examples of antireligious biases in the interpretation of contemporary science—multiverse theory and Darwinian evolution.

Which Universe Do You Live In?

The success of modern cosmology in understanding the history and structure of the universe has led to a profound crisis in the field, which has a curious religious subtext. The topography of the universe discovered by astronomers, physicists, and cosmologists is extraordinary. Our sun, at a distance of 93 million miles, is but a small star in a vast galaxy of some 100 billion stars. This galaxy is but one of 100 billion other galaxies stretching back some 13 billion years at the speed of light into an infinitely dense and infinitely hot originating mystery. It was not until 1922 that the astronomer Edwin Hubble (1889–1954) discovered galaxies and we began to understand the large-scale structure of the universe.

One thing this new cosmology teaches us is that whatever humans in the past believed about God is way too small.[32] Most cosmologists, astronomers, and physicists, however, are not interested in doing God-talk; but those of us who do talk-the-talk should certainly be paying attention to the current cosmos conversation.

The situation is such. Imagine that you walk into a classroom and notice that there is a pencil standing on its point on the table. In all those years in elementary school, no matter how hard you tried, you could not make a pencil stand up on its point. But here, one day in graduate school, you walk into an empty classroom, and there is this pencil standing on its point. So, you call in the physics department to help study this strange occurrence.

One possibility is that there is some strange, invisible force that causes this pencil to stand on its point. Gravity aside, physicists are averse to postulating strange, invisible forces, so perhaps this strange pencil is just a weird, fluky event, however improbable. Physicists, however, do not tend to go for weird, fluky improbabilities.

Such is the case in contemporary cosmology in what is referred to as "the fine-tuning problem." There are a dozen such fine-tuning issues that confound cosmologists. The expansion rate of the universe, the ratio of matter to antimatter in the early universe, the specific values of the weak and strong nuclear forces, the mass ratios between electrons, protons, and neutrons—the list goes on. If any of these variables was ever so slightly different, then none of the complexity we see around or inside us would be possible. In other words, life and consciousness could not have evolved. Where biologists see random drift and natural selection in the messy story of life, physicists see elegant improbabilities in the ordered and intelligible nature of the cosmos.

Some extend the weird role of the observer in fixing the uncertainty in quantum events to apply to the universe as a whole. Perhaps the universe as a whole is a kind of quantum event that requires an observer with something like human consciousness to observe it. "The more I examine the universe and study the details of its architecture," writes the physicist Freeman Dyson, "the more evidence I find that the universe in some sense must have known we were coming."[33] This interpretation is referred to as the anthropic principle. It comes in weak and strong flavors. This interpretation implies a kind of future necessity of our just-so universe, such that present-day consciousness determines past actualities. Physicists, however, are also averse to invisible necessities in which future possibilities determine past realities.

At this point, the normal graduate student trying to figure out why the pencil is standing on its point would probably be happy to reconsider the possibility of an invisible force. Our physicists and cosmologists are very clever with mathematics, which allows them not only to discover realities but also to imagine possibilities that may not be real at all. Such is the case with multiverse theory and its cousin string-theory, the big new fads in contemporary cosmology. The theory goes something like this: we just happen to live in a universe in which the pencil stands on a point. There are an infinite number of parallel universes, in which the pencil realizes every other potential state by falling down. While there are sophisticated mathematical models that might predict the existence of multiple universes, as there have long been for multiple dimensions, it is not clear that we could ever have empirical knowledge of these other universes, if they really exist. As the physicist Paul Davies has observed, in both cases, theism or multiverse theory, we are compelled to postulate an infinite something unseen to account for a finite something that is seen.[34] Multiverse theory has standing within the community of cosmologists; theism has no standing.

Far be it for me, uninitiated and dimly lit, to weigh in on these complex cosmological considerations. I do not understand the math or the physics. "Since our theories are so far ahead of experimental capabilities, we are forced to use mathematics as our eyes," notes Brian Greene, a Columbia University cosmologist and author of a popular text, *The Elegant Universe*. "That's why we follow it [mathematics] where it takes us even if we can't see where we're going."[35]

In the past, mathematics has brought us to many stunning new insights about the universe. There may be compelling reasons to suppose that our universe really is one piece of a vast multiverse, in which case the theists will need to revise the scale of God's exuberant creativity that much more. On the other hand, multiverse theory may be the twenty-first-century equivalent of counting how many angels will fit on the head of a pin. In the latter case, all these sophisticated mathematical contortions are merely a way of avoiding postulating an invisible, intelligent, and conscious force underlying the fine-tuned structures of the universe. This is the antireligious subtext to multiverse theory.

What Is with Evolution?

Charles Darwin (1809–1882) did not invent the idea of evolution. Scientists and philosophers had been interested in evolutionary theories for some time before Darwin arrived on the scene. And yet for some reason in the contemporary scientific and public debates about the meaning of evolution, we have collapsed the distinction between evolution, an observed pattern in natural history, and Darwinism, a theory for how that pattern occurs.[36] There is an important religious subtext in the obfuscation of this distinction.

The evidence in favor of evolution of different species from common ancestors over deep time has grown dramatically in the last century. We must affirm with Theodosius Dobzhansky that "[n]othing in biology makes sense except in the light of evolution."[37] The overwhelming evidence for evolution, however, does not then imply that Darwin's theory of natural selection is necessarily an adequate account of how that process actually occurs.

The logic of natural selection is simple and compelling.[38] Darwin's "long argument" consists of a few simple premises. First, there are among offspring not only similar hereditary characteristics resulting from having the same parents, but there are also variations among offspring from the same parents. Second, every species exhibits an exponential ratio of increase resulting from the number of offspring it is able to produce. Third, this exponential rate of increase results in a universal struggle for survival as individual members of a species compete for food, water, habitat, and mates. Fourth, those variations among offspring that increase the likelihood of survival and reproduction for individual members of a species will tend to persist over time, while those variations that do not increase the likelihood of survival and reproduction will tend to die off. Fifth, the accumulation of all these incremental "selections" over long periods of time, involving also changes in the environment and geographic isolation, will result in the transmutation of one species into others, hence the title of Darwin's revolutionary book *The Origin of Species*. Today, we add the insights from population genetics in what is called the Neo-Darwinian synthesis. The catechism of natural selection is random drift, universal competition, differential survival, differential reproduction, all leading to the transmutation of species into new species, which processes are accentuated by changing environments and geographical isolation of breeding populations over long periods of time.

Darwin's argument is seductively simple, so much so that even philosophers and lay readers can understand the logic. As Alfred North Whitehead warned, however, "[t]he guiding motto in the life of every natural philosopher should be: seek simplicity—and distrust it."[39] Real biology is hugely complicated and context-specific, as any contemporary undergraduate biology textbook reveals. The simple theory becomes a stand-in for having to learn about the incredibly complicated fields of biochemistry, genetics, proteomics, epigenesis, ecology, and so forth.

To reduce evolution to random drift, competition, survival, and reproduction is inadequate in light of new insights arising from developmental biology, ecology, multilevel selection theory, complexity theory, symbiosis, and many other areas. Evolution, as in common descent with modification, has never been more true; but how evolution occurs is now open to serious scientific debate. The typical account of evolution offered in popular literature is inadequate and misleading.[40] When these categories—random drift, competition, survival, and reproduction—are then translated into interpreting the human person, as is done by evolutionary psychology, we are at risk of getting things very confused.

This new integrated developmental perspective on evolution, sometimes referred to as evo-devo or developmental-systems theory, plays havoc with simple Darwinism.[41] The natural selectionist algorithm breaks down into thousands of feedback loops and contextual variables. Complexity and chaos now replace survival and reproduction as the driving force in the evolution of life and, by extension, all the more so in the evolution of human culture, including that dimension of culture that we label religion. Any simple theory of evolution has imploded. We should be all that much more skeptical of simplistic attempts to understand religion and other cultural phenomena in the framework of survival and reproduction, as we explored in chapter 4. Applying Darwinian categories to the study of religion may just be a huge category mistake, like trying to measure the success of computer science and the computer industry by studying the reproductive success of computer programmers.

Particularly pernicious in Darwinism is the use of the terms "random" or "chance." Darwin himself talks about "variations," not "random chance." Evolution is a historical science. We have only one case study of the macroevolution of life on the planet. We cannot run history through multiple iterations as in a laboratory science. We simply cannot tell whether what we observe in the macrohistorical record is "chance" or in some sense "necessity."[42] The same dilemma should also inform our interpretations of the fine-tuning problem in cosmology, which we discussed in the previous section. Distinguishing between random and necessary events requires the possibility of multiple iterations, like flipping a coin. We cannot do that with historical events locked in the past, hence the important distinction between laboratory and historical sciences, which necessarily have different criteria for evidence and validation. What we have access to is an observed pattern in evolutionary history, and we need to distinguish this actual history from the question of how this occurs.

The religious subtext to Darwinism plays out on both sides of the "chance" and "necessity" divide. In emphasizing chance, there is an implied rejection of natural theology in which one argues from "design in nature" to the concept of a "Designer." Many thoughtful religious interpreters, however, embrace this notion of randomness because it provides a way to introduce free will, both human and divine, into the evolutionary epic. A "necessary" evolution is more conducive to deterministic philosophies of science. A necessary evolution is also more conducive to deterministic theologies, for instance, in the Calvinist concept of predestination, in which God is seen as an all-knowing and all-powerful dictator in the sky.

Note that one cannot simply dispense with the theology of nature with a wave of the hand or an invocation of David Hume. Whether for or against some concept of God-by-whatever-name, both atheists and believers are making inference judgments based on science, nature, and lived experiences about the existence and nature of a creator, sustainer, and redeemer God. Inductive generalizations are always tricky when contrasted with deductive logical processes. The interpretation of the whole of science is an inductive process, which science qua science is not qualified to do.

Similarly, the problem of evil is often used as evidence against the existence of God. Of course, this problem of evil existed long before evolutionary theory and modern science. The theodicy argument against the existence or goodness of God has been with us since the beginning of human wonderment. The existence of natural and human evil, much like the question of chance or necessity in evolution, can be interpreted in divergent religious and antireligious ways.

The sciences of evolution challenge the plausibility of certain interpretations of traditional cosmologies, true, but in no way challenge the judgment of whether God-by-whatever-name exists. Evolution and the interpretation thereof do have implications for how we understand the nature of a creator, sustainer, and redeemer God, should one posit the existence of such a God-by-whatever-name for whatever reasons. This will be the topic of the next chapter.

The evolution of the cosmos, life, and humans is not just any old story; it is a privileged narrative. This epic of evolution can be interpreted in many different ways, but it trumps earlier cosmologies of ancient religions. Literal readings of ancient religious cosmologies are a great embarrassment to religions and actually undermine the intellectual integrity of religious movements that are seduced to follow this unfortunate strategy. Mythological interpretations of ancient religious cosmologies, on the other hand, often turn out to be profoundly true to life.

A Privileged Narrative

In the previous chapter, we considered the narrative structure of different religions and ideologies. We engaged in an elaborate philosophical reflection on the hermeneutics of different worldviews and world doings. These metanarratives structure the way people think and even what they consider to be the relevant evidence. We were confronted with the spectra of postmodern relativism in which ideological and religious disagreements could only be solved by a will to power. I developed a hermeneutical approach to adjudicating between these different worldviews by intentionally adopting multiple perspectives, including scientific perspectives, in what I called intellectual nonviolence.

In trying to weave together the many entangled narratives, inhabiting as many different perspectives and truths as possible with our limited intellect and lifespan, it is important to realize that we have now a loom on which to weave the many pieces of truth and goodness that we discover along the way, including the scientific truths. That loom is the history of our species over the last million-plus years, the evolution of life and our planet over the last 4 billion years, and the evolution of the universe over some 13 billion years. This is the story that science has discovered over the last few decades, though it really represents the achievement of all humanity over the millennia. The German physicist Carl Friedrich von Weizsäcker (1912–2007) considered this "history of nature" to be "the most important discovery of modern science."[43]

Few of us have explored what it would mean to integrate this new story of the universe into our own special metanarratives and received traditions. One of the greatest challenges today is to integrate this new, remarkable, and evolving scientific story of the cosmos, society, and self into our diverse, traditional narratives. Science turns out not to be a privileged epistemology but rather a privileged narrative. Some call it "Big History;" others call it "the Epic of Evolution" or "the History of Nature." I prefer to call it "Our Common Story" because it includes all humanity, all plants and animals, the solar system, and the galaxies.[44]

The grand scientific metanarrative is quite new and still evolving, so much so that we do not really have an adequate interpretative tradition surrounding it. In brief outline, this omnicentric universe began some 13 billion years ago as something approaching infinite heat, infinite density, and total symmetry. The universe expanded and evolved into more differentiated and complex structures—forces, quarks, hydrogen, helium, galaxies, stars, heavier elements, complex chemistry, planetary systems. Some 3.5 billion years ago, in a small second- or third-generation solar system, the intricate processes called life began on at least one small planet. Animate matter-energy on Earth presented itself as a marvelous new intensification of the creative dynamic at work in the universe. Then, some 2 million years ago, as if yesterday in the enormous time scales of the universe, protohumans emerged on the savanna of Africa with their enormously heightened capacities for conscious self-reflection, language, and tool making. And this unfolding leads us all the way to today, to this collection of atoms reading this particular book, all of us recycled stardust-become-conscious-beings, engaged in this global conversation about our entangled and competing worldviews, brought to use by ephemeral electrons and photons cascading through the Internet and bouncing off satellites. How then do we interpret this new story of creation and evolution?

Interpreting Science

To our earlier definition of science, we can now add two more points. Science is (8) a cumulatively related body of knowledge (9) that can be organized hierarchically by chronology of emergence, scales of size, and degrees of complexity. The unity of science turns out not to be a privileged epistemology but rather a privileged metanarrative. Science qua science, however, does not authorize any particular grand synthetic interpretation of this new book of nature. The metanarrative is open to multiple interpretations, including robust theistic interpretations, which we will soon explore. Here I am drawing a distinction between the content of science and the interpretation of science, though the distinction will be more like a membrane than a hermetic boundary. There are stories about science and then there is science, which is more than mere story.

Contestations about science are very much part of our entangled world of competing religious and ideological stories, as witnessed by antievolution debates among Christians and Muslims and various ethnosciences proposed in postcolonial societies. Unless we better police the boundaries between science and the interpretations of science, we are bound to get self-defeating confusion. The new metanarrative of science is not open to debate. Some version of deep time and evolution is here to stay. It is a metanarrative in which all our separate stories must necessarily find their home and their partial validity. The metanarrative of science, however, is open to multiple interpretations.

We recall Hayden White's modes of emplotment—romantic, tragic, comic, and ironic. The new universe story is a historiography that includes many tragedies, too immense even to comprehend; but it is also a story of cosmic and comic improbabilities resulting in many fortuitous new possibilities. It is a story with irony, for instance, foisted upon us by our biology and our brains, ironic also because none of the scientists involved in piecing this puzzle together really understood that the collaborative results would be a fantastic and evolving creation story of stunning complexity and grandeur. Finally, it is a story with a great deal of romantic appeal for all its majesty and beauty. Science has done the work of continuing revelation in the twentieth century.

This new story of the universe necessarily includes humans, contrary to the abstractions of the scientists. All our subjective experiences are part of this new objective story of the cosmos. Indeed, subjective experience is the most fundamental way in which we relate to each other and the universe. It is a story in which all the different narratives told by humans around the world have their place within the unfolding plot, all within their appropriate context.

Some say that the story of the universe and humans within it is meaningless, employing an ironic trope. The emplotment of this new universe story, however, is a free choice, first because the data can be read in multiple ways and second because the story itself has not ended. The emplotment can be Jewish, Christian, Muslim, Hindu, Buddhist, secular, and so on. That is a free choice of the interpreter, though the skill of the synthesizer and storyteller will need to be convincing and accurate to the science. Remember Ricoeur's warning in the last chapter: even though we have the same text, not all interpretations are plausible, not all interpretations equal. Today, we have a new, evolving book of nature, and the reading and interpretation of that common text are perhaps the greatest challenges that humans have ever faced. How we interpret the new book of nature will largely determine how we reinvent nature and ourselves in what scientists are now calling the Anthropocene, a new era in the evolution of the planet in which human desires and activities come to dominate the biosphere. Humans turn out to be a Lamarckian wildcard in the epic of evolution. Metaphysics turns out to be politics by other means.

In the end, our entangled religious and ideological narratives must somehow incorporate and answer to the unfolding discoveries of the scientific, evolutionary cosmology. Triumph or tragedy, it is certainly an epic story, an epic of evolution. Hayden White neglected to include epic as a possible trope, assuming that the category is subsumed by one of the other four tropes, but this need not be so. An epic need only be a story that never ends, that has many twists and turns, but just goes on and on.

Every time we use a cell phone, pump 200-million-year-old rainforests into the gas tanks of our cars, travel across the continents in an airplane, or log on to the Internet, we affirm the reality of this new scientific, evolutionary cosmology in deed, if not in thought or understanding. With this common cosmology as a basis, a hermeneutical foundation that also happens to be progressively true, our global civilization would be much better situated to solve the great religious and ideological debates and practical challenges of our time. Of course, we would not all have the same interpretations of this evolutionary cosmology, but we would have a common conversation and a better possibility for a future "fusion of horizons."

This story of the universe and all our separate metanarratives within it are woven together on a cosmic loom, each of us a thread in a greater tapestry of unfolding truth. If we listen carefully to each other and to nature, adopting a hermeneutics of intellectual nonviolence, then our common future may also be a self-transcending process leading to greater truth, beauty, and goodness.

This, then, is the new religion of science. It is a commitment to general scientific literacy, the unity of knowledge, and an open-ended and rigorous dialogue about plausible and probable interpretations of science in conversation with the received and evolved wisdom traditions of humanity.

We have defined science as (1) different methods for detecting patterned phenomena and explaining causal relationships, (2) applied by communities of specialists (3) in rigorous "dialogue" with phenomena, (4) always implicated in lived historical contexts and limitations, (5) resulting in a self-correcting, self-transcending, and progressive learning process that (6) makes strongly objective truth claims, (7) which facts are pragmatically verified in practical applications (8) and cumulatively related in a unified body of knowledge (9) that can be organized hierarchically by chronology of emergence, scales of size, and degrees of complexity. This definition of science embraces pragmatic operationalism, social constructionism, and critical realism, in part by granting the phenomena an active role in the intersubjective communities of science. The latter I have called "symbolic realism" in a phenomenal universe that we understand to be "linguistic" in nature and imbued with "intelligibility/intelligence," as the precondition of any science. I draw a distinction between the content of science and the interpretation of science. In the next chapter, I will offer a religious interpretation of science.

CHAPTER NINE

God-by-Whatever-Name

At the beginning of this exploration, we bracketed the truth claims of religion. As a point of departure in our scientific exploration of religious and spiritual phenomena, it mattered little whether or not God or gods were real, nor whether miracles and supernatural phenomena were possible. What mattered was that people orient their lives around certain sets of beliefs and practices and that these profoundly influence their "moods and motivations," to reference again Clifford Geertz's definition of religion.

In chapter eight, we began to develop elements of a new religious metaphysics from the bottom up, starting from science without reference to any revealed texts and received traditions. In light of contemporary science, we explored natural hierarchies of time, scale, and emergent complexity and, with these hierarchies, the storied nature of the universe, a story that now includes the origins and evolution of humans right up to today and on into the future.

In this chapter, I want to take our bottom-up approach one step farther up the ladder in considering the fundamental intuitions of religions about ultimate reality. Logically, we have three basic options. In the first case, all religions are simply wrong, childish fantasies that should simply be discarded. This, of course, is the position that has been voraciously argued by the so-called New Atheists, but it is really an argument that has been with us for several centuries, if we recall our discussion of Auguste Comte, Karl Marx, Sigmund Freud, and others in chapter two. In the second case, one religion might be true and all others false. This is the position taken by fundamentalist and missionizing religions around the world that seek to convert others to the "one true" path. The third option is that all religions are partly true, depending on how they are interpreted. The truths of these diverse traditions are shaped by specific historical and cultural factors, embedded in profound mythologies, rich symbol systems, and metaphysical intuitions winnowed through centuries of human experimentation and experience. This third view is my point of departure in this chapter. My hunch is that without some deep intuition of sacred truth, an actual correspondence to ultimate reality underlying the diversity of faiths and practices in the world, it would be difficult to understand the ubiquity and persistence of religion in the world. I will label this ultimate reality "God" but leave aside whatever preconception you might have about what the word means.

Before we talk about God, though, we need to acknowledge that some religions do not talk about God at all. Buddhism is technically agnostic. Many gods appear in Buddhist mythology, but they are inferior to the enlightened human, the Buddha. There is no preoccupation in Buddhism with the concept of creation; rather it is salvation that stands at the center of the Buddhist drama. That being so, Buddhism relies on many metaphysical concepts, such as the doctrine of reincarnation, the possibility of nirvana, and the doctrine of *pratitya-samutpada*—a semi-scientific notion of causation driven by universal craving. Confucianism and Taoism are also ambiguous on the use of the God concept. Both of these great Chinese traditions make references to abstract notions of transcendence through concepts such as heaven (*T'ien*), the way (*Tao*), and Energy (*Ch'i*), but these are not personal gods, as typically seen in the theistic and polytheistic traditions. In terms of actual piety, however, Buddhists, Confucianists, and Taoists tend to worship saints and sages as if they were functionally the equivalent of gods. Thus, buddhas, bodhisattvas, Confucius, Lao-Tzu, and other people and concepts are venerated as, sacrificed to, and appealed to in order to receive some divine intervention in people's personal lives. Popular piety looks quite different from the philosophical formulations of these traditions. The philosophical forms of Asian religions, especially as imported in the West, are often motivated by a desire to draw sharp distinctions between the theistic and nontheistic traditions, between East and West. This motivation is partly a reaction against the history of European colonialism and Christian missions in the East, on the one hand, and a disillusionment with Christianity and Judaism in the West, on the other hand.

As discussed in chapter two, I am not sure these distinctions between theism, polytheism, and nontheism are easily drawn or all that important. In Christianity, for instance, we see the proliferation of angels, archangels, saints, and sages, as well as highly abstract concepts of God on the part of theologians and philosophers. So, at the risk of upsetting some of my colleagues in religious studies again, I am going to use the nomenclature "God" as a placeholder for transcendence, purpose, meaning, and hope. By using this term, however, I do not assume that we know what this means or that we somehow already all agree about some definition.

In explicitly theistic traditions, religion is primarily about God-by-some-particular-name. Judaism is the most ambivalent about naming God. Jews use many synonyms—Elohim, Adonai, Mellach HaOlam, and El Shaddai, to name a few. The most sacred name of God is not articulated. Written with the four consonants YHWH, Christians translate this as Jehovah or Yahweh. Today, many Jews writing in English write "G-d" in deference to this ancient prohibition against using God's proper name.

Christians name God as a Trinity—the Father, Son, and the Holy Spirit. Christians pray in the name of Jesus Christ, the Lord and Savior, believing that by no other name can salvation be achieved. Muslims address God as Allah, quickly followed by the declaration that Muhammad is His Prophet and Peace be upon him. Technically, Allah is the same god worshipped by Jews and Christians, albeit with a different foundational myth and revelation. On my Muslim prayer beads are thirty-three beads. A pious Muslim counts out the beads three times round, citing the ninety-nine names of Allah derived from the Qur'an, each name a different attribute. Muslims stop short of one hundred to remind them that there are thousands of names of God, that God cannot be contained in human conceptions. Hindus have many gods—Vishnu, Shiva, Shakti, Devi, Ganesha, and Surya, to name the principals. The Hindu pantheon, however, is also understood to be multiple manifestations of a single, abstract transcendent principle, sometimes referred to as Brahma.

In working from the bottom up, we will not begin with any of these received traditions, nor their sacred scriptures, so I use the phrase *God-by-whatever-name* to make this distinction clear. This is not the only way to approach religion and science. It is also valid and informative to work from the top down, as it were, starting within a particular tradition to see how the scriptures might be reconciled with and inform the interpretation of the universe as described by contemporary science. Sometimes this top-down approach can be quite crass, as in using contemporary science as a proof-text for sacred scriptures. To try to read science back into ancient scriptures is an absurd way to validate a tradition. One will find very little overlap between an introductory college science textbook and sacred scripture. When done well, however, the top-down, tradition-based approach is not about concordance seeking but about interpretation enrichment.

This tradition-based, top-down approach begins with a question: if tradition is true and science is true, then how do we understand each in light of the other. This approach has generated a growing body of scholarly literature within Christianity and other traditions. Our approach, however, is to see how far we can take contemporary science in the direction of some concept of God-by-whatever-name without privileging any revealed tradition at the outset. Of course, in a pluralist and secular society, the approach I am advocating is crucial, even if it misses something unique and precious in the specificity of particular traditions.

Finally, it bears repeating that religions are not just about ideas and beliefs. Religions are as much about performative behaviors as they are about intellectual propositions. Much of what religion communicates is nonverbal, liturgical, and behavioral. Furthermore, we can draw a sharp distinction between beliefs and faith—the latter, I argue, requires uncertainty. In this chapter, we focus on the plausibility of religious beliefs from the bottom up to establish warranted faith, but we should not confuse this intellectual proposition with the totality of religious and spiritual phenomena.

No Language of God

Why talk about God at all, many scientifically minded atheists are inclined to ask? We cannot define God in any rigorous way. Indeed, God-talk is primarily the domain of antiscientific and superstitious supernaturalists, we are told. Many today have an almost allergic reaction to the very word "god." Many others use and misuse the name of God in ways that would certainly justify this negative assessment.

Of course, one of the reasons we need to talk about God is that we propose to study religion scientifically. Religion is an important phenomenon. Religious people talk a lot about God or God-concepts. How can we conduct a science of religion that ignores the central claims of the subjects, a claim made with subjective certainty?

An adequate science of religion needs to develop a phenomenology of God-talk, and this can be separated from the question of whether God exists. The scientific study of religious and spiritual phenomena cannot, as a matter of philosophy, and should not, as a matter of science, be motivated by a desire to prove or disprove the existence of God. The philosophical debate was settled by our medieval ancestors in the form of apophatic theology, which argues that any positive assertion about the character and nature of God is necessarily untrue because "the eternal" and "transcendent" cannot be described by finite human minds with our finite human languages. Apophatic theology is the *Via Negativa* of Christianity, the *En Soph* of Judaism, the *bila kaif* of Islam, the *neti neti* of Hinduism, and the *sunyata* of Buddhism. Under the influence of postmodern philosophy, apophatic theology has made a comeback among thoughtful theologians today. Any "God" that could be discovered or disproved by science simply would not be God. The apophatic God of philosophical theology provides an important point of departure and also a warning. The theologian John Bowker writes:

> It is true that God is not an object *like* a universe, or an object *in* a universe, to be explored and investigated by apparatus and experiments. But it is equally true that God does not depend for his existence or nature on our opinions or concepts about him, and that his reality does set limits on our language about him.... A real cause for alarm would be if theology *could* provide a complete and realistic representation of God, because any such literally accurate 'model' of God would be an idol.[1]

How, then, is God-by-whatever-name to be apprehended? What are the data for and feedback from this God-by-whatever-name that lead humans to conclude that such a transcendent divine force and mind lies beneath, within, and beyond the universe in which we think, live, and act?

What the human sciences can study is the phenomenology of what people think, say, and do in relationship to their perceptions, experiences, beliefs, practices, communities, and values. To locate God in a particular natural phenomenon, "whether in the form of anything that is in heaven above, or that is on earth beneath, or that is in the water under the earth" or even in the form of a particular sacred book or a particular community of faith, is an expression of idolatry. "You shall not make for yourself an image" (Ex. 20:2–17, Deu. 5:6–21). From a biblical perspective, the Ten Commandments prohibit such idolatry, but, ironically, unreflective theists are mostly idolaters in their tendencies to absolutize their particular scriptures, traditions, and faith. When studying humans, including our religions, it helps to have an appreciation of paradox and irony.

Of course, "God" is itself merely another term from one of our finite human languages. The scientifically minded atheist is inclined to ask, If we cannot define it, why not dispense with it completely? An analogy to mathematics at this point can inform our scientific study of religions. Once upon a time, in Indo-Arabian cultures, humans *invented*, *discovered*, and *developed* the concepts of zero and infinity. The mathematical concepts turn out to be very difficult to define. There are many different meanings of zero and many different types of infinity; nevertheless, it would be impossible to do advanced mathematics without 0 and ∞.

God is kind of like zero and infinity. God is a placeholder and concept that humans *invent*, *discover*, and *develop* in order to talk about what the twentieth-century theologian Paul Tillich referred to as "ultimate concern."[2] Proofs of the existence of God have definitely fallen out of favor in contemporary theology. Rather, we should talk about what one means when one talks about "God." Even the atheist has a very particular understanding of the God in whom he does not believe. In this pragmatic and phenomenological view, abolishing God-talk in our civilization might be like abolishing zero and infinity from mathematics. God-talk can be an invitation for a very engaging conversation, not a club used to terminate conversations.

Finally, the scientifically minded atheist will argue, turning the design argument upside down, if there is a creator God, why was he so incompetent or perhaps malevolent in crafting a universe, earth, and humanity so flawed, so filled with suffering, death, and now also moral evil in humans? This is the theodicy argument, and modern science does give it a new edge, even though the problem existed long before Darwinism or contemporary cosmology. The theodicy problem arises because of a particular, logically inconsistent conception of God as omnipotent, omniscient, and omnibenevolent. Note that this formulation is more of a Platonist overlay on traditional theism. The actual Bible or Qur'an presents God as a much more ambiguous and mercurial character in human history.

For instance, there are several verses in the Qur'an that suggest that the good and the bad all come from God (Sura 4:78–79). Similar arguments might be constructed by reading the book of Job or Romans 9. Like any sacred texts worthy of the name, these are not the only relevant citations, but citing them serves a purpose in my argument. What happens if we take out "God" and substitute "universe." The good and the bad all come from the universe. To a scientific mind, that would be self-apparent, without problem. In fact, substituting "universe" for "God" solves nothing. Humans experience a universe filled with *logos* that is the precondition for science, but also with *pathos, eros, filia, ethos,* and *agape*. The universe we encounter is filled with profound ambivalence. The universe giveth and taketh away. The universe is of two minds from our limited perspective—on the one hand, elegant and delightful, on the other, painfully limited and destructive.

Any God that humans could imagine as creator and sustainer of this universe, if we are being observant and honest, would have to include this profound ambivalence. Abolishing God-talk does nothing to solve the theodicy problem; it only relocates it to the universe. Terrible things still happen, and we are still left with existential anguish and outrage. A more interesting place to look for God is in our own unreasonable expectations that life should be otherwise, better than it is, and that we should also be better people than we actually are. This unreasonable hope, which can also be a self-fulfilling prophecy, is where we are most likely to find the religious impulse. In that respect, it is perhaps better to draw a sharp distinction between beliefs and faith. Beliefs are a series of propositions that one holds to be true. Faith is about a series of questions for which one has no answers. Faith requires doubt, not certainty. A leap of faith that does not carry these uncertainties with it is not faith at all.[3] There is no need to pose a false dichotomy between atheism and theism when we can have certainty about neither.

John Bowker argues that God-talk is "indefinitely regressive":

> If God is to have appropriate meaning he must always be slightly beyond human attainment—*Deus semper maior*. For God to be God, to do for men what men have needed emotionally and conceptually and religiously, he must stand beyond the limits of their attainment so far.[4]

Deus semper maior—God is always more! But, then, we can say the same for science—*Sciencia semper maior!* Not only do new scientific discoveries open a seemingly infinite horizon of new questions and new mysteries to contemplate and explore, but science itself is "more than" naturalism. The activity of doing science is an example par excellence of a self-transcending learning process that cannot be reduced to mere social constructions, neurological confabulations, and reproductive fitness reductions. The scientific enterprise is thus "super" natural, not only in discovering a fantastically super, natural order, but also in transcending that order, indeed in empowering humans to significantly restructure that natural order. Science itself is an "intimation of transcendence," as the cosmologist George Ellis suggests.[5] The very possibility of science qua science becomes evidence for some notion of God-by-whatever-name.

Recalling our discussion of induction in the philosophy of science from the previous chapter, we can now understand this God hypothesis to be an induction from the observed data. This inference is certainly plausible, perhaps even probable, but it cannot be deductively proven (much as multiverse theory and natural selection can never be deductively proven.)

Transcendence as an Abstract God

The God hypothesis, however, does not get us very far if we do not explore what meanings lie behind the use of the terminology. What truths may lie behind God-talk as we approach religious notions of transcendence from the bottom up? The first proposition is that some notion of transcendence makes sense from a purely scientific understanding of humans in the universe. I use the term *transcendence* to refer to things that exist apart from individual human opinions and preferences, processes that constrain our choices and possibilities. Affirming transcendence should be the easiest and most obvious proposition to a naturalist and scientist. Most of what scientists study transcends humanity. The laws of physics are transcendent. The evolution of life is transcendent. Our historical and cultural contexts are transcendent. Evolutionary and neuroscientific studies even suggest that much of what we consider to be morally good and aesthetically beautiful may also be transcendent, insofar as the good and the beautiful are instinctive preferences encoded by evolution in our genetic dispositions and biological constitution.

The most transcendent empirical reality that we could contemplate is the set of all phenomena, which we will call "Universe-God." In this formulation, we need to include all past actualities, all present realities, and all future possibilities across all space and time. Universe-God can be thought of as an enormous relational database, the mother of all databases, in which every experience at every level of reality is observed, recorded, and remembered. We do not know how this could be achieved, but we can imagine the possibility thereof. In so doing, we need not postulate anything beyond "naturalism" as understood by contemporary science. Note that this set of all phenomena is an extremely transcendent vision, insofar as this set exists radically apart from our individual and collective existence, opinions, and preferences. Our lives are profoundly constituted and constrained by this set of all phenomena; indeed, we can say in a strictly scientific sense that we are created by this Universe-God.

What, then, is the character of the Universe-God? In the last chapter, we already postulated, based on the actual observed development of the cosmos, of the evolution of life, and of the history of humanity, that the trajectory of the Universe-God is toward greater complexification. Of course, this is an inference based on observation. Such inductive generalizations cannot be proven, but we can provide arguments and evidence to support this inference.[6] So we infer complexification as the expressed purpose of the Universe-God. This by itself does not give us a very robust understanding of God-by-whatever-name, so I turn now to the metaphysical thoughts of Alfred North Whitehead to explore further the metaphysics of contemporary science and the implications for our bottom-up approach to God-by-whatever-name.

Process and Relationship

Alfred North Whitehead (1861–1947) created a comprehensive metaphysical system for understanding science, society, and self. Metaphysics is about making comprehensive inferences about the general structure of reality based on all the facts. These inductions cannot be proven, but they can be plausible or implausible, useful or not, depending on how well they describe the facts. "The theory of Induction is the despair of philosophy," writes Whitehead, "and yet all our activities are based upon it."[7]

The fundamental insights of Whitehead's metaphysics are neatly summarized in the words *process* and *relationship*. Events—not *things*—are fundamentally real. In other words, what constitutes reality is not a collection of nouns, that is, named things, but a series of verbs, that is, temporal activities. All events are relational. They have causal antecedents and causal consequences in webs of varying complexity, significance, and intensity. Events also exhibit some modicum of internal self-creative freedom that is not fully determined by their causal antecedents. More complicated events have greater internal freedom.

Whitehead's process metaphysics does not rely on the usual dualisms that have vexed previous metaphysical systems. We no longer need to be troubled about the distinctions between matter and mind, animate and inanimate, created and evolved, nature and nurture, or reductionism and emergence. The difference between atoms, animals, artifacts, and humans is in the degrees of complexity, the intensity of causal relationships, and the extent of self-creative freedom integrated in these various phenomena, not in any essentialized notions of natural kinds. Most philosophical problems in the metaphysics of contemporary science disappear with Whitehead's event-centered process philosophy, which makes it a very attractive point of departure for our bottom-up approach to God-by-whatever-name.

God is a category that Whitehead feels compelled to invoke in his process philosophy of every "actual occasion," but it is God of all past realities and all future possibilities, the set of all phenomena. The incarnate God is determined by the sum of all past actualities, and the transcendent God is limited within a matrix of future possibilities. Whitehead's God also functions as a persuasive *telos* that draws the universe toward greater complexity, greater integration of these complexities in communion, and greater co-creative freedom within those relational webs. For Whitehead, the one become many and the many one, as the universe and God evolve together.

God in Whitehead's view is this set of all relationships and all processes that we previously discussed. In that sense, Whitehead's God is radically transcendent and radically incarnate at the same time. Instead of Universe-God, we might better call it "Universing-God" or "God-ing-Universe," remembering that this is now a gerund, more of a verb than a thing. God-ing-Universe is a complex distributed system. The technical term used is *panentheism*, everything-in-god, to be distinguished from *pantheism*, everything-is-god. Whiteheadean process metaphysics has given rise to various schools of process theology that have found devotees in numerous seminaries and departments of religion.[8] Indeed, Whitehead is one of the patron saints of the modern dialogue between science and religion.

In Whitehead's view, all being is causally related. This does not mean all beings are equivalent in a flat, relativistic monism without significant distinctions, because being is spun within webs of asymmetrical, multivariable, hierarchically layered, and differentially valued relationships. While Whitehead does not develop an explicit epistemology to go along with his ontology, we may infer that all knowing is also causally related within a web of asymmetrical, multivariable, hierarchically layered, and differentially valued relationships. Epistemology is, thus, improved by adopting the intentional, multiple perspectivalism that I advocated in earlier chapters under the rubric "intellectual nonviolence."

Whitehead's process metaphysics can be understood as reviving Aristotle's notion of natural kinds, albeit in a changing evolutionary context. A nexus of complexity, be it a proton, a protein, or a person, has a temporal "personality" that persists and achieves an emergent identity, a temporary "essence." He combines this evolutionary Aristotelianism with a Platonic notion of an ideal horizon toward which all events tend in the complexification of the universe. This Platonic idea is the persuasive *telos* of the God-ing-Universe, a fusion of horizons toward which all entities tend. Finally, Whitehead adopts a Hegelian notion of history's movement as a kind of progressive incarnation of Spirit in the universe.

Whitehead's event-centered metaphysics will make immediate sense to most practicing scientists, who understand better than most the transitory and relational nature of nature. It is possible to accept process and relationship and its evolutionary Aristotelianism as "self-evident," while rejecting the Platonic concepts of *telos* and the Hegelian concept of progress with its progressive incarnation of Spirit in history. And yet, we can infer and perhaps should conclude a kind of directionality in the observed big history of the universe leading toward greater complexity. Whitehead adds the concepts of increasing integration and freedom to this *telos* of manifest complexification.

Of Mountains and Men

What do we mean when we say that traditional dualism—animate and inanimate, mind and body, human and nonhuman, spirit and matter—disappear in Whitehead's metaphysics? Let us compare a human and a rock. The human is vastly more complex than the rock at a more intensive time scale. A particular human is an extended event, spanning at the maximum a life span of about 120 solar years. Even at this ripe old age, obtained by very few, the span of human life is generally a lot less than that of most rocks. The human, however, is able to integrate exponentially more causal influences in its being than can the rock. Humans are constituted by more complex and dynamic chemistry, including the biochemistry of life. We integrate billions of years of biological evolution in our particular animal bodies and minds. We further integrate human language and culture, which allows for a collective and distributed complexity to accumulate and intensify over many generations. And we integrate the symbolic languages of other natural kinds into our own being through science, as well as other cultural inventions such as art, literature, agriculture, and construction. Humans have exponentially more internal, self-creative freedom than the rock because of this complexity, intensity, and extensity in our temporal being. The rock and the human, however, are not different kinds of essences. Each can be characterized as events, what Whitehead calls "actual entities," that have causal antecedents, a moment of self-creative possibility, and causal consequences in the great chain of becoming.

What exactly is the self-creative freedom of a rock? As acted upon by the wind and the weather, the heat and the cold, we know that the rock will crack and erode. We cannot, however, predict exactly how the rock will break down, either on the mesocosmic scale or the microcosmic scale. Science cannot look inside the "subjective" reality of the rock at this level and predict in advance exactly how the molecules will break apart. This is the internal reality of the rock, its modicum of self-creativity.

Imagine, for a moment, the natural history of a mountain, that is, a large collection of rocks. If we could create a time-lapse movie of the mountain over many tens of thousands of years and play it back on a human time scale of a few hours, then we would observe a very "life-like" process of evolution as the mountain grew and eroded under the force of plate tectonics and volcanism, water and ice, wind and snow, heating and cooling. A similar time-lapse movie of the development of a major urban area over a hundred years played back in the petri dish of a biologist would lead to a similar conclusion, that is, the city is "alive." It has a distributed identity that is greater than the sum of its parts and has a "mind of its own."

In Whitehead's metaphysics, the laws of science are not really immutable "laws"; rather, they are descriptions of reliable patterns in the unfolding of events. The nonhuman events themselves are active participants in an expanded intersubjectivity of our social construction, one in which our human identities and scientific projects are fundamentally relational.

While Whitehead's metaphysics is more wholesome and more compatible with recent scientific insights than all the other leading brands, it also has some problems. The greatest problem with Whitehead is that he invents an impenetrable new terminology to describe his new metaphysics.

Most of his interpreters are equally obscurantist. It is very difficult to decode the meaning of his most important book, *Process and Reality*, which was originally delivered as a Gifford Lecture in Scotland. The book is nearly impossible to read. The story is that, by the last of his lectures in Edinburgh in 1927, the only person left attending was his wife. Many of Whitehead's essays and shorter books, however, are quite accessible, and he can be extremely witty and profound.

Another problem in Whitehead is the tendency to naturalize moral evil in the service of evolution. Whether it be the death of a single child due to disease, starvation, or violence or something on a larger scale like the Rwanda massacre, these past actualities are just part of the unfolding of evolution and the incarnation of God in the universe. There is no outside of history by which such pain, suffering, and death can be "redeemed," as postulated by traditional theism. Moral and natural evil may provoke change, adaptation, and further evolution, that is, progress, but at someone's expense. Whitehead offers no salvation story outside the hoped-for evolution of the universe toward the one, the many, and the beautiful. Thus, Whitehead offers no real solutions to the existential angst over death that motivates much of religious adherence. Morality is further relegated to a subset of aesthetics.

Whitehead's process metaphysics tends to render God impersonal and disconnected from traditional theistic accounts of religion. It is not clear, for instance, why anyone would pray to this God. Nor does Whitehead draw on any of the scriptural sources in theologizing about this new concept of God. Whitehead is disconnected from his own Anglican tradition, in this respect, and will have little appeal to scripturally oriented religious traditionalists. In that sense, he is founding a new religious movement, as witnessed in part by his invention of many neologisms and the cultish behavior of many of his disciples, who tend to frame every topic in terms of "Process Philosophy and..."

On the other hand, an advantage of Whitehead's concept of God is that the theodicy problem disappears because God is no longer omnipotent. This God-ing-Universe suffers with the world, because it is the world; it marvels at its complexity, plays with us, loves with us, and relates with us. God-ing-Universe is a presence all the way up and down the cosmic unfolding of time and scales of emergence. Rendering God no longer omnipotent may render God too emasculated and irrelevant for most traditionalists even to begin considering, but it does solve the theodicy problem. God's "intervention" in the universe is that of a persuasive urging toward the good and the beautiful, not that of a dictator in the sky. A God of love would not be a control freak. And for my mind, humans need to be done with dictatorships, adopting instead limited forms of government and limited forms of theology. God-ing-Universe is a desiring for, suffering with, and remembering of all things in an evolving process. Maybe this is not such a bad reconceptualization after all; indeed, it picks up one of the central Christian concepts of God as the suffering servant and loving companion.

A Moral Order

The observed teleonomy of the universe is increased *differentiation*, increased *communion*, and increased *autopoiesis*. Taken together, these three principles would constitute what Whitehead means by realized beauty. Differentiation, for instance, is promoted by chance and mutation in the evolution of life. Communion is promoted by necessity, symbiosis, and selection. Autopoiesis is promoted by niche creation and choice. We can then move from description to prescription. Human actions and beliefs are true, good, and beautiful when they protect and increase *differentiation*, when they attend to and enjoy *communion*, and when they foster and enhance *autopoiesis*, that is, self-creative freedom. Evil is a corruption of these goods by disproportionately emphasizing one and neglecting the others. The dynamic balance between these tripartite goods constitutes beautiful and ethical behavior.[9]

I find this moral matrix helpful. It would be useful to explore some examples of how this might be applied in political philosophy, bioethics, and environmental ethics. While this framework is not going to give us simple answers to culture-war debates about abortion or homosexuality, national health care or energy policy, it does provide a context for a common moral conversation at least partly grounded in a scientific worldview. In the matrix itself, we see that real ethical problems are often not polar opposites but a conflict of goods that cannot all be maximized at the same time. The great philosophical and moral challenge of our time is to reconcile natural-law philosophy (global ethics) with natural philosophy (contemporary science) in conversation with our received traditions (comparative religions). This is the larger subtext in this book and in my own intellectual and spiritual autobiography.

A Personal God

At this point, we have inferred the possibility, indeed rationality, of postulating God-by-whatever-name, as an abstract set of all phenomena—past, present, and future—that expresses purposes in the universe, which we observe in the trend toward greater differentiation, greater integration, and greater self-creative possibilities. This purpose can be read as a moral order in the universe to which humans can conform or not. Our relationship to this kind of God, however, would be analogous to our relationship to the laws of physics, except that, unlike the laws of physics, it appears that humans have the possibility of violating the universe's purpose, insofar as we may diminish differentiation, integration, and self-creative trends. At this stage, God-by-whatever-name from the bottom up is universal but quite impersonal. This is hardly a God that would inspire liturgies and hymns, temples and cathedrals, prayer and sacrifice. Why pray to the laws of physics?

Is it possible to get from this abstract concept of God to a personal God? To do so requires only that we recognize our own personhood and subjective experience as significant in our bottom-up metaphysics of God-by-whatever-name. Science assiduously tries to minimize the subjective and maximize the objective in its rigorous conversations with natural phenomena, so much so that it often ends up denying subjective experience as essential datum in the metaphysics of science and life. Yet our subjective experiences as persons are essential aspects of our lives, indeed the primary way in which each of us experiences the universe day to day, even for those who work in libraries and laboratories.

Our personhood is a nonreducible and emergent phenomenon, indeed the most important such phenomenon that we must account for in any adequate metaphysics. Every scientist is herself a storied history of teachers and mentors, moods and motivations, adventures and tribulations. Every time a scientist applies for a grant, teaches a class, enters a lab, engages in fieldwork, publishes a paper, and interacts with her colleagues, she expresses personhood. Scientists, like the rest of us, also have lives that are intensely personal and subjective in relationship with parents, friends, lovers, spouses, children, neighbors, colleagues, and others. The universe evolved to create creatures with intense experiences of personality; ergo, the God-ing-Universe is also necessarily personal on some fundamental level. A metaphysics that denies subjective experience does not have an empirical leg to stand on.

In a sense, nothing could be more obvious than that the God-ing-Universe is personal. Just as Whitehead felt compelled by the existence of his own human consciousness to ascribe an aspect of consciousness to all levels of reality, so too we are compelled by our own personhood to ascribe an aspect of personality to all levels of reality. The more complex and integrated the phenomena, the greater the consciousness and personality. God-by-whatever-name as the set of all phenomena would then have the greatest powers of mind and personality, powers that minimally include all our separate human minds and personalities—past, present, and future.

So, we have two aspects of God-by-whatever-name—the abstract and the personal. We should note at this point that scriptural traditions also include both aspects—the impersonal abstract and the personal subjective. In the Bible, for instance, God is sometimes an abstract power over human life and at other times a personal power intensely interested in individual human lives.

Supernaturalism

The question arises whether the God-by-whatever-name can account for miracles and other supernatural events that are described in scriptures and attested to by believers. Here, we need to be a great deal more skeptical.

As already noted, the metaphysics of emergence creates a possibility space for the reality of miracles but hardly a logical necessity. More often, paranormal occurrences are patently falsifiable. In the historical context in which scriptural accounts of miracles were written, humans simply did not have our modern conceptions of natural and supernatural. Science, as we understand it today, did not exist. Through science we have learned that nature is miraculously "super" but probably not "supernatural." The latter we shall better call "unnatural," in order to stigmatize it.

Better that we interpret miracles as psychological and mythological language, rather than as objective and empirical language. The alternative is to insist on an enormous and embarrassing gap between science and religion. For instance, watch what happens when we retell the Christian story with these modern distinctions in mind. We end up saying that an "unnatural" Father did "unnatural" acts to Mary to create an "unnatural" Son who lived an "unnatural" life. Jesus then died an "unnatural" death, experienced an "unnatural" resurrection, and reigns in an "unnatural" heaven. To read this foundational Christian story in this way is to render it implausible and ridiculous, indeed profoundly anti-intellectual and anti-scientific. The psychological, symbolic, and mythological reading of this same story, on the other hand, is profound and transformational. In any case, we today do not have access to events reported to have occurred some two thousand years ago, not through the Bible, not through a forensic laboratory, not through CNN, and not through the supposed realism of a Hollywood portrayal of those events.

There does seem to me one occasion in which we should grant credence to the possibility of miracles, synchronicity, paranormal phenomena, epiphanies, or other kinds of "super" natural occurrences. These occasions are when we personally experience such events. If a person has a religious experience that seems miraculous, one should not immediately discount this important data. A process of testing and discernment is in order, to be sure, but strong subjective experiences are essential datum in our metaphysics and in our lives. If you have a powerful spiritual transformation or an epiphany of some sort, you should not necessarily check in to a mental hospital, especially if that experience is positive and empowering for you. Call it the presence of the Holy Spirit or some other name, but the varieties of religious experience that we detailed in chapter five—interpretative, sensory, revelatory, regenerative, ethical, aesthetic, intellectual, ecstatic, numinous, and oneness —are frequently reported on by our fellow humans and represent vital data in our personal hermeneutics of the self, society, and cosmos. On the other hand, I see no reason to accept evidence of miracles and paranormal events on hearsay, especially as recorded in ancient scriptures. Nor is science ever going to be of much help in establishing the reality of such supernatural occurrences, so do not go looking for science to confirm miracles. If such things exist—and I suppose they do, based on my own experiences and discernment—then the science thereof will necessarily be mute. There are limits to what science can effectively study. Using science to study something "beyond nature" is a category mistake. The interpretation of reported supernatural occurrences is a matter of interpretation, not a matter of rigorous verification.

Life after Death

Much has been written in philosophy, psychology, and theology about the unique existential challenge of anticipating one's own death. To the best that we know, no other species has this existential challenge. Certainly, other animals have emotions, including emotions about the death of family members—for instance, we see grieving over dead ones in elephants and chimpanzees—but to contemplate in advance one's own nonexistence seems uniquely human. For many, perhaps most, the reality of death, one's own death, is a kind of psychic terror. We adapt mostly by denial, but we also adapt by imagining some kind of life after death in the form of reincarnation or resurrection. This imagined afterlife also provides a moral balance to the injustices experienced in this life. In the rewards of heaven, the punishments of hell, or the stages of reincarnation, moral order is imposed on the moral chaos we experience in this world. To some extent, these beliefs also help constrain our passions and desires in this world to the benefit of communities and ourselves. These beliefs also help motivate risk taking and altruistic sacrifices on behalf of others, without which risks and sacrifices no community would long survive.

I am intrigued by the project of reconstructing traditional religions without reference to some afterlife. What happens to Buddhism and Hinduism, for instance, if we drop the doctrine of reincarnation? What happens to Islam, Judaism, or Christianity, if we drop the idea of heaven and hell? Do they still "work"? If so, how? If not, why not? Certainly, we can turn this life into heaven or hell. Certainly, our good and bad actions in this life have a way of reincarnating themselves into the future, even if we are not literally reincarnated. If the sins of the fathers are revisited for seven generations, then so might acts of mercy and kindness reverberate down through the ages. My purpose here, however, is not to reject the concept of the afterlife but rather to show new ways of thinking about it within a scientific worldview.

On first consideration, there is little scientific basis for belief in an afterlife in either the form of reincarnation or resurrection. What we observe is birth, life, and death. In death, breathing and blood circulation stop, brain activity ceases, and bacteria quickly turn the once-living body into a decaying corpse. The corpse itself becomes dangerous to the living, so a variety of rituals have evolved for disposing of human corpses, burial and burning being the most common.

On a molecular level, we can say that the body is recycled, perhaps as food for flora and fauna but always in the form of the atoms that were never really ours to begin with. By mass, we are about 65 percent oxygen,

19 percent carbon, 10 percent hydrogen, and 3 percent nitrogen. To this
we add trace quantities of calcium, phosphorus, potassium, sulfur, chlo-
rine, sodium, magnesium, iron, cobalt, copper, zinc, iodine, selenium,
fluorine, manganese, molybdenum, nickel, and chromium, in roughly
that order.[10] All these elements were created by stars; all have been on earth
for some 4 billion years. Our atoms only temporarily "belonged" to us as
our bodies. Only the calcium in our bones persists for any length of time,
thus giving us skeletal remains that persist for generations in catacombs
and crypts. Indeed, on the atomic level, we are continuously renewing
our bodies throughout life by breathing, drinking, eating, perspiring, and
excreting. The atoms circulate in and out of our epidermis-contained
identities such that we are continuously reconstituted, recreated, and
"reborn" on a daily basis. We are all molecular drops in a huge ocean of
life and matter, a brief nexus of atoms and molecules that constitute a society of 10 trillion cells collaborating to produce consciousness, emotion,
intentionality, discovery, and creativity.

This molecular recycling provides the beginning of a spiritual sense of
immortality, but it does not include our personhood in any identifiable
form. What is it that constitutes the human person? From a scientific
perspective, we would answer that individual humans are the product of
the evolution of our species, that which we share in common, as well as
specific social, cultural, psychological, economic, biological, and historical contexts that constitute each of us as distinct personalities belonging
to multiple group identities. The something more that is added to the
collection of atoms, molecules, and cells can be thought of as information. Scientists do not really have an adequate definition of information;
it means different things in different disciplines. Nor do we have a generic
way to measure information as such, but we can say with some certainty
that what distinguishes a collection of atoms from a living human (or any
other entity) is how the atoms are organized in a persisting pattern. This
persisting pattern, not just of atoms but of embodied experiences and
memories, is your personhood.

Let's imagine God-by-whatever-name again as the "Mother-of-All-
Databases," able to record and remember every actual state of matter-
energy-information in the universe. With this information in hand,
resurrecting or reincarnating a dead human is hardly a problem. The
atoms are already at hand. What one needs is the information content of a
life, the thoughts, the experiences, and the environment.[11]

Now, this information-centered reinterpretation of the afterlife still has
some problems. We still need energy flow for our bodily resurrection or
reincarnation. And we would still have the curious dilemma of debate in
the medieval church of which body, with which mind, and at which age
to be recreated. Youth is wasted on the young (bodies and minds), as the
saying goes. And not all young bodies and minds are healthy bodies, as is
increasingly the case with all older bodies and minds at some point. I suspect most of us would like an upgrade in Self Version x.0 in a glorified

bodily resurrection. Perhaps we can dispense with atoms altogether and retain some kind of afterlife existence as pure information, though we do not really know of such a possibility and what that would mean in any analogical scientific sense.

The point here is not to prove the existence of an afterlife but merely to show that there are scientific ways to imagine the possibility thereof.[12] A different kind of approach to this question looks at space–time–information, instead of matter–energy–information. Time turns out to be really strange in fundamental physics. The microequations of physics operate the same irrespective of time. Forward or backward, the universe does not care. Past, present, and future all exist in the same "space–time" continuum. It is only the Second Law of Thermodynamics, a macrophysical equation, that provides an arrow to time in the universal march of entropy.

Humans, of course, have evolved a very different understanding of time based on birth, life, and death, the daily motions of the sun, the monthly cycles of the moon, and the annual passing of seasons. Our evolved sense of time is very different from the understanding of deep time, space–time, and microscopic time as put forward by modern physics. Our common-sense understanding of time may be an illusion foisted upon us by our biology and our planet. In this new understanding of time, even to talk of an afterlife frames the question the wrong way. Nothing in a timeless universe ever ceases to exist.[13] Everything is eternal. All past actualities and all future possibilities intersect in the present moment, and that is the meaning of eternity.[14]

This quasi-mystical, quasi-scientific understanding of time, information, and the afterlife should be taken analogically, not literally. I am not trying to prove anything, only to open up a possibility and plausibility space for such interpretations within a scientific paradigm. The mystery of death remains. Recognizing that mystery, and our existential terror thereof, is part of the religious impulse. Providing comfort in the face of death is one of the functions of religions. We will know or not when we ourselves cross that divide.

Seeking after God

In political and moral disagreements, invoking God is often done as a power play to end debate and reassure oneself through contrived certainty. Invoking atheism can have the same function in political and moral debates. Instead of speaking for God, we might better orient ourselves toward seeking after God. To say too much about God with too much certainty can be seen as a form of idolatry. "The implication of idolatry is that God cannot be God," writes John Bowker. "[I]dolatry is self-defeating because, by being an attempt to arrive at premature and ostensive definition, it destroys the goodness of God. It destroys what God must be in order to be God."[15]

Bowker argues for an "indefinitely regressive" concept of God, but not necessarily an infinitely regressive concept. In order for God to be God and to serve the psychological, sociological, and philosophical function of God within human life, God-by-whatever-name must be always beyond our reach. It is the seeking, rather than the finding, that is most wholesome and transformative in religion.

Yet if the concept of God is too remote and too unattainable, it would hardly be effective. Somehow there needs to be what Bowker calls "feedback" in his information-systems analysis of God. There must be "sufficiency of effect," if God is to be relevant. George Ellis talks of "intimations of transcendence," which he finds in the universe and upon which he grounds his Quaker commitment to meaningful life guided by the transformational possibilities and real risks of political and spiritual nonviolence.[16] In this approach, God-by-whatever-name is established not as an a priori proposition but through a careful mapping of instantiations, intimations, inferences, and interpretations. The relevant data comes from all science, all human history, our own cultural context (including the religious idioms of those different cultures), our own personal psychology, and our own subjective experiences. "At their most basic level," writes Bowker,

> religions can best be understood as systems organized (in very different ways) for the coding, protection and transmission of information (some of it verbal, but a great deal of it, in the religious case, non-verbal) which has proved to be of worth and which has been tested through many generations. In other words, religions are systems organized for the protection and transmission of the achieved discoveries of human competence.[17]

As information systems that involve coding, channeling, protection, transmission, and reception, religions also require "feedback." Here the concept of symbolic realism comes back into play because religions are hardly the only information system at work in the world today. The feedback is in the form of symbols and signs that can be interpreted as affirmations or refutations of the system. This is an accurate description of genetic processes as well as cultural processes. What are the signs that confirm or refute religious systems? How do religious systems defend their boundaries? We note that throughout the Qur'an, Allah keeps referring to "signs" that can be "read" in nature, signs that confirm the truth contained in the revelation. Is the universe meaningless and purposeless, as the Stoic and existentialist interpretations of science argue, or are there sufficient "signs" in your life and in your science to conclude otherwise? To look for some a priori proof is to frame the question in the wrong way. The God hypothesis is an inductive proposition, and the verification thereof is a matter of a life lived in process and relationship, in interpretation and reinterpretation, which may approach some "fusion of horizons," but a horizon that is also always receding as we approach it. Not every prayer must be answered, but some prayers must be sufficiently answered. Not every liturgy need be motivational, but some liturgies must be. Not every reading of scripture need ring true, but some readings must be profound. Not every religious leader must be saintly and charismatic, but some of them should be.

The behavioral scientist might recognize this pattern as an intermittent-reward pattern, of which gambling provides the classic example. Our brains are apparently hard-wired to chase after rewards, especially when the response is unpredictable. This is why gambling can be so addictive. The earned-reward and punishment methods are by themselves powerful tools in behavior-conditioning experiments with humans and animals, but intermittent rewards are perverse in their ability to mold our behavior toward chasing after some expectation. Perhaps this is part of the reason that religions can be addictive, especially for people already prone to obsessive-compulsive disorders.[18] The fault, however, is not with religion as such but with life itself. Life is an intermittent-reward system, full of unpredictable pleasures and pains. Life is addictive. We should expect no less realism from our religions and our philosophies.

Meaning and Emotion

This book has been largely dispassionate and philosophical, as is appropriate in this genre, but we need to recognize that meaning and emotion are profoundly connected. In our typology of religious experience in chapter five, we saw that many types of religious experiences were highly charged with emotions, and we listed ten types of religious experiences, each of which has different emotional valence and all of which are relational and powerful.

In thinking about the medicine of religion in chapter seven, we explored the deep semiotics of health, noting the power and ubiquity of psychosocial-somatic factors in health and healing. When the standard treatment is ineffective, our complementary-and-alternative-medicine skeptic R. Barker Bausell recommended that you select a CAM treatment and practitioner that suited you and embrace him wholeheartedly. In so doing, the magic of psychosocial-somatic healing has a possibility of taking hold and transforming your sickness and your life.

Here, then, is the dilemma. After all our critical analyses are completed, after we have employed all our new sciences of religion, after we have probed and dissected religious and spiritual phenomena with our critical minds, we must still decide in what we really believe. A plausibility space has been opened up, but how will we live? On what do we ground our sense of hope? What happens to our lives when our hope in the future is built on inadequate foundations? What happens when these foundations crumble? Hope is not just a metaphysical question; it is an

extremely practical question for individuals and societies. We are a species that is profoundly oriented toward the future, a future that is partly
self-fulfilling prophecy, as we learn in thinking about the psychology of
economic markets.

Paul Ricoeur, whom we discussed in chapter seven, talks about a "second naïveté." After all the critical analyses and skepticism, we can go back
into a tradition with a new kind of sophisticated naïveté. We can believe
in religious stories with new insights and more mature understandings.
We can read scriptures not in a way that seeks silly concordances with
science or current events but in ways that allow scriptures to inform our
lives on a deeper level. Which scriptures do we read? How do we choose
in today's Walmart of world religions? How do we reinterpret a scriptural
tradition?

Let us start with the concepts of mercy and compassion, words so often
repeated by Muslims. Let us add the concept of love and forgiveness, so
central to Christians. Let us build upon the idea of covenant and justice, as
Jews try to understand and embody. Let us combine the virtues of wisdom
and compassion as sought by Buddhists. Let these be the hermeneutical
filters through which we re-read and re-interpret our received traditions
in conversation with contemporary science, a global civilization, and a
world of pragmatic problems that we need to solve together. Let these be
the hermeneutical biases that we use to reinvent and transform our individual and collective lives—love, compassion, mercy, forgiveness, covenant, justice, and the wisdom to know the difference.

Religions stand or fall depending on whether there is meaning and
purpose in life. Such purposes must be more than some illusion that we
invent; they must somehow be grounded in the fabric of the universe
in ways that transcend mere opinion and preference. For religions to be
credible and powerful in the twenty-first century, as well as practical and
functional, they must become fully conversant with contemporary science
and competent in the interpretation of science. The content of science
provides an important set of universals upon which to build productive
intra- and interreligious learning and transformations.

Particularist Universalism

We began this book by suggesting that the sciences of religion are to religions what linguistics is to the study of human languages. In spite of the
differences in human languages, there are common structures to language
that can be scientifically studied and philosophically considered. This is
what we attempted to do for religion in part 1, looking at the universal "grammar" of religion with the help of different sciences. These sciences dealt with what we might call the semiotic structures of religion. In
part 2, we shifted to the semantics of religion. What do religions mean?
In what sense might religions be true? Do they have a real reference,

merely an imagined reference, or more probably a dynamic combination of both real and imagined? How do we distinguish between the real and the imagined, between what religions discover and what they invent?[19]

In a world of enormous religious diversity, how does one choose which religion to follow? If you want to probe the deeper meanings and uses of religious language, then you will probably be best served by doing so in your "native tongue." That is not to say that you should not learn another religious language. At a certain level of education and profession, to be monolingual is an embarrassing deficiency. We might say the same about being monoreligious, but real fluency in a foreign language or a foreign religion is a very difficult thing to acquire and is always an incomplete process. Even my native fluency in English is far from perfect.

A story will help illustrate this point. As a young man, I lived abroad twice. I spent my junior year of college at the Hebrew University in Jerusalem, and a few years after college, I found myself working for a year in West Berlin. In both cases, I threw myself into learning the languages—Hebrew and German—and became quite proficient. In both cases, I fell in love with native speakers, an Israeli kibbutznik from Galilee and an East German artist in Leipzig. Negotiating the complexity of romantic relationships in my native English was already difficult enough. My trying to do so in a foreign language was so pitiable as to be humorous. I could negotiate the streets, the offices, the newspapers, and the political debates in Hebrew and German, but not the mysteries and passions of the heart.

Here, then, is the challenge of probing the semantics of religion. Try to find an idiom that works for you, in which you already have some familiarity and proficiency. Some few will convert and immerse themselves in learning a new religious language from scratch, a process that will presumably also involve learning one or more foreign languages. Sometimes such converts can achieve amazing insight and proficiency, more so than even most "native speakers" of that religion. The thoughtful convert is a precious enrichment of a tradition, as such a person does not take anything for granted. He or she analyzes and understands the deep semiotics and profound semantics of a tradition. I think of, for instance, by analogy, of the Polish-born Joseph Conrad and the Russian-born Vladimir Nabokov, both literary geniuses who only learned English as adults and went on to write great works of literature in that foreign idiom. I fear, however, that most converts to foreign religions will be like me, fumbling for words in foreign languages to express romantic infatuations and disappointments.

We now come to the concept of particularist universalism. There is a semantic unity of world religions and semiotic diversity in the lived expression of this unity. "God is one," says the ancient Rig Veda, "but the wise call it by many names" (1.164.46). Here is the dialectic. To get beyond a solipsistic rationality of a single tradition and ground religious faith in multiple rationalities—scientific, historical, and philosophic—it is necessary to posit a common truth that transcends any particular tradition. To explore that common truth in any depth, however, one must enter deeply into the rationality of a single tradition.

The differences matter, as is the case of learning a foreign language, but no less so do the commonalities between religions. Religions, like languages, are structured systems. Like languages, religions evolve through use and interaction. Religions, like languages, borrow from each other over time as they evolve. Religions, like languages, also need to promote, educate, and police the correct usage of their idioms, which is one of the reasons that religions can be as strict and conservative as an elementary-school grammarian with a class of unruly children. But if your religious education ended with that strict and conservative mode of pedagogy in Sunday School, or some different cultural equivalent, then you have missed out on the greatness of religion, which has inspired so much creativity, service, comfort, and good throughout the ages. If you want to understand and fall in love with God-by-whatever-name, you had better have a particular language and a particular name with which to explore that relationship, a relationship that is both intellectual and emotional, a relationship that is both individual and social, a relationship that is sometimes vivid and sometimes mundane, as are the ebbs and flows of all intimate relationships. To converse in this language of hope, love, and charity probably means speaking to God-by-a-particular-name, but it need not in any way diminish others who speak different languages of transcendence in the religions of the world today. Indeed, as we reflect on the trends in globalization and communication, there is an urgent need for all to become conversant in multiple religious traditions, even as we seek to enter more deeply into our own, retesting the received wisdom of the ages and reinterpreting sacred scriptures in dialogue with contemporary science and society.

Science is also a kind of love affair, as I have suggested by defining science as altruistic fidelity to the phenomenon. A scientist begins his or her career by falling in love with some discipline of study, generally mediated by a mentor in school. Without this love, why would one devote long hours of tedious work to studying in detail some small aspect of a vast universe, generally for very modest compensation and a lot of professional insecurity? It is no doubt more difficult to become a scientist with a Ph.D. than to become a Buddhist master, though the two are not mutually exclusive. What happens, I wonder, after a decade or two of hard work, when the scientist may feel that his love is unrequited, when his fascination wanes, when the discipline seems more like a prison and a dead-end career that no longer satisfies or inspires? Perhaps it is possible to sustain a love throughout a lifetime, but not without transformation, growth, and support. Here, I suspect that the long-survived and well-winnowed practical wisdom and metaphysical intuitions of religions may be of great help to the scientist and the scientific enterprise. The mystery of love is that it never really begins with the individual but is always evoked by the phenomena, other humans, and other more-than-human phenomena.

Love may be part of the deeper structure of the universe. Like gravity's giving rise to order in the early universe and igniting the stellar furnaces, love attracts us and binds us together in an inescapable web of mutuality, fascination, and concern.

And here religions may have some useful lessons for science, lessons about the importance of building communities on the one hand and the dangers of intolerance on the other. The New Atheists do not damage religion as much as they do extreme disservice to science in their extremism. Religions surely need critics and skeptics in order to grow and evolve. If Richard Dawkins et al. did not exist, we would need to invent them, not to advance science, which they do not, but to help transform religions. Similarly, the scientific enterprise needs poets and artists, preachers and teachers, and pundits and gurus if it is to grow and evolve in ways that are not just factually true but also practically true. By studying the sciences of religion, we also learn ways to make the religions of science more wholesome and more practical, what dangerous tropes to avoid, and what marketing strategies to employ. Science, like religion, needs a unifying spirit, but not one based on irrational exuberance or cynical caution. Science, like religion, is best served by considered optimism and, when necessary, a prophetic but hopeful pessimism. Yoking science and religion together in a mutually constructive manner may hold the greatest promise for advancing truth and goodness in the twenty-first century.

CHAPTER TEN

Reiterations and Reflections

We began this book by asking several important questions: What is religion? What is spirituality? Are religions functional and healthy for individuals and groups? How do we scientifically study the phenomenon of religion; indeed, how do we even define it? Are religions and spiritualities true and, if so, in what ways? To answer these questions, we took a long journey from the outside in, considering many sciences of religion, and from the bottom up, working from a contemporary scientific worldview toward a concept of God-by-whatever-name. To paraphrase the poet W. H. Auden: to ask hard questions is simple, but the answers are hard, and hard to remember.[1]

The hard answers in this book will be easier to remember if we conduct a brief review. There are five concepts to emphasize in conclusion:

1. nonreductive functionalism in the sciences of religion;
2. entangled narratives and the challenge of comparative interpretation;
3. the interpretation of science as distinct from the content of science;
4. the new metaphysics of science: process, relation, emergence; and
5. particularist universalism in comparative religion.

1. Nonreductive functionalism: The concept of nonreductive functionalism recognizes the multilevel and multivariable complexity of religious and spiritual phenomena. Religions, in this view, can be understood as functional and dysfunctional for individuals and groups with reference to different kinds of secular and psychosocial goods in specific, often-conflicting contexts. This kind of analysis is not particularly concerned with whether the beliefs held and stories told by religious people are true, but rather whether and how they have pragmatic utility in lived circumstances. That being said, nonreductive functionalism holds out the possibility that religious beliefs and practices can be profound, perhaps even profoundly true.

Part 1 of the book primarily dealt with the theory of nonreductive functionalism in the scientific study of religious and spiritual phenomena.

We did so by reviewing economic, evolutionary, neurological, and medical models for understanding religion and spirituality. Within each discipline, we noted a number of debates and a diversity of points of view. Between the disciplines, we also noted that each theoretical orientation acts as a kind of epistemological filter, a set of reading glasses that one puts on, enabling one to foreground certain aspects of the phenomena and not others. In short, there will be no grand unified theory of religion. Nonreductive functionalism celebrates the plurality of perspectives, encouraging researchers to use multiple methodologies in trying to understand the ubiquity and complexity of religious and spiritual phenomena.

2. Entangled narratives: Already in the beginning, when we considered the diversity of religious beliefs and practices around the world and throughout history, we were confronted with the problem of multiple and competing narratives, entangled now in a global economy by mass communication and population migrations. In broadening our definition of religion to include phenomenologically similar processes such as primary subcultures, ideologies, and nationalism, we also came to understand (1) the narrative nature of human nature and (2) the difficulty of adjudicating between these different worldviews. Each metanarrative that we enumerated structures what people think is true and good and what people recognize as the relevant evidence in supporting that metanarrative. Thus, these metanarratives provide a powerful orientation for thinking and acting in the world. These insights lead to the postmodern moment in contemporary scholarship and world affairs, where we are reduced either to a troubling relativism or a more troubling will to power. A critical and humble hermeneutics helps to negotiate this new reality of competing and entangled worldviews and world doings. Our best hope for sorting out this muddle is to adopt what I call "intellectual nonviolence," in other words, intentionally adopting multiple perspectives, inhabiting multiple rationalities, as structured by different metanarratives in reference to many data sets. I likened this to the multiple methodologies advocated by nonreductive functionalism in the scientific study of religion. I likened it also to the very ideals of science, which I characterized as altruistic fidelity to the phenomena. Multiple methodologies, multiple worldviews, and multiple perspectives hold the greatest promise for discerning larger truths and pragmatics goods.

3. The interpretation of science: It may be a difficult boundary to police, but it is essential that we maintain a distinction between the facts of science and the interpretation of science. To interpret science responsibly requires that we understand the philosophy of science as well as the cumulative content of many sciences in diverse disciplines. I defined science as (1) different methods for detecting patterned phenomena and explaining causal relationships, (2) applied by communities of specialists (3) in rigorous "dialogue" with phenomena, (4) always implicated in

lived historical contexts and limitations, (5) resulting in a self-correcting, self-transcending, and progressive learning process that (6) makes strongly objective truth claims, (7) which facts are pragmatically verified in practical applications (8) and cumulatively related in a unified body of knowledge (9) that can be organized hierarchically by chronology of emergence, scales of size, and degrees of complexity.

Science, I argued, can no longer be thought of as a privileged epistemology, but is nonetheless a unified body of knowledge, knowledge that now presents itself as a privileged metanarrative. The new evolutionary cosmology must now replace earlier religious cosmologies. The latter might be interpreted metaphorically and metaphysically, but in no sense, can we think of religious cosmologies in a literal sense. Reading sacred scriptures as science textbooks, for instance, is a huge and embarrassing category mistake.

The interpretation of science, in its parts and as an epic whole, is open to numerous strategies. The Stoic and Existentialist interpretation favored by some contemporary oracles of science is but one of many strategies. Theistic interpretations of the new cosmology are not only plausible but are more probable than the Stoic and Existentialist interpretation, which, I argue, is self-refuting. A theistic interpretation of the Epic of Evolution, however, requires that we also reinterpret our traditional understandings of God and the universe.

4. The new metaphysics: Interpretations of science always involve metaphysical assumptions, for instance, in defining terms like *natural* and *supernatural*, *phenomena* and *epiphenomena*, or *material* and *nonmaterial*. These terms are also implicated in our understanding of religious and spiritual phenomena and whether and how they might be true. Metaphysical arguments are inductive generalizations on a grand scale that attempt to characterize the fundamental nature of ultimate reality. We can provide evidence for or against some particular metaphysical interpretation, but we cannot simply prove that one metaphysical interpretation is true or not. Nevertheless, some metaphysical systems may be more plausible, more practical, and more pleasing than others, depending on how well they account for the totality of evidence.

In our bottom-up approach to religion and spirituality, we encountered a dialectic between reductionism and holism in contemporary science. We noted that the concept of materialism deconstructs itself in contemporary physics and stressed the importance of information as a new metaphysical category in our contemporary scientific understandings of natural processes. We also considered hierarchies of explanation in science, as well as hierarchies of size, chronology, and complexity in the universe. We postulated that the phenomena of emergence provide an entry point for concepts of transcendence, including a logical possibility space for emergent phenomena that might be characterized as "miracles" or other kinds of "supernatural" events, albeit with many caveats and doubts noted. This bottom-up approach also gave us new concepts of information and time that provide new ways of thinking about the possibilities of an afterlife, whether it be thought of as a resurrection or a reincarnation. None of this was to prove the existences of miracles or the reality of an afterlife, only to show logical possibilities for these religious beliefs to be plausible interpretations within a contemporary scientific framework.

We noted that it was now possible to postulate a concept of God-by-whatever-name as the set of all events—past, present, and future—and that which also transcends the known universe. In this set theory of the transcendence, God would be characterized by process and relations, manifested through the emergent properties of the universe, including the emergence of human persons and personalities. This is not simply an abstract conception of God because, insofar as the universe has given rise to persons and insofar as our own personhood is epistemically and existentially central to our own human perspectives, God-ing-Universe must also in some sense include personality and subjectivity. This view of God is fully consistent with contemporary science and may also help in recovering neglected and more authentic interpretations of sacred scriptures. In this view, the religions of the world represent intuitions and discoveries by humans into the nature of this ultimate reality, accumulated, filtered, and passed on over millennia of human experimentation in diverse historical and cultural contexts.

Finally, we noted that God-by-whatever-name, as understood from the bottom up, seems to desire in the universe the increased complexification of entities (differentiation), increased integration of entities (communion), and increased self-creative "freedom" of entities (autopoiesis). This provides a kind of expressed teleology and purpose in the universe and, with it, a natural moral order for humans. In other words, God's purposes are served when humans preserve and increase complexity, recognize and intensify communion, and defend and extend freedoms. Thus, from our theology of nature, working from the bottom up, it is possible to derive a natural law philosophy based on contemporary science.

5. Particularist universalism: At different times in this book, I have made analogies between the sciences of religion and the field of linguistics. I have argued that, in spite of the diversity of religious beliefs and practices, it may be possible to decode universal patterns of thoughts and behaviors, much as linguistics is able to do between diverse human languages. This possibility and some empirical examples led me to speculate that there is more functional diversity inside a major religious tradition than between traditions.

Later, I took the linguistic analogy even further, by suggesting that the philosophy of science may be akin to linguistics. Just as one could speak a human language and know nothing of formal grammar and linguistics, so too could one practice a science and know nothing of the philosophy of science. The philosophy of science, however, is necessary and useful in trying to understand how the sciences actually work across different domains.

I took the analogy one step further when I suggested that the universe is, in some sense, already linguistic, as manifested in the intelligibility of nature to scientific investigation, as well as other kinds of human representation. I called this "symbolic realism" and noted that this was one of the intuitions we have inherited from many religious traditions. The deep semiotics of nature is an intimation of a deeper semantics to the universe, emergent meaning and purpose that both religion and science can help us to understand better.

The linguistics analogy, however, also suggests that we must return from abstract generalities to speaking particular human languages, even as we discuss common patterns and features between different human languages. Here we have the dialectic between generalization and specialization, synthesis and analysis. We can practice only particular sciences, not sciences in general. And if this analogy holds, then whatever truths and profundities are intuited by world religions can themselves only be approached inside particular religious idioms, even as we can only speak a single human language at a time. To really appreciate religion, one must be "competent" in a particular religion, entering into the richly informative and emotive rationalities and practices of one great religion and scriptural tradition. The "magic" of religion requires deep emotional and social commitments, much like the "magic" of placebos that we discussed in chapter six also requires psychosocial-somatic reinforcement. In practice, religion is more about prayer and liturgy than about philosophy and theology. The magic of religion is more performative than intellectual. Indeed, belief and faith might better be thought of as antonyms because the latter requires consequential action within the context of uncertainty.

If one hopes to go beyond the superficiality of abstract religion without a lived practice (this would be an absurd impossibility in linguistics), then one must probably commit to entering the religious idiom of a particular tradition. Multireligious fluency is a possibility, but it is no doubt difficult to acquire, especially because the wisdom of religions is as much about embodied practice as it is about ideas, concepts, and beliefs. After all the critical analysis is done from the imagined outside looking in, what is most true and most important about religion will only be encountered from within. This, then, is Ricoeur's concept of "the second naïveté": after all the demythologizing and deconstruction, there comes a moment of remythologizing and reconstruction. The term *particularist universalism* tries to capture some of that dynamic of universal verities that can be discovered only through particular religious idioms.

Of course, like languages, religions also evolve. To say that we should fully commit to a single religious tradition to probe the wisdom therein must not blind us to the ways that religions evolve by interacting with other traditions and changing social circumstances. The evolution of religious idioms is demonstrable in past history and is to be expected even more so in the future, especially given the globalization of our civilization. Religions, like languages, borrow from their neighbors, even as they seek to maintain the boundaries of correct usage. Maintaining those boundaries, however, need not mean disparaging other religions as inferior or mistaken. If religions are not all partly right in intuiting something profound about the universe and humans, then they are all probably completely wrong on their most fundamental commitments. Religious exclusivism is not only dangerous in a world of weapons of mass destruction, it also undermines the intellectual plausibility of any religion's making ontologically valid truth claims.

★   ★   ★

I have employed the metaphor of *outside in* to explore what might be entailed in the new sciences of religion. I have similarly employed the metaphor of *bottom up* to develop a new religious metaphysics of science. In the end, these metaphors can and should be deconstructed. There is no objective outside from which to observe the human drama; there is no bottom from which to build up that does not presuppose finite human perspectives at the top. And yet this hermeneutical move, what Ricoeur called *distanciation*, is a powerful technique for transforming a solipsistic hermeneutical circle into a spiral of new possibilities and new insights. This book as a whole is an example of such a hermeneutics, a hermeneutic of multiple methodologies and perspectives entered into in a spirit of intellectual nonviolence.

This long argument is inconclusive, perhaps disappointing. The new sciences of religion offer some interesting insights, but over and over again, we see that they are limited and contextually dependent. We are humbled in the face of the complexity of the phenomena we study from the outside. We are all "participant observers" in the sense that we cannot really avoid certain existential, ethical, and metaphysical questions that are traditionally part of the domain of religions. When we study religion from the outside, we typically employ disciplines such as sociology, psychology, and anthropology. I have largely ignored these fields, but this is not meant to be a disparagement. Indeed, I still find archetypal psychoanalytic interpretations of religion in Freudian, Jungian, and other schools to be powerfully illuminating, though I have not discussed these in this book. Instead, I have used disciplines such as evolutionary psychology, economics, game theory, linguistics, and philosophy. Of course, it is not enough to theorize from outside; one also needs to check the validity of the theories with the data from inside.

Many of those who purport to offer us a new science of religion are still encumbered with the old Enlightenment animus toward religion. They seek to explain religion away and enthrone science as sacred. They detest the category that they purport to study scientifically. In the case of some, I am reminded of the proverbial armchair anthropologist who sits in his university study theorizing about some tribe in Borneo or Brazil but who has never done any field work. He is not going to live among the natives, learn their languages, eat their food, play with their children, and talk with their elders. This Victorian-era anthropologist is certainly not going to be a "participant observer." Furthermore, this contemporary scientist of religion is studying the tribe with the intention of ensuring its extinction because he detests the "ignorant heathens." So, at least, appear to me some of the New Atheists, who seek to explain religion away, but that, of course, is because they are missionaries promoting what should really be understood as a new religious movement. When understood as such, as one "religion" among many, they are more than welcome at the table of interreligious dialogue.

Others who promote a scientific study of religion do so with apologetic biases, trying to revalorize religion, generally their own tradition, through studies that show the secular utility of religion in promoting human health and well-being. These religiously motivated social scientists at least love what they study, but that love presents a curious dilemma and a potentially problematic distortion.

It is not clear to me that scientists can ever legitimately study something—animal, vegetable, or mineral—that they do not on some level believe is intrinsically fascinating and beautiful, worthy of respect, and a great deal of their efforts. Actually, we should all be fascinated with religion for a variety of reasons. It is a powerful and enduring human phenomenon; it is an important part of our common history; it inspires great works of art and literature; it motivates the best and the worst things that humans do in the world; it raises profound questions about meaning and purpose; it proposes answers to those questions.

The normal course of a scientific career begins by falling in love with the phenomena that one then studies in excruciating detail for years, if not decades. How could one devote so much effort to something that one detests? True science is best understood as altruistic fidelity to the phenomena, and it matters not whether the phenomena are particles, proteins, or people. If the phenomena are going to be religion and spirituality, then the science thereof is going to need to begin with deep empathy and engaged fascination. Now comes the rub: in order for it to be a science, this empathy and fascination must also include a certain distance, rigor, and objectivity. At every stage, we must resist the seduction of filtering our sciences of religion through ideological and apologetic filters, which invariably predetermine the results of our studies. Beware of rotten fruit in sheep's clothing, to mix Jesus's mixed metaphors, and radical-atheist scientists purporting to study religion. The corollary is to beware of devoted religionists purporting to study religion scientifically. In both cases, we will get different forms of apologetics with predetermined conclusions.

This book is also a kind of apologia, true, but one that seeks to be fair and balanced. E. O. Wilson writes in his book *Consilience* that "science faces in ethics and religion its most interesting and possibly humbling challenge, while religion must somehow find the way to incorporate the discoveries of science in order to retain credibility." This is a sage observation and sound advice for both sides. Wilson continues, "[T]he eventual result of the competition between the two world views, I believe, will be the secularization of the human epic and of religion itself." This is a statement of Wilson's own faith and not a necessary or even obvious conclusion to be drawn from science or history. Indeed, given the resurgence of religion in the world today, Wilson's hope appears utopic and counterfactual. He concludes, "However the process plays out, it demands open discussion and unwavering intellectual rigor in an atmosphere of mutual respect."[2] This, of course, I affirm; but the new sciences of religion still have a long way to go in fostering an atmosphere of mutual respect, open discussion, and unwavering intellectual rigor. I hope this book has helped contribute to such a dialogue.

The late Pope John Paul II weighed in on this very subject as well:

> Science can purify religion from error and superstition; religion can purify science from idolatry and false absolutes. Each can draw the other into a wider world, a world in which both can flourish.[3]

I would only add that error, superstition, idolatry, and false absolutes seem to be shared in different measures on both sides of the science and religion ledger. The corrective is certainly to be found in more and better science and in more and better religion, but especially in vigorous, open-ended exploration between both domains.

If I were to reduce the religious impulse to one word, it would be hope. Without some faith in the future, a sense of meaning and purpose that transcends the past and motivates the present, there would be no reason and no need for religion. In the first chapter of Genesis, God declares that life is "good," indeed "very good" when considered as a whole. That goodness is not a scientific statement, but a statement of faith that sooner or later will be put to the test in a world also filled with trials and tribulations, suffering and death. This transcendent hope gives meaning to the past, value to the present, and purpose to the future. Of course, as a nonreductive functionalist, I am not allowed to reduce religion to any one thing or word, but still I remain hopeful against all evidence to the contrary and see therein something of the magic and reality of the spiritual intuitions handed down to us by religions.

What is thought to be on the inside of religion and what is thought to be outside is something we should continually question. We need to be pushing on these boundaries, testing certain assumptions and prejudices. Religious people should be the first to erase the boundary. There is no reason to fear any of the sciences of religion. These are just an enlargement of the relevant curriculum and can be helpmates in the hermeneutics of authenticity that every religion confronts from the inside.

Nor can the scientifically minded atheist or secular society simply avoid existential, ethical, and metaphysical questions that are normally thought to be in the domain of religions. Indeed, in encountering these questions, scientists should expect to learn much from thousands of years of human experimentation and reflection by religions at different times and in different cultures. To my colleagues in the sciences, please do push the scientific envelope as far as possible but be humble and self-critical, as religious people must also be. And whether we are working from the top down or the bottom up, from the inside out or the outside in, we can hope to meet some day in the middle with many beautiful, good, and true stories to tell each other.

NOTES

Introduction

1. Google searches conducted on July 28, 2009.
2. Pascal Boyer, *Religion Explained: The Evolutionary Origins of Religious Thought* (New York: Basic Books, 2001); Richard Dawkins, *The God Delusion* (New York: Houghton Mifflin, 2006); Victor J. Stenger, *God: The Failed Hypothesis: How Science Shows That God Does Not Exist* (New York: Prometheus Books, 2007); Daniel C. Dennett, *Breaking the Spell: Religion as a Natural Phenomenon* (New York: Viking, 2006); Dean H. Hamer, *The God Gene: How Faith Is Hardwired into Our Genes* (New York: Anchor, 2005); Sam Harris, *The End of Faith: Religion, Terror, and the Future of Reason* (New York: W. W. Norton, 2004); Harris, *Letter to a Christian Nation* (New York: Knopf, 2006); David Sloan Wilson, *Darwin's Cathedral: Evolution, Religion, and the Nature of Society* (Chicago: University of Chicago Press, 2002).
3. *Nonreductive functionalism* is a term of art in the philosophy of mind. David Chalmers popularized the concept in his 1996 book *The Conscious Mind.* He argues that "consciousness can only be understood within a non-reductionist science of the mind." Consciousness is "supervenient" on physical states of the brain. Chalmers argues for "property dualism," that is, mental states cannot be fully reduced to and understood through biochemical, neuron-level analyses of the brain, contrary to the ambitions of physicalist reductionists such as John Searle and Daniel Dennett. See David J. Chalmer, *The Conscious Mind: In Search of a Fundamental Theory* (New York: Oxford University Press, 1996). My use of the term is related but greatly expanded beyond the domain of the cognitive sciences and the philosophy of mind.
4. Edwin A. Abbott, *Flatland: A Romance of Many Dimensions* (Project Gutenberg, 1884).
5. Alfred North Whitehead, *Science and the Modern World* (New York: Free Press, [1925] 1967), 51.
6. "Metanexus Institute," http://www.metanexus.net.
7. "Television" and "automobile" are examples of other modern bastard combinations of Greek and Latin words.
8. Edwin Schrödinger, "What Is Life?" http://whatislife.stanford.edu/Homepage/LoCo_files/What-is-Life.pdf.

1   The Challenge of Comparative Religion

1. "Adherents.Com: National & World Religion Statistics," http://www.adherents.com/Religions_By_Adherents.html.
2. Another source puts the number of distinct religions in the world at ten thousand, of which 150 have 1 million or more members. These statistics are put together to support Christian missionaries in David Barrett, George Kurian, and Todd Johnson, *World Christian Encyclopedia* (New York: Oxford University Press, 2001). The authors count some 33,830 denominations within Christianity.
3. Anthony F. C. Wallace, *Revitalizations and Mazeways: Essays on Culture Change*, ed. Robert S. Grumet, vol. 1 (Lincoln: University of Nebraska Press, 2003).
4. Daniel L. Overmyer, "Chinese Religion: An Overview," in *Encyclopedia of Religion*, ed. Lindsay Jones (New York: Macmillan Reference, 2005).

5. See, for instance, Sam Harris, *The End of Faith: Religion, Terror, and the Future of Reason* (New York: W. W. Norton, 2004); Harris, *Letter to a Christian Nation* (New York: Knopf, 2006); Richard Dawkins, *The God Delusion* (New York: Houghton Mifflin, 2003); Christopher Hitchens, *God Is Not Great: How Religion Poisons Everything* (New York: Hachette Books, 2007). For a thoughtful rebuttal, see John Haught, *God and the New Atheism: A Critical Response to Dawkins, Harris, and Hitchens* (Louisville, KY: Westminister John Knox Press, 2008).
6. Donald E. Brown, *Human Universals* (New York: McGraw-Hill, 1991).
7. See Mircea Eliade, *Patterns in Comparative Religion* (New York: Sheed & Ward, 1958); Eliade, *The Sacred and the Profane: The Nature of Religion*, trans. Willard R. Trask (New York: Harper Torchbooks, 1961); Eliade, *The Myth of the Eternal Return: Cosmos and History*, trans. Willard R. Trask (Princeton, NJ: Princeton University Press, 1971); and Eliade, *Myths, Rites, Symbols: A Mircea Eliade Reader*, ed. Wendell C. Beane and William G. Doty, vol. 2 (New York: Harper Colophon, 1976). For critics of Eliade, see G. S. Kirk, *Myth: Its Meaning and Functions in Ancient and Other Cultures* (Berkeley: University of California Press, 1973); Kirk, *The Nature of Greek Myths* (Harmondsworth: Penguin Books, 1974); Guilford Dudley III, *Religion on Trial: Mircea Eliade & His Critics* (Philadelphia: Temple University Press, 1977).
8. Carl Gustav Jung, *Psychology and Religion* (New Haven, CT: Yale University Press, [1938] 1966); *The Portable Jung*, ed. Joseph Campell (New York: Penguin, 1971).
9. It is not the case that Christianity and other religions necessarily reject the validity of other faiths, even as they might argue for their own superiority over other approaches. Part of the genius of Hindu civilization is its ability to absorb and incorporate many diverse religions and incompatible philosophies into its synthesizing spirit. Jews understand themselves to be a chosen people with a special covenant with God, but this is not to say that God does not also relate to other peoples and faiths. Islam also affirms the diversity of faiths as part of God's plan: "We have created you male and female, and have made you nations and tribes that you may know one another. The noblest of you, in the sight of Allah, is the best in conduct" (Qu'ran, Sura 49:13). These are complex texts and traditions, so other verses and examples also can be cited to contradict this implied inclusivity. At this stage, I need only note that particular religions recognize and sometimes affirm the legitimacy of other particular religions. Concerns about orthodoxy and heterodoxy are historically mostly matters internal to particular traditions, not so much between traditions.
10. George Santayana, *Life of Reason*, vol. 3, *Reason in Religion* (New York: Prometheus Books, [1905–06] 1998).
11. John Bowker, *The Sense of God* (Oxford: Oneworld Publications, [1973] 1995), x.
12. Paul Ricoeur, *Interpretation Theory: Discourse and the Surplus of Meaning* (Fort Worth: Texas Christian University Press, 1976).
13. Jack Miles, *God: A Biography* (New York: Alfred A. Knopf, 1995).
14. Stanley H. Ambrose, "Late Pleistocene Human Population Bottlenecks, Volcanic Winter, and Differentiation of Modern Humans," *Journal of Human Evolution* 34, no. 6 (1998); Ambrose, "Volcanic Winter, and Differentiation of Modern Humans," Bradshaw Foundation, http://www.bradshawfoundation.com/stanley_ambrose.php. Accessed June 12, 2009.

2　The Old Sciences of Religion

1. Michel Bourdeau, "Auguste Comte," in *Stanford Encyclopedia of Philosophy*, ed. Edward N. Zalta (Palo Alto, CA: Stanford University, 2008).
2. Ibid.; Frederick Ferré, *Introduction to Positive Philosophy Auguste Comte* (New York: Bobbs-Merrill Company, 1970); Andrew Wernick, *Auguste Comte and the Religion of Humanity: The Post-Theistic Program of French Social Theory* (New York: Cambridge University Press, 2001); Henri de Lubac, *The Drama of Atheist Humanism*, trans. Edith M. Riley and Anne Englund Nash (San Francisco: Ignatious Press, [1944] 1983); Gertrud Lenzer, "Introduction: Auguste Comte and Modern Positivism," in *Auguste Come and Positivism: The Essential Writings,* ed. Gertrud Lenzer (New Brunswick, NJ: Transaction Publishers, 2008).
3. Auguste Comte, "Plans for the Scientific Operations Necessary for Reorganizing Society" (1822), in *The Crisis in Industrial Civilization: The Early Writings of Auguste Comte*, ed. Ronald Fletcher (London: Heinemann, 1974), 144.

4. Ibid., 134.

5. Comte, "Philosophical Considerations on the Sciences and Savants" (1825), in *The Crisis in Industrial Civilization: The Early Writings of Auguste Comte*, ed. Ronald Fletcher (London: Heinemann, 1974), 192.

6. Comte, "Plans for the Scientific Operations," 134.

7. Comte, "Philosophical Considerations," 185.

8. Auguste Comte, *The Positive Philosophy*, trans. Harriet Martineau (New York: AMS Press, [1842] 1974), 558.

9. Comte, "Philosophical Considerations," 185.

10. Ibid., 187.

11. Ibid.

12. Comte, *Positive Philosophy*, 36.

13. Auguste Comte, "Considerations on the Spiritual Power" (1826), in *The Crisis of Industrial Civilization: The Early Essays of Auguste Comte*, ed. Ronald Fletcher (London: Heinemann, 1974), 236.

14. Ibid., 241.

15. Comte, "Philosophical Considerations," 199.

16. Comte, *System of Positive Polity, or Treatise on Sociology: Instituting the Religion of Humanity*, trans. Frederic Harrison, 3 vols., vol. 2 (New York: B. Franklin, [1852] 1968), 47.

17. Ibid., 296.

18. Richard McCarty, "Comte's Positivist Calendar," East Carolina University, http://personal.ecu.edu/mccartyr/pos-cal.html.

19. Comte, *System of Positive Polity*, 45.

20. John Stuart Mill, *Auguste Comte and Positivism* (Project Gutenberg, 1865).

21. This analysis of Comte's significance in ten points in the thinking of other nineteenth- and early twentieth-century theorists of religion draws on primary-source material as well as the following books: Daniel L. Pals, *Eight Theories of Religion*, 2nd ed. (New York: Oxford University Press, 2006); Eric J. Sharpe, *Comparative Religion: A History*, 5th ed. (Chicago, IL: Open Court Publishing, 1986); J. Samuel Preus, *Explaining Religion: Criticism and Theory from Bodin to Freud*, ed. Terry Godlove, Texts and Translation Series, American Academy of Religion (Atlanta, GA: Scholars Press, 1996); and Ronald Fletcher, ed. *The Crisis of Industrial Civilization: The Early Essays of Auguste Comte* (London: Heinemann Educational Books,1974).

22. Sigmund Freud, *Totem and Taboo* (New York: Prometheus Books, [1918] 2000); Freud, *Future of an Illusion* ([1927]); Freud, *Civilization and Its Discontents* (New York: W.W. Norton, [1930] 1961).

23. Ludwig Feuerbach, *The Essence of Christianity*, trans. George Eliot (New York: Harper Torchbooks, 1843 [1957]); Karl Marx and Friedrich Engels, *Basic Writings on Politics and Philosophy*, ed. Lewis S. Feuer (New York: Doubleday, 1959).

24. J. H. Brooke, *Science and Religion: Some Historical Perspectives* (Cambridge: Cambridge University Press,1999); Richard Boyd, Philip Gasper, and J. D. Trout, eds., *The Philosophy of Science* (Cambridge, MA, and London: MIT Press,1991).

25. In Plato's *Republic* we get a similar account of religion in the need for a Noble Lie to motivate the service and sacrifice of the Guardians.

26. Émile Durkheim, *The Elementary Forms of the Religious Life*, trans. Joseph Ward Swain (New York: The Free Press, [1912] 1915), 44.

27. Clifford Geertz, *The Interpretation of Cultures* (New York: Harper, 1973).

28. Mary Midgley, *Science as Salvation: A Modern Myth and Its Meaning* (New York: Routledge, 1994).

29. George M. Marsden, *Soul of the American University: From Protestant Establishment to Established Nonbelief* (New York: Oxford University Press, 1996); David A. Hollinger, *Science, Jews, and Secular Culture: Studies in Mid-Twentieth-Century American Intellectual History* (Princeton, NJ: Princeton University Press, 1996).

30. Freud, *Totem and Taboo*; Freud, *Civilization and Its Discontents*.

31. Maximillian Weber, *The Protestant Ethic and the Spirit of Capitalism* (New York: Charles Scribner's Sons, [1905] 1958); Weber, *The Sociology of Religion*, trans. Ephraim Fischoff (Boston, MA: Beacon Press, [1922] 1963); Weber, *The Religion of India*, trans. Hans Gerth and Don Martindale (Glencoe, IL: Free Press, [1920] 1958); Weber, *The Religion of China*, trans. Hans Gerth (Glencoe, IL: Free Press, [1920] 1951).

32. Andrew Dickson White, *A History of the Warfare of Science with Theology in Christendom* (Project Gutenberg, 1896).
33. William James, *Varieties of Religious Experience* (New York: Macmillian, [1902] 1961).
34. Geertz, *Interpretation of Cultures*, 90.
35. E. B. Tylor, *Religion in Primitive Culture* (New York: Harper Torchbooks, [1871] 1958), 9.
36. Walter Burkert, *Creation of the Sacred: Tracks of Biology in Early Religion* (Cambridge, MA: Harvard University Press, 1996), 177.
37. Scott Atran, *In Gods We Trust: The Evolutionary Landscape of Religion* (New York: Oxford University Press, 2002), 4.
38. Pascal Boyer, *Religion Explained: The Evolutionary Origins of Religious Thought*, 7, 307.
39. See for instance, Stephen M. Kossyln, "A Science of the Divine," *Edge*, http://www.edge.org/q2006/q06_9.html#kosslyn.
40. For background on transhumanism, see Nick Bostrom et al., "H+: Transhumanism Answers Its Critics," *Metanexus*, http://www.metanexus.net/magazine/PastIssues/tabid/126/Default.aspx?PageContentID=33. For a critique of transhumanism, see Hava Tirosh-Samuelson et al., "Special Issue on Transhumanism," *Metanexus*, http://www.metanexus.net/magazine/PastIssues/tabid/126/Default.aspx?PageContentID=27.
41. For an excellent analysis of these authors, see John Haught, *God and the New Atheism: A Critical Response to Dawkins, Harris, and Hitchens* (Louisville, KY: Westminister John Knox Press, 2008).

3   The Economics of Religion

1. These are 2008 estimates. See Central Intelligence Agency, "The World Factbook," https://www.cia.gov/library/publications/the-world-factbook/geos/xx.html. See also Eric D. Beinhocker, *The Origin of Wealth: Evolution, Complexity, and the Radical Remaking of Economics* (Cambridge, MA: Harvard Business Press, 2006), 9.
2. The question of limits of growth and sustainable development are real and serious. See J. Robert McNeill, *Something New under the Sun: An Environmental History of the Twentieth-Century World* (New York: W. W. Norton, 2000); J. Robert McNeill and William H. McNeill, *The Human Web: A Bird's-Eye View of World History* (New York: W. W. Norton, 2003). See also William J. Grassie, "Re-Reading Economics: In Search of New Economic Metaphors for Biological Evolution," *Metanexus* (2007), http://www.metanexus.net/Magazine/ArticleDetail/tabid/68/id/9932/Default.aspx.
3. Beinhocker, *Origin of Wealth*.
4. Robert Wright, *Non-Zero: The Logic of Human Destiny* (New York: Pantheon, 2000).
5. See, for instance, D. Stephen Long, *Divine Economy: Theology and the Market* (New York: Routledge, 2000).
6. One can also argue that religions are *discovered*, that religions offer fundamental insights about the nature of ultimate reality, while at the same time recognizing that religions create and invent new forms of thought and behavior.
7. The term *social capital* first appeared in 1916. The term *human capital* first appeared in a 1961 article by the Nobel Prize–winning economist Theodore W. Shultz. See also Robert D. Putnam, *Making Democracy Work* (Princeton, NJ: Princeton University Press, 1993) and Putnam, *Bowling Alone: The Collapse and Revival of American Community* (New York: Simon & Schuster, 2000). For other citations and a review of the literature, see Theodore Roosevelt Malloch, "Social, Human, and Spiritual Capital in Economic Development," *Metanexus*, http://www.metanexus.net/spiritual_capital/research_articles.asp.; and Laurence R. Iannaccone and Jonathan Klick, "Spiritual Capital: An Introduction and Literature Review," *Metanexus*, http://www.metanexus.net/spiritual_capital/research_review.asp.
8. At the Metanexus Institute, I helped manage a major grants project on "spiritual capital" with funding from the John Templeton Foundation. We loosely defined spiritual capital as "the effects of spiritual and religious practices, beliefs, networks and institutions that have a measurable impact on individuals, communities and societies."
9. "Spiritual Capital," *Metanexus*, http://www.metanexus.net/spiritual_capital.
10. See "Society for the Scientific Study of Religion," http://www.sssrweb.org/, and "Association for the Study of Religion, Economics and Culture," http://www.religionomics.com/.

11. Weber, *The Protestant Ethic and the Spirit of Capitalism* (New York: Charles Scribner's Sons, [1905] 1958); Weber, *The Sociology of Religion,* trans. Ephraim Fischoff (Boston, MA: Beacon Press, [1922] 1963). See also Peter L Berger and Robert W. Hefner, "Spiritual Capital in Comparative Perspective," *Metanexus,* http://www.metanexus.net/spiritual_capital/pdf/Berger.pdf.

12. Rodney Stark, *The Victory of Reason: How Christianity Led to Freedom, Capitalism, and Western Success* (New York: Random House, 2006).

13. Peter L. Berger et al., *The Desecularization of the World: Resurgent Religion and World Politics* (New York: Wm. B. Eerdmans, 1999).

14. Francis Fukuyama, "Social Capital," in *Culture Matters: How Values Shape Human Progress,* ed. Lawrence Harrison and Samuel P. Huntington (New York: Basic Books, 2000), 106.

15. Rodney Stark, *The Victory of Reason.*

16. Timur Kuran, *Islam & Mammon: The Economic Predicaments of Islamism* (Princeton, NJ: Princeton University Press, 2004).

17. United Nations Development Programme, "Arab Human Development Report," http://www.arab-hdr.org., 2004, 2005, #940.

18. Bernard Lewis, *What Went Wrong? The Clash between Islam and Modernity in the Middle East* (New York: Oxford University Press, 2002).

19. Korinna Horta, "Dateline Chad: Return of the 'Resource Curse'?" *The Globalist,* August 25, 2006.

20. Kuran, *Islam & Mammon,* 58.

21. Ibid., 21.

22. Ibid., 16.

23. Ibid., 20–21.

24. Notes from a lecture given by Timur Kuran, "The Role of Islamic Law in the Economic Evolution of the Middle East," at the Association of the Study of Religion, Economics and Culture (ASREC), Rochester, NY, 2005.

25. David Landes, "Culture Makes Almost All the Difference," in Harrison and Huntington, *Culture Matters,* 2–13.

26. Jen'nan Ghazal Read, "Muslims in America," *Contexts: Understanding People in their Social Worlds,* Fall 2008, 37–41.

27. Deirdre N. McCloskey, *The Bourgeois Virtues: Ethics for an Age of Commerce* (Chicago: University of Chicago Press, 2007). See also McCloskey, "What Would Jesus Spend? Why Being a Good Christian Won't Hurt the Economy," John Templeton Foundation, http://www.incharacter.org/article.php?article=8.

28. Adam Smith, *The Theory of Moral Sentiments,* 1790 ed. (London: A. Millar, 1759).

29. Adam Smith, *An Inquiry into the Nature and Causes of the Wealth of Nations* (London: Methuen and Co., 1776), book 1, ch. 1, p. 4.

30. The term *sacred canopy* is taken from Peter L. Berger, *The Sacred Canopy: Elements of a Sociological Theory of Religion* (New York: Doubleday, 1967).

31. I would argue that the religious impulse expresses itself in Western Europe in new forms like Communism and environmentalism, recalling our earlier discussion of "primary subgroup identity."

32. Gary Becker, "Keynote Address," paper presented at the "Spiritual Capital Conference," Cambridge, MA, October 9, 2003. Reprinted in *Spiritual Capital* (Philadelphia, PA: Metanexus Institute, 2003); Laurence R. Iannaccone, "The Economics of Religion: A Survey of Recent Work," *Journal of Economic Literature* 36 (September1998): 1465–1496.

33. Robert Woodbury, "Missionary Data (1813–1968) as a Resource for Testing Religious Economies and Secularization Theory," paper presented at the Association for the Study of Religion, Economics and Culture, Rochester, NY, November 4, 2005.

34. Rodney Stark, *The Rise of Christianity: How the Obscure, Marginal Jesus Movement Became the Dominant Religious Force* (New York: HarperCollins, 1997).

35. As quoted by Beinhocker, *Origin of Wealth,* 52.

36. Rodney Stark and Roger Finke, *Acts of Faith: Explaining the Human Side of Religion* (Berkeley: University of California Press, 2000), 121, 123.

37. David Sloan Wilson, *Darwin's Cathedral: Evolution, Religion, and the Nature of Society* (Chicago: University of Chicago Press, 2002).

38. A survey of paper topics recently presented at one of the annual meetings of the Association for the Study of Religion, Economics and Culture (ASREC) gives us some idea of the wealth of

empirical and theoretical insights derived from this new research program in the field of economics, sociology, and political science. I can only list a few here and refer you to the website for the details:

- Spirituality, Socially Referenced Preferences, and the Afterlife
- Efficiency Comparison between Conventional Development Aid and Missionary Work
- Religion, Attitudes toward Working Mothers and Wives' Full-time Employment: Evidence for Germany, Italy, and the UK
- Did Religion Have Anything to Do with Success and Failure in the Post-Communist Transition?
- Greedy Sects and the Jealous States: The Political Logic of Religious Regulation
- Egalitarianism and Economics: American Jewish Families
- Does Low Religious Market Share Boost Recruitment Efforts?
- The Marketplace of Religion: Reflections on the Rise of the Dge lugs School in Tibet
- The Afterlife as a Disciplinary Device: On Purgatory and the Credibility of Postmortem Prayers in Medieval Christian Chantries
- Religion and Economic Development: Weber was Right!
- Cultural Transformations and "Islamic Capitalism" in Malaysia from 1971 to the Present
- Performance Incentives and Contracts for Clergy Labor
- Moving on Over: Geographic Mobility as a Predictor of Switching and Attendance Frequency in American Religion

This list is presented to illustrate that there are lots of interesting questions and research projects that can result from using economic models to study religious behavior. See ASREC, http://www.religionomics.com/asrec/asrec07_program.html.

39. Robert H. Nelson, *Economics as Religion: From Samuelson to Chicago and Beyond* (State College: Penn State University Press, 2001).

40. Plato, *The Last Days of Socrates: Euthyphro, Apology, Crito, Phaedo*, trans. Hugh Tredennick and Harold Tarrant (New York: Penguin Classics, 1993), 53. Of course, Job would disagree! He was a righteous man who suffered of no fault of his own. Jesus and Buddha are also ambivalent on this point. Goodness, in their view, leads to voluntary poverty. A cross to bear!

4　The Evolution of Religion

1. McNeill and McNeill, The Human Web: A Bird's-Eye View of World History (New York: W.W. Norton, 2003); Jared Diamond, Guns, Germs, and Steel: The Fates of Human Societies (New York: W. W. Norton, 1997, 1999); Ian Tattersall, Becoming Human: Evolution and Human Uniqueness (New York: Harcourt Brace, 1998); David Christian, Maps of Time: An Introduction to Big History (Berkeley: University of California Press, 2004).

2. Phineas Taylor Barnum (1810–1891) was an American showman who founded a circus that is known today as "The Ringling Brothers and Barnum & Bailey Circus—The Greatest Show on Earth." In another age, P. T. Barnum might have been a very successful religious entrepreneur. The quote that is ascribed to him, apocryphally, makes the point. People believe and pass on lots of hearsay that is not true, though it quickly becomes taken for granted.

3. In this discussion, I follow a similar overview presented by Pascal Boyer, *Religion Explained: The Evolutionary Origins of Religious Thought* (New York: Basic Books, 2001), 1–50.

4. See, for instance, John Cartwright, *Evolution and Human Behavior: Darwinian Perspectives on Human Nature* (New York: Palgrave Macmillan, 2000).

5. See Donald E. Brown, *Human Universals* (New York: McGraw-Hill, 1991).

6. When traced on the male side through the Y-chromosome, our earliest common male ancestor appeared about sixty thousand years ago. When traced on the female side through mitochondrial DNA, our earliest common female ancestor would be about 140,000 years old. "Adam" and "Eve," if we want to be playful, did not know each other, not in the biblical sense or otherwise; and they would not have been lonely, as there would have been lots of other human around in their respective tribes. For more information on our common ancestors, see Richard Dawkins, *The Ancestors' Tale: A Pilgrimage to the Dawn of Evolution* (New York: Houghton Mifflin, 2004).

7. Stanley H. Ambrose, "Late Pleistocene Human Population Bottlenecks, Volcanic Winter, and Differentiation of Modern Humans," *Journal of Human Evolution* 34, no. 6 (1998): 623–51; Ambrose, "Volcanic Winter, and Differentiation of Modern Humans," Bradshaw Foundation, http://www.bradshawfoundation.com/stanley_ambrose.php.

8. See William H. Durham, *Coevolution: Genes, Culture, and Human Diversity* (Palo Alto, CA: Stanford University Press, 1992).

9. Take the Asian elephant as an example. With an average life span of sixty years, it reaches sexual maturity around twelve years of age. Pregnancy lasts for about 1.5 years, followed by three years of nursing. If we assume a female fertility of forty years, a single female is capable of giving birth to perhaps ten offspring in her lifetime. That is a growth rate of .25 per year over forty years, which with compound exponential growth would "take off" in a steep climb within a hundred years, thus covering the entire island of Sri Lanka with elephants shoulder to shoulder. The same calculations taken for the tiny aphids in the corner of the room show that aphids would cover the entire surface of the planet within a year of unconstrained reproduction.

10. Charles Darwin, *The Origin of Species* (1859). http://www.gutenberg.org/etext/2009.

11. See Edward J. Larson, *Summer of the Gods: The Scopes Trial and America's Continuing Debate over Science and Religion* (Cambridge, MA: Harvard University Press, 1997).

12. See Edward O. Wilson, *Sociobiology: The New Synthesis* (Cambridge, MA: Harvard University Press, 1975); Wilson, *On Human Nature* (Cambridge, MA: Harvard University Press, 1978).

13. See Cartwright, *Evolution and Human Behavior.*

14. Charles Darwin, *The Descent of Man* (1871). http://www.gutenberg.org/etext/2300.

15. Wilson, *On Human Nature.*

16. Luke 10:29–37. See also Holmes Rolston, "The Good Samritan and His Genes," *Metanexus* (1999), http://www.metanexus.net/Magazine/tabid/68/id/3021/Default.aspx.

17. Richard Dawkins, *The Selfish Gene* (New York: Oxford University Press, 1976).

18. William D. Hamilton, "The Genetical Evolution of Social Behavior," *Journal of Theoretical Biology* 7 (1964): 1–16.

19. This is an example of the Nash equilibrium, also known as an evolutionary stable strategy. Prisoner A defects and Prisoner B defects, and that's that.

20. Paul Ekman, *Emotions Revealed: Recognizing Faces and Feelings to Improve Communication and Emotional Life* (New York: Times Books, 2003).

21. Michael T. Ghiselin, *The Economy of Nature and the Evolution of Sex* (Berkeley: University of California Press, 1974).

22. Wilson, *On Human Nature,* 167.

23. See Pitrim A. Sorokin, *The Ways and Power of Love: Types, Factors, and Techniques of Moral Transformation* (Conshohocken, PA: Templeton Foundation Press, [1954] 2002); Stephen G. Post, *Unlimited Love: Altruism, Compassion, and Service* (Conshohocken, PA: Templeton Foundation Press, 2003); Stephen G. Post et al., eds., *Research on Altruism and Love: An Annotated Bibliography of Major Studies in Psychology, Sociology, Evolutionary Biology, and Theology* (Conshohocken, PA: Templeton Foundation Press,2003).

24. Mary Midgley, *The Ethical Primate: Humans, Freedom, and Morality* (New York: Routledge, 1994).

25. Daniel C. Dennett, "Review of Burkert's Creation of the Sacred,"(1996), http://philpapers.org/rec/DENROB.

26. Two recent anthologies bring this literature and many of the scholars together in edited volumes. See Joseph Bulbulia et al., eds., *The Evolution of Religion: Studies, Theories, & Critiques* (Santa Margarita, CA: Collins Foundation Press, 2008), and Jay R. Feierman, ed, *The Biology of Religious Behavior: The Evolutionary Origins of Faith and Religion* (Westport, CT: Praeger, 2009).

27. Dawkins, *Selfish Gene.*

28. Susan Blackmore, *The Meme Machine* (New York: Oxford University Press, 1999).

29. Richard Dawkins, *Unweaving the Rainbow: Science, Delusion, and the Appetite for Wonder* (Boston, MA: Houghton Mifflin, 1998).

30. Richard Dawkins, *A Devil's Chaplain: Reflections on Hope, Lies, Science, and Love* (Boston, MA: Houghton Mifflin, 2003).

31. Stephen Jay Gould and R. D. Lewontin, "The Spandrels of San Marco and the Panglossian Paradigm: A Critique of the Adaptationist Programme," *Proceedings of the Royal Society of London* 205 (1979).

32. Boyer, *Religion Explained,* 50.

33. Ilkka Pyysiäinen and Veikko Anttonen, eds., *Current Approaches in the Cognitive Science of Religion* (New York: Continuum, 2002).
34. The analysis of the Balinese Water Temple system might be applied also to understanding the role of Buddhism in the distributed maintenance of the irrigation system in ancient Sri Lanka civilization.
35. David Sloan Wilson, *Darwin's Cathedral: Evolution, Religion, and the Nature of Society* (Chicago: University of Chicago Press, 2002), 217.
36. Ibid., 228.
37. Ibid., 230.
38. Jean Baptiste Lamarck (1744–1829) was a French biologist who advanced a theory of evolution prior to Darwin. Lamarck theorized that acquired characteristics of species striving in their environments would be passed on to the next generation. This turns out not to be true in nature, at least not directly, but it is certainly true of human culture.

5   The Neurosciences of Religion

1. Boyer, *Religion Explained: The Evolutionary Origins of Religious Thought* (New York: Basic Books, 2001).
2. F. A. Azevedo et al., "Equal Numbers of Neuronal and Nonneuronal Cells Make the Human Brain an Isometrically Scaled-up Primate Brain," *Journal of Comparative Neurology* 513, no. 5 (2009); R. W. Williams and K. Herrup, "The Control of Neuron Number," *Annual Review of Neuroscience* 11 (1988).
3. Andrew Newberg, "Religious and Spiritual Practices: A Neurochemical Perspective," in *Where God and Science Meet*, ed. Patrick McNamara (Westport, CT: Praeger, 2006).
4. David B. Larson et.al., "Religious Content in the Dsm-Iii-R Glossary of Technical Terms," *American Journal of Psychiatry* 150 (1993).
5. David J. Hufford, "An Analysis of the Field of Spirituality, Religion, and Health," *Metanexus* (2005), http://www.metanexus.net/metanexus_online/show_article2.asp?id=9387.
6. V. S. Ramachandran and Sandra Blakeslee, *Phantoms in the Brain* (New York: HarperCollins, 1998).
7. V. S. Ramachandran, "Beyond Belief 2006 Conference Lecture," *TSN: The Science Network*, http://thesciencenetwork.org/programs/beyond-belief-science-religion-reason-and-survival.
8. David J. Hufford, *The Terror That Comes in the Night: An Experience-Centered Study of Supernatural Assault Traditions* (Philadelphia: University of Pennsylvania Press, 1982).
9. See Ian Barbour, *Myths, Models, and Paradigms* (New York: Harper and Row, 1974).
10. Paul Ricoeur, *Interpretation Theory: Discourse and the Surplus of Meaning* (Fort Worth: Texas Christian University Press, 1976).
11. Ramachandran and Blakeslee, *Phantoms in the Brain*.
12. Julian Jaynes, *The Origin of Consciousness in the Breakdown of the Bicameral Mind* (New York: Houghton Mifflin, 1976).
13. John Horgan, *Rational Mysticism* (New York: Houghton Mifflin, 2003).
14. Andrew Newberg and Eugene D'Aquili, *The Mystical Mind* (Minneapolis, MN: Fortress Press, 1999); Newberg and D'Aquili, "The Neuropsychology of Religious and Spiritual Experience," *Journal of Consciousness Studies* 7, nos. 11–12 (2000).
15. Andrew Newberg and Eugene D'Aquili, *Why God Won't Go Away: Brain Science and the Biology of Belief* (New York: Ballantine Books, 2001).
16. Ronald Siegel, *Intoxication* (New York: E. P. Dutton, 1989).
17. Horgan, *Rational Mysticism*.
18. Ibid.
19. Jeremy Sherman, "Meditation and Future Pharmaceuticals: A Short Science Fiction," *Metanexus* (1999), http://www.metanexus.net/Magazine/tabid/68/id/3062/Default.aspx.
20. D. Kelemen, "Are Children "Intuitive Theists"?: Reasoning About Purpose and Design in Nature," *Psychological Science* 15 (2004); Justin L. Barrett, *Why Would Anyone Believe in God?* (Lanham, MD: Altamira, 2004); Paul Bloom, "Is God an Accident?" *Atlantic Monthly*, December 2005, http://www.theatlantic.com/doc/200512/god-accident.
21. Candace S. Alcorta, "Religion and the Life Course: Is Adolescence An 'Experience Expectant' Period for Religious Transmission?" in McNamara, *Where God and Science Meet*.

22. This is a compilation of different typologies of religious experience. See Ian Barbour, *Religion in an Age of Science: The Gifford Lectures 1989–1991*, vol. 1 (San Francisco: Harper, 1990), 36–38; Carolyn F. Davis, *The Evidential Force of Religious Experience* (New York: Oxford University Press, 1989), ch 2; and James Fowler, *Stages of Faith: The Psychology of Human Development and the Quest for Meaning* (San Francisco: Harper, 1981).
23. John B. S. Haldane, "When I Am Dead," in *Possible Worlds and Other Essays* (London: Chatto and Windus, [1927] 1932).
24. B. Allan Wallace, *The Taboo of Subjectivity: Towards a New Science of Consciousness* (New York: Oxford University Press, 2000).
25. Petr Janata is conducting these kinds of studies at UC Davis with funding from the Metanexus Institute and the John Templeton Foundation. Petr Janata, Center for Mind and Brain, UC Davis, http://atonal.ucdavis.edu.
26. Horgan, *Rational Mysticism*.
27. William J. Grassie, "Useless Arithmetic and Inconvenient Truths: A Review," *Metanexus* (2007), http://www.metanexus.net/Magazine/tabid/68/id/9854/Default.aspx.
28. Jaron Lanier, "One-Half of a Manifesto: Why Stupid Software Will Save the Future from Neo-Darwinian Machines," *WIRED* 8, no.12 (1999).
29. William James, *A Pluralistic Universe* (Cambridge, MA: Harvard University Press, [1909] 1977), 142.
30. William James, *Varieties of Religious Experience* (New York: Macmillian, [1902] 1961), 456.

6 The Medicine of Religion

1. H. G. Koenig, M E. McCullough, and D. B. Larson, *Handbook of Religion and Health* (New York: Oxford University Press, 2001), 18.
2. Peter C. Hill and Ralph W. Hood, *Measures of Religiosity* (Birmingham, AL: Religious Education Press, 1999).
3. Fetzer Institute, "Multidimensional Measurement of Religiousness/Spirituality for Use in Health Research"(1999), http://www.fetzer.org/research/248-dses.
4. R. Barker Bausell, *Snake Oil Science: The Truth about Complementary and Alternative Medicine* (New York: Oxford University Press, 2007), 41–42.
5. Ibid., 169.
6. For a review of religion and mortality studies, see Koenig, McCullough, and Larson, *Handbook of Religion and Health*, 318–30.
7. Robert D. Putnam, *Bowling Alone: The Collapse and Revival of American Community* (New York: Simon & Schuster, 2000).
8. Metanexus Institute ran a multidimensional scientific study of spiritual transformation. One of the interesting results was survey work that suggested that 50 percent of people in the United States have had such a dramatic spiritual transformation. Tom W. Smith, "The National Spiritual Transformation Study," *Journal for the Scientific Study of Religion* 45, no. 2 (2006).
9. Edward F. Kelly et al., *Irreducible Mind: Toward a Psychology for the 21st Century* (Lanham, MD: Rowan & Littlefield, 2007), 367–422.
10. Koenig, McCullough, and Larson, *Handbook of Religion and Health*.
11. J. D. Kark et al., "Does Religious Observance Promote Health? Mortality in Secular vs. Religious Kibbutzim in Israel," *American Journal of Public Health* 86, no. 3 (1996). This study is also reviewed in Koenig, McCullough, and Larson, *Handbook of Religion and Health*, 327–28.
12. G. Ironson, R. Stuetzle et al., "View of God Is Associated with Disease Progression in HIV," in *Society of Behavioral Medicine* (San Francisco: Annals of Behavioral Medicine, 2006). See also Gail Ironson, R. Stuetzle R, and M. A. Fletcher, "An Increase in Religiousness/Spirituality Occurs after HIV Diagnosis and Predicts Slower Disease Progression over 4 Years in People with HIV," *Journal of General Internal Medicine*, no. 5 (2006); G. Ironson, O'Cleirigh et al., "Psychosocial Factors Predict Cd4 and Vl Change in Men and Women with Human Immunodeficiency Virus in the Era of Highly Active Antiretroviral Treatment," *Psychosomatic Medicine* 67, no. 6 (2005); G. Ironson, G. F. Solomon et al., "The Ironson-Woods Spirituality/Religiousness Index Is Associated with Long Survival, Health Behaviors, Less Distress, and Low Cortisol in People with HIV/AIDS," *Annals of Behavioral Medicine* 24, no. 1 (2002); and Gail Ironson, Heidemarie

Kremer, and Dale Ironson, "Spirituality, Spiritual Experiences, and Spiritual Transformation in the Face of HIV," in *Spiritual Transformation and Healing*, ed. Philip and Joan D. Koss-Chioino Hefner (Lanham, MD: Altamira Press, 2006).

13. L. Roberts et al., "Intercessory Prayer for the Alleviation of Ill Health," *Cochrane Database System Review* 2, no. CD000368 (2009).

14. H. .Benson et al., "Study of the Therapeutic Effects of Intercessory Prayer (Step) in Cardiac Bypass Patients: A Multicenter Randomized Trial of Uncertainty and Certainty of Receiving Intercessory Prayer," *American Heart Journal* 151, no. 4 (2006).

15. Benedict Carey, "Can Prayers Heal? Critics Say Studies Go Past Science's Reach," *New York Times*, October 10, 2004.

16. Richard P. Sloan, "Field Analysis of the Literature on Religion, Spirituality, and Health," *Metanexus* (2005), http://www.metanexus.net/metanexus_online/show_article2.asp?id=9467.

17. Stephen G. Post, ed., *Altruism and Health: Perspectives from Empirical Research* (New York: Oxford University Press, 2007).

18. Herbert Benson, "Institute for Mind-Body Medicine," http://www.mbmi.org/; Benson, *Timeless Healing* (New York: Fireside, Simon and Schuster, 1996); Benson, *The Relaxation Response* (New York: Harper, 1975).

19. Jon Kabat-Zinn, "Center for Mindfulness in Medicine, Health Care, and Society," University of Massachusetts Medical School, http://www.umassmed.edu/Content.aspx?id=41252; Kabat-Zin, *Wherever You Go You Are There* (New York: Hyperion, 1995).

20. Noah Schachtman, "Army's New PTSD Treatment: Yoga, Reiki, 'Bioenergy,'" *WIRED*, March 25, 2008; Schachtman, "Walter Reed Using Yoga to Fight PTSD," *WIRED*, May 6, 2008.

21. Dolores Krieger, *The Therapeutic Touch: How to Use Your Hands to Help or Heal* (Englewood Cliffs, NJ: Prentice-Hall, 1979); , "Therapeutic Touch: The Imprimatur of Nursing," *American Journal of Nursing* 75 (1975).

22. David J. Hufford, "An Analysis of the Field of Spirituality, , Religion, and Health," *Metanexus* (2005), http://www.metanexus.net/metanexus_online/show_article2.asp?id=9387.

23. Koenig, McCullough, and Larson, *Handbook of Religion and Health*, 5.

24. NIH Consensus Development Program, "Acupuncture—Consensus Development Conference Statement," May 15, 1997, http://consensus.nih.gov/1997/1997Acupuncture107html.htm.

25. Bausell, *Snake Oil Science*.

26. Arthur K. Shapiro and Elaine Shapiro, "The Placebo: Is It Much Ado About Nothing?" in *The Placebo Effect: An Interdisciplinary Exploration*, ed. Anne Harrington (Cambridge, MA: Harvard University Press, 1997).

27. Howard L. Fields and Donald D. Price, "Toward a Neurobiology of Placebo Analgesia," in Harrington, *The Placebo Effect*; P. Petrovic et al., "Placebo and Opioid Analgesia—Imaging a Shared Neuronal Network," *Science* 295, no. 5560 (2002).

28. Esther Sternberg, *The Balance Within: The Science Connecting Health and Emotions* (New York: W.H. Freeman, 2001).

29. National Institutes of Health, "The Science of the Placebo," http://placebo.nih.gov.

30. Ibid.

31. In 1955, H. K. Beecher claimed a 35 percent placebo effect in fifteen studies; Henry K. Beecher, "The Powerful Placebo," *Journal of the American Medical Association* 159 (1955). This study and others were reanalyzed in 2001 and 2004 by Hrobjartsson and Gotzsche, who found no significant placebo effect. Improved health outcomes were instead "due to spontaneous improvements, fluctuation of symptoms, regression to the mean, additional treatment, conditional switching of placebo treatment, scaling bias, irrelevant response variables, answers of politeness, experimental subordination, conditioned answers, neurotic or psychotic misjudgment, psychosomatic phenomena, misquotation, etc." Note that many of the confounders listed in their study are actually placebo-linked variables, for example, "answers of politeness, conditioned answers, psychosomatic phenomena." A. Hrobjartsson and P. Gotzsche, "Is the Placebo Powerless? An Analysis of Clinical Trial Comparing Placebo with No Treatment," *New England Journal of Medicine* 344 (2001): 1594–1602 ; Hrobjartsson and Gotzsche, "Is the Placebo Powerless? Update of a Systematic Review of 52 New Randomized Trials Comparing Placebo with No Treatment," *Journal of Internal Medicine* 256 (2004): 91–100.

32. Sissela Bok, "The Ethics of Giving Placebos," *Scientific American* 231 (1975).
33. Patricia Leigh-Brown, "A Doctor for Disease, a Shaman for the Soul," *New York Times*, September 19, 2009, http://www.nytimes.com/2009/09/20/us/20shaman.html?_r=1&hp.
34. Koenig, McCullough, and Larson, *Handbook of Religion and Health.*
35. Richard P. Sloan, *Blind Faith: The Unholly Alliance of Religion and Medicine* (New York: St. Martin's Press, 2006), 4.
36. Christopher Peterson and Martin E. P. Seligman, *Character Strengths and Virtues* (New York: Oxford University Press, 2004); Martin E. P. Seligman, *Authentic Happiness: Using the New Postive Psychology to Realize Your Potential for Lasting Fulfillment* (New York: Free Press, 2002).
37. Sloan, "Field Analysis of the Literature on Religion, Spirituality, and Health."
38. See N.A. Christakis and J.H. Fowler. *Connected: The Surprising Power of Our Social Networks and How They Shape Our Lives.* (New York: Little, Brown and Company, 2009); Clive Thompson, "Are Your Friends Making You Fat?" *New York Times Magazine,* September 10, 2009, http://www.nytimes.com/2009/09/13/magazine/13contagion-t.html?ref=magazine.
39. See Anne Harrington, *The Cure Within: A History of Mind-Body Medicine* (New York: W.W. Norton, 2008); Anne Harrington et al., "The Science of the Placebo: Toward an Interdisciplinary Research Agenda," paper presented at the NIH, Bethesda, MD, 2000, http://placebo.nih.gov; and Harrington, *The Placebo Effect.*
40. T. J. Kaptchuk et al., "Sham Device V Inert Pill: Randomised Controlled Trial of Two Placebo Treatments," *British Medical Journal* 132, no. 7538 (2006): 391–97; A. J. M. de Craen, P. J. Roos et al., "Effect of Colour of Drugs: Systematic Review of Perceived Effect of Drugs and of Their Effectiveness," *British Medical Journal* 313, no. 7072 (1996).
41. Bausell, *Snake Oil Science,* 291–94.
42. Thomas Szasz, *The Second Sin* (Garden City, NY: Doubleday, 1974), 128.

7   The Narratives of Religion

1. Robert Wright provides a thorough review of the historical critical perspective on sacred texts in his new book *The Evolution of God* (New York: Little, Brown, 2009).
2. "Catechism of the Catholic Church," http://www.scborromeo.org/ccc.htm.
3. Charles Taylor, *Sources of the Self* (Cambridge, MA: Harvard University Press, 1989). Paul Ricoeur, *Time and Narrative,* trans. Kathleen and David Pellauer McLauglin, 3 vols. (Cambridge: Cambridge University Press, 1984, 1985, 1986); Christian Smith, *Moral, Believing Animals: Human Personhood and Culture* (New York: Oxford University Press, 2003).
4. Jerome Bruner, "The Narrative Creation of Self," in *The Handbook of Narrative Psychotherapy: Practice, Theory, and Research,* ed. Lynne E. and McLeod Angus, John (Thousand Oaks, CA: Sage, 2002).
5. Taylor, *Sources of the Self.*
6. John Rawls, *A Theory of Justice* (Cambridge, MA: Harvard University Press, 1971).
7. Paul C. Vitz, "The Uses of Stories in Moral Development: New Psychological Reasons for an Old Education Method," *American Psychologist* 45 (1990).
8. Paul Ricoeur, "Hermeneutics and the Critique of Ideology," in *Hermeneutics and the Human Sciences,* ed. John P. Thompson (New York: Cambridge University Press, [1973] 1981).
9. Smith, *Moral, Believing Animals,* 87.
10. Ibid., 85–86.
11. Thomas Berry and Brian Swimme, *The Universe Story: From the Primordial Flaring Forth to the Ecozoic Era* (San Francisco: Harper, 1992).
12. Eric Hobsbawn, *On History* (New York: The New Press, 1997).
13. Smith, *Moral, Believing Animals,* 71.
14. Elsewhere I have argued that interpretation is central to the natural sciences as well. See William J. Grassie, "Reinventing Nature: Science Narratives as Myths for an Endangered Planet," Ph.D. diss., Temple University, 1994; and Grassie, "Hermeneutics in Science and Religion," in *The Encyclopedia of Religion and Science,* ed. Wentzel Van Huysstenn (New York: Macmillan, 2003).
15. Hans Georg Gadamer, *Truth and Method,* trans. J. Weinsheimer and D.G. Marshall (New York: Crossroad, 1989).

16. Jurgen Habermas, *The Theory of Communicative Action*, vol. 1, *Reason and the Rationalization of Society*, trans. T. McCarthy (Boston, MA: Beacon, 1984); Habermas, *The Theory of Communicative Action*, vol. 2, *Lifeworld and System*, trans. T. McCarthy (Boston, MA: Beacon, 1987).

17. Paul Ricoeur, *Interpretation Theory: Discourse and the Surplus of Meaning* (Fort Worth: Texas Christian University Press, 1976).

18. Abdolkarim Soroush, *Reason, Freedom, and Democracy in Islam*, trans. Mahmoud Sadri and Ahmad Sadri (New York: Oxford University Press, 2000).

19. Ralph W. Hood, Peter C. Hill, and William Paul Williamson, *The Psychology of Religious Fundamentalism* (New York: Guilford Press, 2005).

20. Paul Ricoeur, *Lectures on Ideology and Utopia* (New York: Columbia University Press, 1986).

21. Ibid., 2.

22. See Tim LaHaye and Jerry B. Jenkins, *Left Behind: A Novel of the Earth's Last Days*, 16 vols. (Wheaton, IL: Tyndale House Publishers, 1995–2007). As of 2007, some 42 million copies of the books had been sold. The series inspired a movie version, a video game, and many other products. For more information, go to www.leftbehind.com.

23. Alasdair MacIntyre, *Three Rival Versions of Moral Enquiry: Encyclopaedia, Genealogy, and Tradition* (Notre Dame, IN: University of Notre Dame Press, 1990). 81.

24. Gustavo Gutiérrez, *A Theology of Liberation: History, Politics, Salvation* (Maryknoll, NY: Orbis Books, [1971] 1973).

25. G. W. F. Hegel, *The Phenomenology of Spirit*, trans. A. V. Miller (Oxford: Clarendon Press, [1807] 1977).

26. Sandra Harding, *The Science Question in Feminism* (Ithaca, NY: Cornell University Press, 1986).

27. Hayden White, *Tropics of Discourse: Essays in Cultural Criticism* (Baltimore: Johns Hopkins University Press, 1978). White's four plots may not be enough. See, for instance, Christopher Booker, *The Seven Basic Plots: Why We Tell Stories* (New York: Continuum, 2004).

28. Richard Rorty, *Contingency, Irony, and Solidarity* (New York: Cambribge University Press, 1989).

29. For an extended discussion of Niebuhr's understanding of sin, see chapters 7, 8, and 9 in volume 1 of Reinhold Niebuhr, *The Nature and Destiny of Man* (Louisville, KY: Westminster John Knox Press, [1941] 1996).

30. Jeffrey Stout, *Democracy and Tradition* (Princeton, NJ: Princeton University Press, 2004), 287–88.

31. Reinhold Niebuhr, *Moral Man and Immoral Society: A Study in Ethics and Politics* (New York: Charles Scribner's Sons, [1932] 1960).

32. Ricoeur, *Lectures on Ideology and Utopia*, 313.

33. Ibid., 312.

8   The New Religion of Science

1. Richard E. Rubenstein, *Aristotle's Children: How Christians, Muslims, and Jews Rediscovered Ancient Wisdom and Illuminated the Middle Ages* (New York: Harcourt, 2003); Norbert M. Samuelson, *Judaism and the Doctrine of Creation* (Cambridge: Cambridge University Press, 1994); Samuelson, *Jewish Faith and Modern Science: On the Death and Rebirth of Jewish Philosophy* (New York: Rowman and Littlefield, 2009).

2. Carolyn Merchant, *The Death of Nature: Women, Ecology, and the Scientific Revolution* (New York: Harper & Row, 1980).

3. See, for instance, Sandra Harding, ed., *The "Racial" Economy of Science* (Bloomington: Indiana University Press, 1993); Harding, *The Science Question in Feminism* (Ithaca, NY: Cornell University Press, 1986).

4. The corollary of this is that someone might be competent in linguistics and quite incompetent in learning foreign languages. Similarly, one can be competent in the philosophy of science and not really be an expert in any particular science.

5. Aristotle, "Physics," MIT, http://classics.mit.edu/Aristotle/physics.2.ii.html.

6. For a discussion of the Aristotle's four causes as they pertain to the modern scientific revolution, see Holmes Rolston, *Science and Religion: A Critical Survey* (Philadelphia: Temple University Press, 1987), 34–36; and Merchant, *Death of Nature*, 11–12.

7. This presentation of the scientific method was taught to me in middle school. As the discussion below indicates, what science really is as a methodology is not so clear. For an excellent collection of essays on the philosophy of science, see Richard Boyd, Philip Gasper, and J. D. Trout, eds., *The Philosophy of Science* (Cambridge, MA, and London: MIT Press, 1991).

8. Alfred North Whitehead, *Science and the Modern World* (New York: Free Press, [1925] 1967), 35.

9. Boyd, Gasper, and Trout, *Philosophy of Science.*

10. Thomas S. Kuhn, *The Structure of Scientific Revolutions* (Chicago: University of Chicago Press, [1962] 1972), 92–94.

11. See, for instance, Trevor Pinch, "Theory Testing in Science—The Case of Solar Neutrinos: Do Crucial Experiments Test Theories or Theorists?" *Philosophy of Sociology of Science* 15 (1985); H. M. Collins and T. J. Pinch, "The Construction of the Paranormal: Nothing Unscientific Is Happening," in *On the Margins of Science: The Social Construction of Rejected Knowledge,* ed. Roy Wallis (Keele: The Sociological Review, 1978); Ronald N. Giere, "The Philosophy of Science Naturalized," *Philosophy of Science* 52 (1985); and Paul Thagard, "The Conceptual Structure of the Chemical Revolution," *Philosophy of Science* 57 (1990). For a bibliography and review of the literature, see Steve Fuller, "The Philosophy of Science since Kuhn: Readings on the Revolution That Has yet to Come," *Choice* 27 (1989).

12. Kuhn responds to his critics in a Postscript to *The Structure of Scientific Revolutions,* 174–75.

13. Perhaps Ludwig Wittgenstein is the background here. In the *Tractatus* (1921), Wittgenstein is a logical positivist, indeed an active member of the Vienna School along with Moritz Schlick. Late in his life, Wittgenstein wrote *Philosophical Investigations* (1953), in which he promotes the idea of incommensurate "language games." One could talk about rationality and irrationality within particular language games, but comparing language games was comparing other-rationalities. Ludwig Wittgenstein, *The Wittgenstein Reader,* ed. Anthony Kenny (Oxford: Blackwell, 1994).

14. Carl Sagan, *The Demon-Haunted World: Science as a Candle in the Dark* (New York: Ballantine Books, 1996).

15. David Abram prefers the term "more-than-human" in his effort to build a nature-centric understanding of human language. See David Abram, *The Spell of the Sensuous: Perception and Language in a More-Than-Human World* (New York: Pantheon, 1996).

16. Here I am drawing on the synthetic philosophy of Paul Ricoeur, which I discussed in chapter three of my dissertation. William J. Grassie, "Reinventing Nature: Science Narratives as Myths for an Endangered Planet," Ph.D. diss., Temple University, 1994.

17. See Abram, *Spell of the Sensuous*; and Terrence W. Deacon, *The Symbolic Species: The Co-Evolution of Language and the Brain* (New York: Norton, 1997).

18. Bill Bryson, *A Short History of Nearly Everything: Special Illustrated Edition* (New York: Broadway Books, 2003, 2005), 477–78.

19. Scott F. Gilbert and David Epel, *Ecological Developmental Biology: Integrating Epigenetics, Medicine, and Evolution* (Sunderland, MA: Sinauer Associates, 2009), 98.

20. Paul Shepard and Daniel McKinley, eds., *The Subversive Science: Essays toward an Ecology of Man* (Boston, MA: Houghton-Mifflin, 1969).

21. Robert B. Laughlin, "Fractional Quantisation," *Review of Modern Physics* 71, no. 4 (1998).

22. *Naturalism* is a similarly tricky term, an abstraction that defines itself largely by what it opposes. In other words, "naturalism" is anything that is not "supernaturalism," so we are thrown back into metaphysics. This is one of the reasons that I spurn the use of the term "supernatural" in my preferred definition of religion. If God exists, then God is completely "natural" and only works through emergent "natural" processes. Mythological stories are not description of real events in history but profound metaphorical interpretations produced by prescientific peoples.

23. Varadaraja V. Raman, *Truth and Tension in Science and Religion* (Center Ossipee, NH: Beech River Books, 2009), 115.

24. David Harel, *Computers Ltd.: What They Really Can't Do* (New York: Oxford University Press, 2000); John D. Barrow, *Impossibility: The Limits of Science and the Science of Limits* (New York: Oxford University Press, 1999); Orrin H. Pilkey and Linda Pilkey-Jarvis, *Useless Arithmetic: Why Environmental Scientists Can't Predict the Future* (New York: Columbia University Press, 2007); William Grassie, "Useless Arithmetic and Inconvenient Truths: A Review," *Metanexus* (2007), http://www.metanexus.net/Magazine/tabid/68/id/9854/Default.aspx.

25. John Horgan, *The End of Science: Facing the Limits of Knowledge in the Twilight of the Scientific Age* (New York: Addison-Wesley, 1996).

26. For a discussion of emergent hierarchies in science, see George F. R. Ellis and Nancey Murphy, *On the Moral Nature of the Universe: Theology, Cosmology, and Ethics* (Minneapolis, MN: Fortress Press, 1996).

27. Joel R. Primack and Nancy Ellen Abrams, *The View from the Center of the Universe: Discovering Our Extraordinary Place in the Cosmos* (New York: Riverhead, 2006).

28. Eric Chaisson, *Epic of Evolution : Seven Ages of the Cosmos* (New York: Columbia University Press, 2006).

29. Chaisson, *Cosmic Evolution: The Rise of Complexity in Nature* (Cambridge, MA: Harvard University Press, 2001), 139; Chaisson, *Epic of Evolution*, 293—96; Christian, *Maps of Time: An Introduction to Big History* (Berkeley: University of California Press, 2004).

30. One possible exception to the second law of thermodynamics is the impact of gravity in giving structure to the early universe. By drawing clouds of hydrogen and helium together into denser and denser regions, gravity ignited stellar fusion. Once stellar fusion begins, the second law applies to the life cycle of a star, but apparently not before.

31. This interpretation has been advanced by physicist-turned-theologian John Polkinghorne. See, for instance, John C. Polkinghorne, *Science and Providence* (London: SPCK, 1989); Polkinghorne, *Faith of a Physicist, The: Reflections of a Bottom-up Thinker*, Gifford Lectures for 1993–4 (Princeton, NJ: Princeton University Press, 1994); Polkinghorne, *Belief in God in an Age of Science* (New Haven, CT: Yale University Press, 1998).

32. Hindu cosmologies are the only ones in traditional religion that approach the scale of our contemporary understanding of the universe, albeit framed in unbelievable characters and details that have nothing to do with science.

33. Freeman Dyson, *Disturbing the Universe* (New York: Basic Books, 1979), 250.

34. Paul C. W. Davies, "Science and Religion in the 21st Century," *Metanexus* (2000), http://www.metanexus.net/magazine/tabid/68/id/2592/Default.aspx.

35. As quoted by Dennis Overbye, "Pure Math, Pure Joy," *New York Times*, June 29, 2003, http://www.nytimes.com/2003/06/29/weekinreview/29OVER.html.

36. The pre-Socratic philosopher Heraclitus (ca. 535–475 B.C.E.) famously proposed an early vision of a universe characterized by transformation and change. Certainly, Buddhism, arising in a different place around the same time, also promoted a concept of endless change as the fundamental characteristic of reality. In the modern Europe, we encounter the French philosopher Denis Diderot (1713–1784) speculating about evolution in a 1769 book. The French biologist Jean Baptiste Lamarck (1744–1829) proposed a theory of evolution prior to Darwin's theory of natural selection in the first decade of the nineteenth century. In 1803, Erasmus Darwin, Charles's grandfather, invoked evolutionary concepts in his book *The Temple of Nature*. Erasmus appeals to his Muse to tell him "how rose from elemental strife / Organic forms, and kindled into life." The Muse responds with an evolutionary story of how "imperious man, who rules the bestial crowd, / . . . Arose from rudiments of form and sense." Richard Lewontin, "Why Darwin?" *New York Review of Books* 56, no. 9 (2009).

37. Theodosius Dobzhansky, "Biology, Molecular and Organismic," *American Zoology* 4 (1964): 443.

38. See, for instance, Daniel C. Dennett, *Darwin's Dangerous Idea: Evolution and the Meaning of Life* (New York: Simon & Schuster, 1995).

39. A. N. Whitehead, *The Concept of Nature* (Cambridge: Cambridge University Press, 1926), 163.

40. See a standard introductory biology textbook, for instance, William K. Purves et al., *Life: The Science of Biology* (Sunderland, MA: Sinauer Associates, 1998). For discussions of the inadequacies of natural selection as explanation, see David Depew and Bruce Weber, *Darwinism Evolving: Systems Dynamics and the Genealogy of Natural Selection* (Cambridge, MA: MIT Press, 1996); Robert Wesson, *Beyond Natural Selection* (Cambridge, MA: MIT Press, 1991); Simon Conway Morris, *Life's Solution: Inevitable Humans in a Lonely Universe* (New York: Cambridge University Press, 2003); Ian Stewart, *Life's Other Secret: The New Mathematics of the Living World* (New York: Wiley & Sons, 1998). See especially Gilbert and Epel, *Ecological Developmental Biology*.

41. For a discussion of the philosophical implications of developmental systems theory, see the coda in Gilbert and Epel, *Ecological Developmental Biology*.

42. Jacques Monod, *Chance and Necessity: An Essay on the Natural Philosophy of Modern Biology*, trans. Austryn Wainhouse (New York: Alfred A. Knopf, 1971).

43. Carl Friedrich von Weizsaecker, *Die Geschichte Der Natur* (Frankfurt: Vandenhoeck & Ruprecht, 1962), cited in the foreword to Bernd-Olaf Küppers, *Der Ursprung biologischer*

Information (Munich: R. Piper and Co., 1986); Küppers, *Information and the Origin of Life*, trans. Paul Wooley (Cambridge, MA: MIT Press, 1990), xi.

44. Christian, *Maps of Time*; Cynthia Stokes Brown, *Big History : From the Big Bang to the Present* (New York: New Press : Distributed by W.W. Norton, 2007); Chaisson, *Epic of Evolution*; McNeill and McNeill, *The Human Web: A Bird's-Eye View of World History* (New York: W.W. Norton, 2003); Bryson, *A Short History of Nearly Everything*; Primack and Abrams, *The View from the Center of the Universe*; Berry and Swimme, *The Universe Story*.

9   God-by-Whatever-Name

1. John Bowker, *Is Anybody out There? Religion and Belief in God in the Contemporary World* (Westminster, MD: Christian Classics, 1987), 74.
2. Paul Tillich, *Dynamics of Faith* (New York: HarperCollins, [1957] 2001).
3. Wilfred Cantwell Smith, *Faith and Belief: The Difference between Them* (Princeton, NJ: Princeton University Press, 1987).
4. Bowker, *The Sense of God* (Oxford: Oneworld Publications, [1973] 1995), 94.
5. George F. R. Ellis and Nancey Murphy, *On the Moral Nature of the Universe: Theology, Cosmology, and Ethics* (Minneapolis, MN: Fortress Press, 1996).
6. Holmes Rolston, for instance, argues that the observed pattern of evolution of life on the planet, in spite of a number of setbacks, favors this interpretation of increasing complexity. See Holmes Rolston, *Genes, Genesis, and God: Values and Their Origins in Natural and Human History* (New York: Cambridge University Press, 1998).
7. A. N. Whitehead, *Science and the Modern World* (New York: Free Press, [1925] 1967), 35.
8. Whitehead developed this metaphysical system in *Process and Reality* (1929). This is a very difficult text to read, so it is advised to start with an introductory book. See, for instance, C. Robert Mesle, *Process-Relational Philosophy* (West Conshohocken, PA: Templeton Foundation Press, 2008). Whitehead's process philosophy has been very influential in theology. Claremont School of Theology, for instance, is host to the Center for Process Studies http://www.ctr4process. org/.
9. Thomas Berry and Brian Swimme, *The Universe Story: From the Primordial Flaring Forth to the Ecozoic Era* (San Francisco, CA: Harper, 1992). For my discussion of Berry and Swimme's ethics, see chapter five of my dissertation, Grassie, "Reinventing Nature: Science Narratives as Myths for an Endangered Planet," Ph.D. diss., Temple University, 1994.
10. Raymond Chang, *Chemistry*, 9th ed. (New York: McGraw-Hill, 2007), 52.
11. This interpretation of information is a common theme in the writings of John Polkinghorne. See Polkinghorne, *Faith of a Physicist, The: Reflections of a Bottom-up Thinker*, Gifford Lectures for 1993–94 (Princeton, NJ: Princeton University Press, 1994); and Polkinghorne, *Belief in God in an Age of Science* (New Haven, CT: Yale University Press, 1998).
12. Martin Gardner (1914–), a founding member of the Committee for the Scientific Investigation of Claims of the Paranormal (CSICOP) and a regular contributor to the organization's periodical, *The Skeptical Inquirer*, campaigned tirelessly against pseudoscience and yet maintained a very open mind toward some of the religious interpretations articulated in this chapter. His book *The Whys of a Philosophical Scrivener* makes a number of these arguments, with chapters titles such as "Why I Am Not an Ethical Relativist," "Why I Am Not an Atheist," "Prayer, Why I Do Not Think It Foolish," "Immortality, Why I Am Not Resigned, Why I Do Not Think It Strange, Why I Do Not Think It Impossible," and "Why I Do Not Believe God's Existence Can Be Demonstrated." Michael Gardner, *The Whys of a Philosophical Scrivener* (New York: St. Martin's Press, [1983] 1999).
13. Julian Barbour, *The End of Time: The Next Revolution in Physics* (New York: Oxford University Press, 1999).
14. I picked up this expression in graduate school and have long attributed this sentence to Alfred North Whitehead, but have never been able to find the actual citation in his writings. For the insight, I am certainly in debt to Whitehead.
15. Bowker, *Sense of God*, 113–14.
16. Ellis and Murphy, *On the Moral Nature of the Universe*.
17. Bowker, *Sense of God*, x.
18. For a discussion of religion and obsessive-compulsive disorder, see Sigmund Freud, "Obsessive Actions and Religious Practices," in *The Standard Edition of the Complete Psychological Works of*

Sigmund Freud, Volume 9 (1906–1908): *Jensen's 'Gradiva' andOther Works,* 115–128 (London: Hogarth Press, [1907] 1959); S. Dulaney and A. P.Fiske, "Cultural Rituals and Obsessive-Compulsive Disorder: Is There a Common Psychological Mechanism?" *Ethos* 22, no. 3 (1994); and Pascal Boyer and P. Lienard, "Why Ritualized Behavior? Precaution Systems and Action Parsing in Developmental, Pathological, and Cultural Rituals," *Behavioral and Brain Sciences* 29, no. 595–650 (2006).

19. The founder of modern linguistics, Ferdinand de Saussure, is noted for separating the semiotic structure of language from the semantic meaning or *parole.* Saussure held that a science of language could be obtained by ignoring the individual uses of language in different contexts and focusing only on the systematic structure of signs. In his discussion of Saussure, Paul Ricoeur argues for a dialectic between the semiotic structure of language and the semantic uses of language. Without the latter, we would not be able to account for how languages evolved and continue to evolve. I am making the same distinction here between the semiotics of religion and the semantics of religion. See Ricoeur, *Interpretation Theory: Discourse and the Surplus of Meaning* (Fort Worth: Texas Christian University Press, 1976).

10   Reiterations and Reflections

1. W.H. Auden, *W. H. Auden: Selected Poems,* ed. Edward Mendelson (New York: Faber & Faber, 1979), 17.
2. Edward O. Wilson, *Consilience: The Unity of Knowledge* (New York: Knopf, 1998), 265.
3. John Paul II, "Letter to Reverend George V. Coyne, S.J.," June 1, 1988, http://clavius.as.arizona.edu/vo/R1024/ppt-Message.html.

BIBLIOGRAPHY

Abbott, Edwin A. *Flatland: A Romance of Many Dimensions*: Project Gutenberg, 1884.
Abram, David. *The Spell of the Sensuous: Perception and Language in a More-Than-Human World*. New York: Pantheon, 1996.
"Adherents.Com: National & World Religion Statistics." http://www.adherents.com/Religions_By_Adherents.html.
Alcorta, Candace S. "Religion and the Life Course: Is Adolescence An 'Experience Expectant' Period for Religious Transmission?" In *Where God and Science Meet*, edited by Patrick McNamara, 55–80. Westport, CT: Praeger, 2006.
Ambrose, Stanley H. "Late Pleistocene Human Population Bottlenecks, Volcanic Winter, and Differentiation of Modern Humans." *Journal of Human Evolution* 34, no. 6 (1998): 623–51.
———. "Volcanic Winter, and Differentiation of Modern Humans." Bradshaw Foundation, http://www.bradshawfoundation.com/stanley_ambrose.php.
Aristotle. "Physics." MIT, http://classics.mit.edu/Aristotle/physics.2.ii.html.
Association for the Study of Religion, Economics and Culture. http://www.religionomics.com/asrec/asrec07_program.html.
"Association for the Study of Religion, Economics and Culture." http://www.religionomics.com.
Atran, Scott. *In Gods We Trust: The Evolutionary Landscape of Religion*. New York: Oxford University Press, 2002.
Auden, W. H. *W. H. Auden: Selected Poems*. Edited by Edward Mendelson. New York: Faber & Faber, 1979.
Azevedo F. A., L. R. Carvalho, L. T. Grinberg, J. M. Farfel, R. E. Ferretti, R. E. Leite, W. Jacob Filho, R. Lent, and S. Herculano-Houzel. "Equal Numbers of Neuronal and Nonneuronal Cells Make the Human Brain an Isometrically Scaled-up Primate Brain." *Journal of Comparative Neurology* 513, no. 5 (2009): 532–41.
Barbour, Ian. *Myths, Models, and Paradigms*. New York: Harper and Row, 1974.
———. *Religion in an Age of Science: The Gifford Lectures 1989–1991*. Volume 1. San Francisco: Harper, 1990.
Barbour, Julian. *The End of Time: The Next Revolution in Physics*. New York: Oxford University Press, 1999.
Barrett, David, George Kurian, and Todd Johnson. *World Christian Encyclopedia*. New York: Oxford University Press, 2001.
Barrett, Justin L. *Why Would Anyone Believe in God?* Lanham, MD: Altamira, 2004.
Barrow, John D. *Impossibility: The Limits of Science and the Science of Limits*. New York: Oxford University Press, 1999.
Bausell, R. Barker. *Snake Oil Science: The Truth about Complementary and Alternative Medicine*. New York: Oxford University Press, 2007.
Becker, Gary. "Keynote Address." paper presented at the "Spiritual Capital Conference," Cambridge, MA, October 9, 2003. Reprinted in *Spiritual Capital* (Philadelphia, PA: Metanexus Institute, 2003).
Beecher, Henry K. "The Powerful Placebo." *Journal of the American Medical Association* 159, (1955): 1602–06.

Beinhocker, Eric D. *The Origin of Wealth: Evolution, Complexity, and the Radical Remaking of Economics.* Cambridge, MA: Harvard Business School Press, 2006.

Benson H., J. A. Dusek, J. B. Sherwood, P. Lam, C. F. Bethea, W. Carpenter, S. Levitsky, P. C. Hill, D. W. Clem Jr., M. K. Jain, D. Drumel, S. L. Kopecky, P. S. Mueller, D. Marek, S. Rollins, and P. L. Hibberd. "Study of the Therapeutic Effects of Intercessory Prayer (Step) in Cardiac Bypass Patients: A Multicenter Randomized Trial of Uncertainty and Certainty of Receiving Intercessory Prayer." *American Heart Journal* 151, no. 4 (2006): 934–42.

Benson, Herbert. "Institute for Mind-Body Medicine." http://www.mbmi.org/.

———. *The Relaxation Response.* New York: Harper, 1975.

———. *Timeless Healing.* New York: Fireside, Simon and Schuster, 1996.

Berger, Peter L., and Robert W. Hefner. "Spiritual Capital in Comparative Perspective." *Metanexus* (2003). http://www.metanexus.net/spiritual_capital/pdf/Berger.pdf.

Berger, Peter L, Jonathan Sacks, David Martin, Tu Weiming, George Weigel, Grace

Davie, and Abdullahi A. An-Na'im. *The Desecularization of the World: Resurgent Religion and World Politics.* New York: Wm. B. Eerdmans, 1999.

Berger, Peter L. *The Sacred Canopy: Elements of a Sociological Theory of Religion.* New York: Doubleday, 1967.

Berry, Thomas, and Brian Swimme. *The Universe Story: From the Primordial Flaring Forth to the Ecozoic Era.* San Francisco: Harper, 1992.

Blackmore, Susan. *The Meme Machine.* New York: Oxford University Press, 1999.

Bloom, Paul. "Is God an Accident?" *Atlantic Monthly*, December 2005, http://www.theatlantic.com/doc/200512/god-accident.

Bok, Sissela. "The Ethics of Giving Placebos." *Scientific American* 231 (1975): 17–23.

Booker, Christopher. *The Seven Basic Plots: Why We Tell Stories.* New York: Continuum, 2004.

Bostrom, Nick, Natasha Vita-More, Audrey de Grey, Max More, Russell Blackford, Sky Marsen, Michael LaTorra, Mark Walker, Amara Graps, and Martine Rothblatt. "H+: Transhumanism Answers Its Critics." *Metanexus* (2009). http://www.metanexus.net/magazine/PastIssues/tabid/126/Default.aspx?PageContentID=33.

Bourdeau, Michel. "Auguste Comte." In *Stanford Encyclopedia of Philosophy*, edited by Edward N. Zalta. Palo Alto, CA: Stanford University Press, 2008.

Bowker, John. *Is Anybody out There? Religion and Belief in God in the Contemporary World.* Westminster, MD: Christian Classics, 1987.

———. *The Sense of God.* Oxford: Oneworld Publications, [1973] 1995.

Boyd, Richard, Philip Gasper, and J. D. Trout, eds. *The Philosophy of Science.* Cambridge, MA, and London: MIT Press, 1991.

Boyer, Pascal. *Religion Explained: The Evolutionary Origins of Religious Thought.* New York: Basic Books, 2001.

Boyer, Pascal, and P. Lienard. "Why Ritualized Behavior? Precaution Systems and Action Parsing in Developmental, Pathological, and Cultural Rituals." *Behavioral and Brain Sciences* 29, no. 595–650 (2006): 595–650.

Brooke, J. H. *Science and Religion: Some Historical Perspectives.* Cambridge: Cambridge University Press, 1999.

Brown, Cynthia Stokes. *Big History : From the Big Bang to the Present.* New York: New Press; Distributed by W. W. Norton, 2007.

Brown, Donald E. *Human Universals.* New York: McGraw-Hill, 1991.

Bruner, Jerome. "The Narrative Creation of Self." In *The Handbook of Narrative Psychotherapy: Practice, Theory, and Research*, edited by Lynne E. Angus and John McLeod, 3–14. Thousand Oaks, CA: SAGE, 2002.

Bryson, Bill. *A Short History of Nearly Everything: Special Illustrated Edition.* New York: Broadway Books, 2003, 2005.

Bulbulia, Joseph, Richard Sosis, Erica Harris, Russell Genet, Cheryl Genet, and Karen Wyman, eds. *The Evolution of Religion: Studies, Theories, & Critiques.* Santa Margarita, CA: Collins Foundation Press, 2008.

Burkert, Walter. *Creation of the Sacred: Tracks of Biology in Early Religion.* Cambridge, MA: Harvard University Press, 1996.

Carey, Benedict. "Can Prayers Heal? Critics Say Studies Go Past Science's Reach." *New York Times*, October 10, 2004.

Cartwright, John. *Evolution and Human Behavior: Darwinian Perspectives on Human Nature*. New York: Palgrave Macmillan, 2000.

"Catechism of the Catholic Church." http://www.scborromeo.org/ccc.htm.

Central Intelligence Agency. "The World Factbook." https://www.cia.gov/library/publications/the-world-factbook/geos/xx.html.

Chaisson, Eric. *Cosmic Evolution: The Rise of Complexity in Nature*. Cambridge, MA: Harvard University Press, 2001.

————. *Epic of Evolution : Seven Ages of the Cosmos*. New York: Columbia University Press, 2006.

Chalmer, David J. *The Conscious Mind: In Search of a Fundamental Theory*. New York: Oxford University Press, 1996.

Chang, Raymond. *Chemistry*. 9th ed. New York: McGraw-Hill, 2007.

Christian, David. *Maps of Time: An Introduction to Big History*. Berkeley: University of California Press, 2004.

Collins, H. M., and T. J. Pinch. "The Construction of the Paranormal: Nothing Unscientific Is Happening." In *On the Margins of Science: The Social Construction of Rejected Knowledge*, edited by Roy Wallis, 237–70. Keele: The Sociological Review, 1978.

Comte, Auguste. "Considerations on the Spiritual Power." In *The Crisis of Industrial Civilization: The Early Essays of Auguste Comte*, edited by Ronald Fletcher, 214–45. London: Heinemann, [1826] 1974.

————. "Philosophical Considerations on the Sciences and Savants." 1825. In *The Crisis in Industrial Civilization: The Early Writings of Auguste Comte*, edited by Ronald Fletcher, 182–213. London: Heinemann, 1974.

————. "Plans for the Scientific Operations Necessary for Reorganizing Society." 1822. In *The Crisis in Industrial Civilization: The Early Writings of Auguste Comte*, edited by Ronald Fletcher, 111–81. London: Heinemann, 1974.

————. *System of Positive Polity, or Treatise on Sociology: Instituting the Religion of Humanity*. Translated by Frederic Harrison. 3 vols. Vol. 2. New York: B. Franklin, [1852] 1968.

————. *The Positive Philosophy*. Translated by Harriet Martineau. New York: AMS Press, [1842] 1974.

Darwin, Charles. *The Descent of Man*. 1871. http://www.gutenberg.org/etext/2300.

————. *The Origin of Species*. 1859. http://www.gutenberg.org/etext/2009.

Davies, Paul C. W. "Science and Religion in the 21st Century." *Metanexus* (2000). http://www.metanexus.net/magazine/tabid/68/id/2592/Default.aspx.

Davis, Carolyn F. *The Evidential Force of Religious Experience*. New York: Oxford University Press, 1989.

Dawkins, Richard. *A Devil's Chaplain: Reflections on Hope, Lies, Science, and Love*. Boston, MA: Houghton Mifflin, 2003.

————. *The Ancestors' Tale: A Pilgrimage to the Dawn of Evolution*. New York: Houghton Mifflin, 2004.

————. *The God Delusion*. New York: Houghton Mifflin, 2006.

————. *The Selfish Gene*. New York: Oxford University Press, 1976.

————. *Unweaving the Rainbow: Science, Delusion, and the Appetite for Wonder*. Boston, MA: Houghton Mifflin, 1998.

de Craen, A. J. M., P. J. Roos, A. Leonard de Vries, and J. Kleijnen. "Effect of Colour of Drugs: Systematic Review of Perceived Effect of Drugs and of Their Effectiveness." *British Medical Journal* 313, no. 7072 (1996): 1624–26.

de Lubac, Henri. *The Drama of Atheist Humanism*. Translated by Edith M. Riley and Anne Englund Nash. San Francisco: Ignatius Press, [1944] 1983.

Deacon, Terrence W. *The Symbolic Species: The Co-Evolution of Language and the Brain*. New York: Norton, 1997.

Dennett, Daniel C. *Breaking the Spell: Religion as a Natural Phenomenon*. New York: Viking, 2006.

————. *Darwin's Dangerous Idea: Evolution and the Meaning of Life*. New York: Simon & Schuster, 1995.

Dennett, Daniel C. "Review of Burkert's *Creation of the Sacred.*" *PhilPapers* (1996), http://philpapers. org/rec/DENROB .

Depew, David, and Bruce Weber. *Darwinism Evolving: Systems Dynamics and the Genealogy of Natural Selection.* Cambridge, MA: MIT Press, 1996.

Diamond, Jared. *Guns, Germs, and Steel: The Fates of Human Societies.* New York: W. W. Norton, 1997, 1999.

Dobzhansky, Theodosius. "Biology, Molecular and Organismic." *American Zoology* 4, (1964): 443–52.

Dudley III, Guilford. *Religion on Trial: Mircea Eliade & His Critics.* Philadelphia: Temple University Press, 1977.

Dulaney, S., and A. P. Fiske. "Cultural Rituals and Obsessive-Compulsive Disorder: Is There a Common Psychological Mechanism?" *Ethos* 22, no. 3 (1994): 243–83.

Durham, William H. *Coevolution: Genes, Culture, and Human Diversity.* Palo Alto, CA: Stanford University Press, 1992.

Durkheim, Émile. *The Elementary Forms of the Religious Life.* Translated by Joseph Ward Swain. New York: The Free Press, [1912] 1915.

Dyson, Freeman. *Disturbing the Universe.* New York: Basic Books, 1979.

Ekman, Paul. *Emotions Revealed: Recognizing Faces and Feelings to Improve Communication and Emotional Life.* New York: Times Books, 2003.

Eliade, Mircea. *Myths, Rites, Symbols: A Mircea Eliade Reader.* Edited by Wendell C. Beane and William G. Doty. Vol. 2. New York: Harper Colophon, 1976.

———. *Patterns in Comparative Religion.* New York: Sheed & Ward, 1958.

———. *The Myth of the Eternal Return: Cosmos and History.* Translated by Willard R. Trask. Princeton, NJ: Princeton University Press, 1971.

———. *The Sacred and the Profane: The Nature of Religion.* Translated by Willard R. Trask. New York: Harper Torchbooks, 1961.

Ellis, George F. R., and Nancey Murphy. *On the Moral Nature of the Universe: Theology, Cosmology, and Ethics.* Minneapolis, MN: Fortress Press, 1996.

Feierman, Jay R., ed. *The Biology of Religious Behavior: The Evolutionary Origins of Faith and Religion.* Westport, CT: Praeger, 2009.

Ferré, Frederick. *Auguste Comte: Introduction to Positive Philosophy.* New York: Bobbs-Merrill Company, 1970.

Fetzer Institute. "Multidimensional Measurement of Religiousness/Spirituality for Use in Health Research." 1999. http://www.fetzer.org/research/248-dses.

Feuerbach, Ludwig. *The Essence of Christianity.* Translated by George Eliot. New York: Harper Torchbooks, [1843] 1957.

Fields, Howard L., and Donald D. Price. "Toward a Neurobiology of Placebo Analgesia." In *The Placebo Effect: An Interdisciplinary Exploration,* edited by Anne Harrington, 93–116. Cambridge, MA: Harvard University Press, 1997.

Fletcher, Ronald, ed. *The Crisis of Industrial Civilization: The Early Essays of Auguste Comte.* London: Heinemann Educational Books, 1974.

Fowler, James. *Stages of Faith: The Psychology of Human Development and the Quest for Meaning.* San Francisco: Harper, 1981.

Freud, Sigmund. *Civilization and Its Discontents.* New York: W. W. Norton, [1930] 1961.

———. *Future of an Illusion.* Seattle, WA: Pacific Publishing Studio, [1927] 2010.

———. "Obsessive Actions and Religious Practice." Trans. R. C. McWatters. In *The Standard Edition of the Complete Psychological Works of Sigmund Freud,* Volume 9 (1906–1908): *Jensen's 'Gradiva' and Other Works,* pp. 115–28. London: Hogarth Press, [1907] 1959.

———. *Totem and Taboo.* New York: Prometheus Books, [1918] 2000.

Fukuyama, Francis. "Social Capital." In *Culture Matters: How Values Shape Human Progress,* edited by Lawrence Harrison and Samuel P. Huntington, 98–111. New York: Basic Books, 2000.

Fuller, Steve. "The Philosophy of Science since Kuhn: Readings on the Revolution That Has yet to Come." *Choice* 27 (1989): 595–601.

Gadamer, Hans Georg. *Truth and Method.* Translated by J. Weinsheimer and D. G. Marshall. New York: Crossroad, 1989.

Gardner, Michael. *The Whys of a Philosophical Scrivener.* New York: St. Martin's Press, [1983] 1999.

Geertz, Clifford *The Interpretation of Cultures.* New York: Harper, 1973.

Ghiselin, Michael T. *The Economy of Nature and the Evolution of Sex.* Berkeley: University of California Press, 1974.

Giere, Ronald N. "The Philosophy of Science Naturalized." *Philosophy of Science* 52 (1985): 331–56.

Gilbert, Scott F., and David Epel. *Ecological Developmental Biology: Integrating Epigenetics, Medicine, and Evolution.* Sunderland, MA: Sinauer Associates, 2009.

Gould, Stephen Jay, and R. D. Lewontin. "The Spandrels of San Marco and the Panglossian Paradigm: A Critique of the Adaptationist Programme." *Proceedings of the Royal Society of London* 205 (1979): 581–98.

Grassie, William J. "Re-Reading Economics: In Search of New Economic Metaphors for Biological Evolution." *Metanexus* (2007). http://www.metanexus.net/Magazine/ArticleDetail/tabid/68/id/9932/Default.aspx.

———. "Reinventing Nature: Science Narratives as Myths for an Endangered Planet." Ph.D. diss., Temple University, 1994.

———. "Useless Arithmetic and Inconvenient Truths: A Review." *Metanexus* (2007). http://www.metanexus.net/Magazine/tabid/68/id/9854/Default.aspx.

Guess, H. A., Kleinman, A., Kuzek, J. W., & Engel, L. W. (Eds.). *The Science of the Placebo: Toward an Interdisciplinary Research Agenda.* London: BMJ Books, 2002.

Gutiérrez, Gustavo. *A Theology of Liberation: History, Politics, Salvation.* Maryknoll, NY: Orbis Books, [1971] 1973.

Habermas, Jurgen. *The Theory of Communicative Action.* Vol. 1: *Reason and the Rationalization of Society.* Translated by T. McCarthy. Boston, MA: Beacon, 1984.

———. *The Theory of Communicative Action.* Vol. 2: *Lifeworld and System.* Translated by T. McCarthy. Boston, MA: Beacon, 1987.

Haldane, J. B. S. "When I Am Dead." In *Possible Worlds and Other Essays*, 204–10. London: Chatto and Windus, [1927] 1932.

Hamer, Dean H. *The God Gene: How Faith Is Hardwired into Our Genes.* New York: Anchor, 2005.

Hamilton, William D. "The Genetical Evolution of Social Behavior." *Journal of Theoretical Biology* 7 (1964): 1–16.

Harding, Sandra, ed. *The "Racial" Economy of Science.* Bloomington: Indiana University Press, 1993.

———. *The Science Question in Feminism.* Ithaca: Cornell University Press, 1986.

Harel, David. *Computers Ltd.: What They Really Can't Do.* New York: Oxford University Press, 2000.

Harrington, Anne. *The Cure Within: A History of Mind-Body Medicine.* New York: W. W. Norton, 2008.

———, ed. *The Placebo Effect: An Interdisciplinary Exploration.* Cambridge, MA: Harvard University Press, 1997.

———. "Seeing the Placebo Effect: Historical Legacies and Present Opportunities." In H. A. Guess, A. Kleinman, J. W. Kuzek, and L. W. Engel, eds., *The Science of the Placebo: Toward an Interdisciplinary Research Agenda*, 35–52. London: BMJ Books, 2002.

Harris, Sam. *Letter to a Christian Nation.* New York: Knopf, 2006.

———. *The End of Faith: Religion, Terror, and the Future of Reason.* New York: W. W. Norton, 2004.

Haught, John. *God and the New Atheism: A Critical Response to Dawkins, Harris, and Hitchens.* Louisville, KY: Westminister John Knox Press, 2008.

Hegel, G. W. F. *The Phenomenology of Spirit.* Translated by A.V. Miller. Oxford: Clarendon Press, [1807] 1977.

Hill, Peter C., and Ralph W. Hood. *Measures of Religiosity.* Birmingham, AL: Religious Education Press, 1999.

Hitchens, Christopher. *God Is Not Great: How Religion Poisons Everything.* New York: Hachette Books, 2007.

Hobsbawn, Eric. *On History.* New York: 1997.

Hollinger, David A. *Science, Jews, and Secular Culture: Studies in Mid-Twentieth-Century American Intellectual History*. Princeton, NJ: Princeton University Press, 1996.

Hood, Ralph W., Peter C. Hill, and William Paul Williamson. *The Psychology of Religious Fundamentalism*. New York: Guilford Press, 2005.

Horgan, John. *The End of Science: Facing the Limits of Knowledge in the Twilight of the Scientific Age*. New York: Addison-Wesley, 1996.

———. *Rational Mysticism*. New York: Houghton Mifflin, 2003.

Horta, Korinna. "Dateline Chad: Return of the 'Resource Curse'?" *The Globalist*, August 25, 2006.

Hrobjarsson, A., and P. Gotzsche. "Is the Placebo Powerless? An Analysis of Clinical Trial Comparing Placebo with No Treatment." *New England Journal of Medicine* 344 (2001): 1594–602.

———. "Is the Placebo Powerless? Update of a Systematic Review of 52 New Randomized Trials Comparing Placebo with No Treatment." *Journal of Internal Medicine* 256 (2004): 91–100.

Hufford, David J. "An Analysis of the Field of Spirituality, Religion, and Health." *Metanexus* (2005). http://www.metanexus.net/metanexus_online/show_article2.asp?id=9387.

———. *The Terror That Comes in the Night: An Experience-Centered Study of Supernatural Assault Traditions*. Philadelphia: University of Pennsylvania Press, 1982.

Iannaccone, L. R. (1998). The Economics of Religion: A Survey of Recent Work. *Journal of Economic Literature* 36 (September 1998): 1465–196.

Iannaccone, Laurence R., and Jonathan Klick. "Spiritual Capital: An Introduction and Literature Review." *Metanexus* (2003). http://www.metanexus.net/spiritual_capital/research_review.asp

Ironson, Gail, Heidemarie Kremer, and Dale Ironson. "Spirituality, Spiritual Experiences, and Spiritual Transformation in the Face of Hiv." In *Spiritual Transformation and Healing: Anthropological, Theological, Neuroscientific and Clinical Perspectives*, edited by Joan D. Koss-Chioino and Philip Hefner, 241–62. Lanham, MD: Altamira Press, 2006.

Ironson, G., C. O'Cleirigh, M.A. Fletcher, J. P. Laurenceau, E. Balbin, and N. Klimas "Psychosocial Factors Predict Cd4 and Vl Change in Men and Women with Human Immunodeficiency Virus in the Era of Highly Active Antiretroviral Treatment." *Psychosomatic Medicine* 67, no. 6 (2005): 1013–21.

Ironson, G., G. F. Solomon, E. G. Balbin, C. O'Cleirigh, A. George, and M. Kumar. "The Ironson-Woods Spirituality/Religiousness Index Is Associated with Long Survival, Health Behaviors, Less Distress, and Low Cortisol in People with Hiv/Aids." *Annals of Behavioral Medicine* 24, no. 1 (2002): 34–48.

Ironson, Gail, R. Stuetzle, and M.A. Fletcher. "An Increase in Religiousness/Spirituality Occurs after Hiv Diagnosis and Predicts Slower Disease Progression over 4 Years in People with Hiv." *Journal of General Internal Medicine,* no. 5 (2006): S62–8.

Ironson, G., R. Stuetzle, M. A. Fletcher, and D. Ironson. "View of God Is Associated with Disease Progression in Hiv." In *Annals of Behavioral Medicine*, S074. San Francisco: Society of Behavioral Medicine, 2006.

James, William. *A Pluralistic Universe*. Cambridge, MA: Harvard University Press, [1909] 1977.

———. *Varieties of Religious Experience*. New York: Macmillian, [1902] 1961.

Janata, Petr. "Center for Mind and Brain." UC Davis, http://atonal.ucdavis.edu.

Jaynes, Julian. *The Origin of Consciousness in the Breakdown of the Bicameral Mind*. New York: Houghton Mifflin, 1976.

John Paul II. "Letter to Reverend George V. Coyne, S. J." June 1, 1988 http://clavius.as.arizona.edu/vo/R1024/ppt-Message.html.

Jung, Carl Gustav. *Psychology and Religion*. New Haven, CT: Yale University Press, [1938] 1966.

———. *The Portable Jung*. Edited by Joseph Campell. New York: Penguin, 1971.

Kabat-Zinn, Jon. "Center for Mindfulness in Medicine, Health Care, and Society." University of Massachusetts Medical School, http://www.umassmed.edu/Content.aspx?id=41252.

———. *Wherever You Go You Are There*: New York: Hyperion, 1995.

Kaptchuk, T. J., W. B. Stason, R. B. Davis, A. R. Legedza, R. N. Schnyer, C. E. Kerr, D. A. Stone, B. H. Nam, I. Kirsch, and R. H. Goldman. "Sham Device V Inert Pill: Randomised Controlled Trial of Two Placebo Treatments." *British Medical Journal* 132, no. 7538 (2006): 391–97.

Kark, J. D., G. Shemi, Y. Friedlander, O. Martin, O. Manor, and S.H. Blondheim. "Does Religious Observance Promote Health? Mortality in Secular vs. Religious Kibbutzim in Israel." *American Journal of Public Health* 86, no. 3 (1996): 341–46.

Kelemen, D. "Are Children "Intuitive Theists"? Reasoning about Purpose and Design in Nature." *Psychological Science* 15 (2004): 295–301.

Kelly, Edward F., Emily Williams Kelly, Adam Crabtree, Alan Gauld, Michael Grosso, and Bruce Greyson. *Irreducible Mind: Toward a Psychology for the 21st Century.* Lanham, MD: Rowan and Littlefield, 2007.

Kirk, G. S. *Myth: Its Meaning and Functions in Ancient and Other Cultures.* Berkeley: University of California Press, 1973.

———. *The Nature of Greek Myths.* Harmondsworth: Penguin Books, 1974.

Koenig, H. G., M. E. McCullough, and D. B. Larson. *Handbook of Religion and Health.* New York: Oxford University Press, 2001.

Kossyln, Stephen M. "A Science of the Divine." *Edge,* 2006. http://www.edge.org/q2006/q06_9.html#kosslyn.

Krieger, Dolores. *The Therapeutic Touch: How to Use Your Hands to Help or Heal.* Englewood Cliffs, NJ: Prentice-Hall, 1979.

———. "Therapeutic Touch: The Imprimatur of Nursing." *American Journal of Nursing* 75, (1975): 784–87.

Kuhn, Thomas S. *The Structure of Scientific Revolutions.* Chicago: University of Chicago Press, [1962] 1972.

Kuran, Timur. *Islam & Mammon: The Economic Predicaments of Islamism.* Princeton, NJ: Princeton University Press, 2004.

———. "The Role of Islamic Law in the Economic Evolution of the Middle East." Paper presented at the conference of the Association of the Study of Religion, Economics and Culture (ASREC), Rochester, NY, November 5, 2005.

LaHaye, Tim, and Jerry B. Jenkins. *Left Behind: A Novel of the Earth's Last Days.* 16 vols. Wheaton, IL: Tyndale House Publishers, 1995–2007.

Landes, David. "Culture Makes Almost All the Difference." In *Culture Matters: How Values Shape Human Progress,* edited by Lawrence E. Harrison and Samuel P. Huntington, 2–13. New York: Basic Books, 2002.

Lanier, Jaron. "One-Half of a Manifesto: Why Stupid Software Will Save the Future from Neo-Darwinian Machines." *WIRED* 8.12 (1999). http://www.wired.com/wired/archive/8.12/lanier.html.

Larson, David B., S. B.Thielman, M. A. Greenwold, J. S. Lyons, and S. G. Post, "Religious Content in the *DSM-III-R* Glossary of Technical Terms." *American Journal of Psychiatry* 150 (1993): 1884–85.

Larson, Edward J. *Summer of the Gods: The Scopes Trial and America's Continuing Debate over Science and Religion.* Cambridge, MA: Harvard University Press, 1997.

Laughlin, Robert B. "Fractional Quantisation." *Review of Modern Physics* 71, no. 4 (1998): 863–74.

Leigh-Brown, Patricia. "A Doctor for Disease, a Shaman for the Soul." *New York Times,* September 19, 2009. http://www.nytimes.com/2009/09/20/us/20shaman.html?_r=1&hp.

Lenzer, Gertrud. "Introduction: Auguste Comte and Modern Positivism." In *Auguste Comte and Positivism: The Essential Writings,* edited by Gertrud Lenzer, xxxi–lxxxii. New Brunswick, NJ: Transaction Publishers, 2008.

Lewis, Bernard. *What Went Wrong? The Clash between Islam and Modernity in the Middle East.* New York: Oxford University Press, 2002.

Lewontin, Richard. "Why Darwin?" *New York Review of Books* 56, no. 9 (2009). http://www.nybooks.com/articles/archives/2009/may/28/why-darwin-2.

Long, D. Stephen. *Divine Economy: Theology and the Market.* New York: Routledge, 2000.

MacIntyre, Alasdair. *Three Rival Versions of Moral Enquiry: Encyclopaedia, Genealogy, and Tradition.* Notre Dame: University of Notre Dame Press, 1990.

Malloch, Theodore Roosevelt. "Social, Human, and Spiritual Capital in Economic Development." *Metanexus* (2003). http://www.metanexus.net/spiritual_capital/research_articles.asp.

Marsden, George M. *Soul of the American University: From Protestant Establishment to Established Nonbelief.* New York: Oxford University Press, 1996.

Marx, Karl, and Friedrich Engels. *Basic Writings on Politics and Philosophy.* Edited by Lewis S. Feuer. New York: Doubleday, 1959.

McCarty, Richard. "Comte's Positivist Calendar." East Carolina University, http://personal.ecu.edu/mccartyr/pos-cal.html.

McCloskey, Deirdre N. *The Bourgeois Virtues: Ethics for an Age of Commerce.* Chicago: University of Chicago Press, 2007.

———. "What Would Jesus Spend? Why Being a Good Christian Won't Hurt the Economy." John Templeton Foundation, http://archive.incharacter.org/article.php?article=8.

McNeill, J. Robert, and William H. McNeill. *The Human Web: A Bird's-Eye View of World History.* New York: W. W. Norton, 2003.

McNeill, J. Robert. *Something New under the Sun: An Environmental History of the Twentieth-Century World.* New York: W.W. Norton & Company, 2000.

Merchant, Carolyn. *The Death of Nature: Women, Ecology, and the Scientific Revolution.* New York: Harper & Row, 1980.

"Metanexus Institute." http://www.metanexus.net.

Midgley, Mary. *Science as Salvation: A Modern Myth and Its Meaning.* New York: Routledge, 1994.

———. *The Ethical Primate: Humans, Freedom, and Morality.* New York: Routledge, 1994.

Miles, Jack. *God: A Biography.* New York: Alfred A. Knopf, 1995.

Mill, John Stuart. *Auguste Comte and Positivism*: Project Gutenberg, 1865.

Monod, Jacques. *Chance and Necessity: An Essay on the Natural Philosophy of Modern Biology.* Translated by Austryn Wainhouse. New York: Alfred A. Knopf, 1971.

Morris, Simon Conway. *Life's Solution: Inevitable Humans in a Lonely Universe.* New York: Cambridge University Press, 2003.

National Institutes of Health. NIH Consensus Development Program. "Acupuncture— Consensus Development Conference Statement." 1997. http://consensus.nih.gov/1997/1997Acupuncture107html.htm.

———. "The Science of the Placebo." Paper presented at a conference at the National Institutes of Health, Bethesda, MD, November 19–21, 2000. http://placebo.nih.gov.

Nelson, Robert H. . *Economics as Religion: From Samuelson to Chicago and Beyond.* State College, PA: Penn State University Press, 2001.

Newberg, Andrew. "Religious and Spiritual Practices: A Neurochemical Perspective." In *Where God and Science Meet,* edited by Patrick McNamara, 15–32. Westport, CT: Praeger, 2006.

Newberg, Andrew, and Eugene D'Aquili. *The Mystical Mind.* Minneapolis, MN: Fortress Press, 1999.

———. "The Neuropsychology of Religious and Spiritual Experience." *Journal of Consciousness Studies* 7, nos. 11–12 (2000): 251–66.

———. *Why God Won't Go Away: Brain Science and the Biology of Belief.* New York: Ballantine Books, 2001.

Niebuhr, Reinhold. *Moral Man and Immoral Society: A Study in Ethics and Politics.* New York: Charles Scribner's Sons, [1932] 1960.

———. *The Nature and Destiny of Man.* 2 vols. Louisville, KY: Westminster John Knox Press, [1941] 1996.

Overbye, Dennis. "Pure Math, Pure Joy." *New York Times,* June 29, 2003, http://www.nytimes.com/2003/06/29/weekinreview/29OVER.html.

Overmyer, Daniel L. "Chinese Religion: An Overview." In *Encyclopedia of Religion,* edited by Lindsay Jones. New York: Macmillan Reference, 2005.

Pals, Daniel L. *Eight Theories of Religion.* 2nd ed. New York: Oxford University Press, 2006.

Peterson, Christopher, and Martin E. P. Seligman. *Character Strengths and Virtues.* New York: Oxford University Press, 2004.

Petrovic, P., E. Kalso, K. M. Petersson, and M. Ingvar. "Placebo and Opioid Analgesia— Imaging a Shared Neuronal Network." *Science* 295, no. 5560 (2002): 1737–40.

Pilkey, Orrin H., and Linda Pilkey-Jarvis. *Useless Arithmetic: Why Environmental Scientists Can't Predict the Future.* New York: Columbia University Press, 2007.

Pinch, Trevor. "Theory Testing in Science—The Case of Solar Neutrinos: Do Crucial Experiments Test Theories or Theorists?" *Philosophy of Sociology of Science* 15 (1985): 267–87.

Plato. *The Last Days of Socrates: Euthyphro, Apology, Crito, Phaedo.* Translated by Hugh Tredennick and Harold Tarrant. New York: Penguin Classics, 1993.

Polkinghorne, John C. *Belief in God in an Age of Science.* New Haven, CT: Yale University Press, 1998.

———. *The Faith of a Physicist: Reflections of a Bottom-up Thinker.* Gifford Lectures for 1993–94. Princeton, NJ: Princeton University Press, 1994.

———. *Science and Providence.* London: SPCK, 1989.

Post, Stephen G., ed. *Altruism and Health: Perspectives from Empirical Research.* New York: Oxford University Press, 2007.

———. *Unlimited Love: Altruism, Compassion, and Service.* Conshohocken, PA: Templeton Foundation Press, 2003.

Post, Stephen G., Byron Johnson, Jeffrey P. Schloss, and Michael E. McCullough, eds. *Research on Altruism and Love: An Annotated Bibliography of Major Studies in Psychology, Sociology, Evolutionary Biology, and Theology.* Conshohocken, PA: Templeton Foundation Press, 2003.

Preus, J. Samuel. *Explaining Religion: Criticism and Theory from Bodin to Freud.* Edited by Terry Godlove, Texts and Translation Series, American Academy of Religion. Atlanta, GA: Scholars Press, 1996.

Primack, Joel R., and Nancy Ellen Abrams. *The View from the Center of the Universe: Discovering Our Extraordinary Place in the Cosmos.* New York: Riverhead, 2006.

Purves, William K., H. Gordon, H. Orians, Craig Heller, and David Sadava. *Life: The Science of Biology.* Sunderland, MA: Sinauer Associates, 1998.

Putnam, Robert D. *Bowling Alone: The Collapse and Revival of American Community.* New York: Simon & Schuster, 2000.

———. *Making Democracy Work.* Princeton, NJ: Princeton University Press, 1993.

Pyysiäinen, Ilkka, and Veikko Anttonen, eds. *Current Approaches in the Cognitive Science of Religion.* New York: Continuum, 2002.

Ramachandran, V. S. "Beyond Belief 2006 Conference Lecture." TSN: The Science Network, http://thesciencenetwork.org/programs/beyond-belief-science-religion-reason-and-survival.

Ramachandran, V.S., and Sandra Blakeslee. *Phantoms in the Brain.* New York: HarperCollins, 1998.

Raman, Varadaraja V. *Truth and Tension in Science and Religion.* Center Ossipee, NH: Beech River Books, 2009.

Rawls, John. *A Theory of Justice.* Cambridge, MA: Harvard University Press, 1971.

Read, Jen'nan Ghazal. "Muslims in America." *Contexts: Understanding People in their Social Worlds* (Fall 2008): 37–41.

Ricoeur, Paul. "Hermeneutics and the Critique of Ideology." In *Hermeneutics and the Human Sciences,* edited by John P. Thompson, 63–100. New York: Cambridge University Press, [1973] 1981.

———. *Interpretation Theory: Discourse and the Surplus of Meaning.* Fort Worth: Texas Christian University Press, 1976.

———. *Lectures on Ideology and Utopia.* New York: Columbia University Press, 1986.

———. *Time and Narrative.* Translated by Kathleen McLauglin and David Pellauer. 3 vols. Cambridge: Cambridge University Press, 1984, 1985, 1986.

Roberts L., I. Ahmed, S. Hall, A. Davison. "Intercessory Prayer for the Alleviation of Ill Health." *Cochrane Database System Review* 2, no. CD000368 (2009).

Rolston, Holmes. *Genes, Genesis, and God: Values and Their Origins in Natural and Human History.* New York: Cambridge University Press, 1998.

———. *Science and Religion: A Critical Survey.* Philadelphia, PA: Temple University Press, 1987.

———. "The Good Samaritan and His Genes." *Metanexus* (1999). http://www.metanexus.net/Magazine/tabid/68/id/3021/Default.aspx.

Rorty, Richard. *Contingency, Irony, and Solidarity.* New York: Cambribge University Press, 1989.

Rubenstein, Richard E. *Aristotle's Children: How Christians, Muslims, and Jews Rediscovered Ancient Wisdom and Illuminated the Middle Ages.* New York: Harcourt, 2003.

Sagan, Carl. *The Demon-Haunted World: Science as a Candle in the Dark.* New York: Ballantine Books, 1996.

Samuelson, Norbert M. *Jewish Faith and Modern Science: On the Death and Rebirth of Jewish Philosophy.* New York: Rowman and Littlefield, 2009.

———. *Judaism and the Doctrine of Creation.* Cambridge: Cambridge University Press, 1994.

Santayana, George. *Life of Reason.* Vol. 3, *Reason in Religion.* New York: Prometheus Books, [1905–06] 1998.

Schachtman, Noah. "Army's New Ptsd Treatment: Yoga, Reiki, 'Bioenergy.' " *WIRED*, March 25, 2008.

———. "Walter Reed Using Yoga to Fight Ptsd." *WIRED*, May 6, 2008.

Schrödinger, Edwin. *What Is Life?* 1944. http://whatislife.stanford.edu/Homepage/LoCo_files/What-is-Life.pdf.

Seligman, Martin E.P. *Authentic Happiness: Using the New Postive Psychology to Realize Your Potential for Lasting Fulfillment.* New York: Free Press, 2002.

Shapiro, Arthur K., and Elaine Shapiro. "The Placebo: Is It Much Ado about Nothing?" In *The Placebo Effect: An Interdisciplinary Exploration,* edited by Anne Harrington, 12–36. Cambridge, MA: Harvard University Press, 1997.

Sharpe, Eric J. *Comparative Religion: A History.* 5th ed. Chicago: Open Court Publishing, 1986.

Shepard, Paul, and Daniel McKinley, eds. *The Subversive Science: Essays toward an Ecology of Man.* Boston, MA: Houghton-Mifflin, 1969.

Sherman, Jeremy. "Meditation and Future Pharmaceuticals: A Short Science Fiction." *Metanexus* (1999). http://www.metanexus.net/Magazine/tabid/68/id/3062/Default.aspx.

Siegel, Ronald. *Intoxication.* New York: E. P. Dutton, 1989.

Sloan, Richard P. *Blind Faith: The Unholly Alliance of Religion and Medicine.* New York: St. Martin's Press, 2006.

———. "Field Analysis of the Literature on Religion, Spirituality, and Health." *Metanexus* (2006). http://www.metanexus.net/metanexus_online/show_article2.asp?id=9467.

Smith, Adam. *An Inquiry into the Nature and Causes of the Wealth of Nations.* London: Methuen and Co., 1776. http://www.econlib.org/LIBRARY/Smith/smWN.html.

———. *The Theory of Moral Sentiments.* 1790 ed. London: A. Millar, 1759. http://www.econlib.org/LIBRARY/Smith/smMS.html.

Smith, Christian. *Moral, Believing Animals: Human Personhood and Culture.* New York: Oxford University Press, 2003.

Smith, Tom W. "The National Spiritual Transformation Study." *Journal for the Scientific Study of Religion* 45, no. 2 (2006): 283–96.

Smith, Wilfred Cantwell. *Faith and Belief: The Difference between Them.* Princeton, NJ: Princeton University Press, 1987.

"Society for the Scientific Study of Religion." http://www.sssrweb.org.

Sorokin, Pitrim A. *The Ways and Power of Love: Types, Factors, and Techniques of Moral Transformation.* Conshohocken, PA: Templeton Foundation Press, [1954] 2002.

Soroush, Abdolkarim. *Reason, Freedom, and Democracy in Islam.* Translated by Mahmoud Sadri and Ahmad Sadri. New York: Oxford University Press, 2000.

"Spiritual Capital." Metanexus Institute, http://www.metanexus.net/spiritual_capital.

Stark, Rodney. *The Rise of Christianity: How the Obscure, Marginal Jesus Movement Became the Dominant Religious Force.* New York: HarperCollin, 1997.

———. *The Victory of Reason: How Christianity Led to Freedom, Capitalism, and Western Success.* New York: Random House, 2006.

Stark, Rodney, and Roger Finke. *Acts of Faith: Explaining the Human Side of Religion.* Berkeley, CA: University of California Press, 2000.

Stenger, Victor J. *God: The Failed Hypothesis: How Science Shows That God Does Not Exist.* New York: Prometheus Books, 2007.

Sternberg, Esther. *The Balance Within: The Science Connecting Health and Emotions.* New York: W. H. Freeman, 2001.

Stewart, Ian. *Life's Other Secret: The New Mathematics of the Living World.* Hoboken, NJ: Wiley & Sons, 1998.

Stout, Jeffrey. *Democracy and Tradition.* Princeton, NJ: Princeton University Press, 2004.

Szasz, Thomas. *The Second Sin.* Garden City, NY: Doubleday, 1974.

Tattersall, Ian. *Becoming Human: Evolution and Human Uniqueness.* New York: Harcourt Brace, 1998.

Taylor, Charles. *Sources of the Self.* New York: Harvard University Press, 1989.

Thagard, Paul. "The Conceptual Structure of the Chemical Revolution." *Philosophy of Science* 57 (1990): 183–209.

Thompson, Clive. "Are Your Friends Making You Fat?" *New York Times Magazine,* September 10, 2009. http://www.nytimes.com/2009/09/13/magazine/13contagion-t.html?ref=magazine.

Tillich, Paul. *Dynamics of Faith.* New York: HarperCollins, [1957] 2001.

Tirosh-Samuelson, Hava, Don Ihde, Jean-Pierre Dupuy, Katherine Hayles, Andrew Pickering, and Ted Peters. "Special Issue on Transhumanism." *Metanexus*(2008). http://www.metanexus.net/magazine/PastIssues/tabid/126/Default.aspx?PageContentID=27.

Tylor, E. B. *Religion in Primitive Culture.* New York: Harper Torchbooks, [1871] 1958.

United Nations Development Programme. "Arab Human Development Report 2009." http://www.arab-hdr.org.

Vitz, Paul C. "The Uses of Stories in Moral Development: New Psychological Reasons for an Old Education Method." *American Psychologist* 45 (1990): 709–20.

von Weizsaecker, Carl Friedrich. *Die Geschichte Der Natur.* Frankfurt: Vandenhoeck & Ruprecht, 1962.

Wallace, Anthony F. C. *Revitalizations and Mazeways: Essays on Culture Change.* Edited by Robert S. Grumet. Vol. 1. Lincoln: University of Nebraska Press, 2003.

Wallace, B. Allan. *The Taboo of Subjectivity: Towards a New Science of Consciousness.* New York: Oxford University Press, 2000.

Weber, Maximillian. *The Protestant Ethic and the Spirit of Capitalism.* New York: Charles Scribner's Sons, [1905] 1958.

———. *The Religion of China.* Translated by Hans Gerth. Glencoe, IL: Free Press, [1920] 1951.

———. *The Religion of India.* Translated by Hans Gerth and Don Martindale. Glencoe, IL: Free Press, [1920] 1958.

———. *The Sociology of Religion.* Translated by Ephraim Fischoff. Boston: Beacon Press, [1922] 1963.

Wernick, Andrew. *Auguste Comte and the Religion of Humanity: The Post-Theistic Program of French Social Theory.* New York: Cambridge University Press, 2001.

Wesson, Robert. *Beyond Natural Selection.* Cambridge, MA: MIT Press, 1991.

White, Andrew Dickson. *A History of the Warfare of Science with Theology in Christendom*: Project Gutenberg, 1896.

White, Hayden. *Tropics of Discourse: Essays in Cultural Criticism.* Baltimore: Johns Hopkins University Press, 1978.

Whitehead, Alfred North. *Science and the Modern World.* New York: Free Press, [1925] 1967.

Williams, R. W., Herrup, K. "The Control of Neuron Number." *Annual Review of Neuroscience* 11 (1988): 423–53.

Wilson, David Sloan. *Darwin's Cathedral: Evolution, Religion, and the Nature of Society.* Chicago: University of Chicago Press, 2002.

Wilson, Edward O. *Consilience: The Unity of Knowledge.* New York: Knopf, 1998.

———. *On Human Nature.* Cambridge, MA: Harvard University Press, 1978.

———. *Sociobiology: The New Synthesis.* Cambridge, MA: Harvard University Press, 1975.

Wittgenstein, Ludwig. *The Wittgenstein Reader.* Edited by Anthony Kenny. Oxford: Blackwell, 1994.

Woodbury, Robert. "Missionary Data (1813–1968) as a Resource for Testing Religious Economies and Secularization Theory." Paper presented at the Association for the Study of Religion, Economics and Culture, Rochester, NY, November 4, 2005.

Wright, Robert. *Non-Zero: The Logic of Human Destiny.* New York: Pantheon, 2000.

———. *The Evolution of God.* New York: Little, Brown and Company, 2009.

INDEX